SHAKESPEARE IN PERFORMANCE

Shakespeare

ജ *in* ൙

Performance

Inside the Creative Process

൙

MICHAEL FLACHMANN

In Honor of the Utah Shakespeare Festival's Fiftieth Anniversary

THE UNIVERSITY OF UTAH PRESS
Salt Lake City

The Defiance House Man colophon is a registered trademark
of the University of Utah Press. It is based upon a four-foot-tall,
Ancient Puebloan pictograph (late PIII) near Glen Canyon, Utah.

15 14 13 12 11   1 2 3 4 5

LIBRARY OF CONGRESS CATALOGING-IN-PUBLICATION DATA
Flachmann, Michael.
 Shakespeare in performance : inside the creative process / Michael Flachmann.
   p. cm.
 "In honor of the Utah Shakespeare Festival's fiftieth anniversary."
 Includes bibliographical references.
   ISBN 978-1-60781-128-2 (pbk. : alk. paper)
 1. Shakespeare, William, 1564–1616—Dramatic production. 2. Shakespeare,
William, 1564–1616—Stage history—Utah. 3. Theater—Utah—History. 4. Utah
Shakespeare Festival. I. Title.
 PR3105.F53 2011
 792.9'5—dc22

2010050748

Cover: Melinda Pfundstein as Audrey and Michael David Edwards as Touchstone
in the Utah Shakespeare Festival's 2002 production of *As You Like It*. Photograph
by Karl Hugh. Cover design by Phil Hermansen.

Printed and bound by Sheridan Books, Inc., Ann Arbor, Michigan.

For Fred and Barbara Adams

Contents

Illustrations

INTRODUCTION

The following pages chronicle a thirty-year love affair with theatre, during which I've had the privilege of being on the design teams for more than one hundred professional Shakespearean productions, principally at the Tony Award–winning Utah Shakespeare Festival but also at the Oregon Shakespeare Festival, the La Jolla Playhouse, and many other first-rate theatrical organizations throughout the United States. This unique and intimate acquaintance with the way plays are produced and performed has given me unprecedented insider access to a wide range of fascinating information about how directors, designers, actors, and other key theatre personnel make artistic decisions that bring audiences to their feet cheering at the conclusion of a brilliant show.

Though my interest in Shakespeare started with a BA, MA, and PhD in English literature and many years' experience teaching at the university level, my theatrical apprenticeship really began when my dear friend Libby Appel, longtime artistic director at the Oregon Shakespeare Festival (OSF), asked me to assist her on a production of *A Midsummer Night's Dream* she was directing at the Utah Shakespeare Festival (USF) in 1986. I had known Libby from earlier work at the now-defunct California Shakespearean Festival in Visalia, where we both assisted artistic director Mark Lamos on a number of shows, but the invitation to join her in Utah was my first real dramaturgical job, the results of which are documented in the initial essay of this collection, "Dream Making in Cedar City."

During that first summer in Utah, I became friends with the delightful Fred Adams, then artistic director of the theatre, who took a chance on an inexperienced kid from California and hired me as the first (and so far the *only*) staff dramaturg at the USF. Between Fred's kind encouragement and Libby's patient on-the-job training, I slowly learned how my background in literature and research methods could be useful in this exciting new world of professional theatre, where the collaborative and pragmatic demands of mounting a production far outweigh the solitary pleasures of reading Shakespeare's plays in the comfort of your own study. What we were dealing with, Libby taught me, were "scripts designed for performance," where every black mark floating softly on the pristine white page offered tantalizing hints about the way specific words should be pronounced, lines could be delivered, blocking might be choreographed, and entire scenes could be staged.

I was immediately enchanted with this living, breathing artistic process that seamlessly united my love of Shakespeare with my strong desire to reach out to a wider audience as a teacher and scholar. As my theatrical "classroom" expanded, so, too, did my fledgling dramaturgical skills, which soon included the construction of a huge research binder for each play, complete with scholarly articles, production reviews, information about place names and historical personages, and other relevant material that might be useful during rehearsal. Later, I began receiving invitations to all the early production meetings, where the shows first take nascent shape through creative dialogue among the directors, designers, and stage technicians responsible for turning conceptual visions into theatrical reality. I soon learned how to write song lyrics and program notes; how to edit scripts so the curtain came down on time; and how to explore the text of a play with actors, always searching for subtle clues that might translate into interesting and truthful production choices.

Because of the incredible generosity of Fred, Libby, and so many others who took me under their dramatic wings, I feel as if I've earned a second doctorate in theatre to complement my earlier degrees in literature. I still teach during the school year, but my summer theatre work enhances, inspires, and informs my academic life with a vast array of perceptive insights that I happily share with my students. In fact, this unique combination of dramaturgy and pedagogy has even earned me a few teaching awards, the most prestigious of which was being named United States Professor of the Year by the Carnegie Foundation in 1995, which honored me for "extraordinary dedication to undergraduate teaching." I would not be the educator I am today without this real-world experience in professional theatre to supplement the previous training I had in the study of literature.

This book is divided into seven principal parts: (1) Dramaturgy, (2) The Comedies, (3) The Histories, (4) The Tragedies, (5) The Romances, (6) Shakespeare's Contemporaries and Other Playwrights, and (7) Acting Shakespeare: Roundtable Discussions with Actors and Directors. An appendix acknowledges the original source of each essay. The book begins with "The Birth of a Festival," an account of the very first year of the USF based on several interviews with Fred Adams, its founder and longtime artistic director. It sets the stage for the essays that follow, most of which are notes from Shakespearean festival programs written for specific productions and a general audience of readers and theatregoers. Some of the other articles—including "The Merchant of Ashland," "'Swear by Your Double Self,'" "Parrot, Parody, and Paronomasia," "The Rhythm of the Kiss," "*Cymbeline* in the Wooden O," and "The Kindest Cut of All"—appeared first in a variety of literary and theatrical journals. All act, scene, and line numbers in the articles are taken from the Arden edition of Shakespeare's plays.[1]

The last of the seven sections, "Acting Shakespeare: Roundtable Discussions with Actors and Directors," contains edited transcripts of conversations recorded as the culminating event of the USF's Wooden O Symposium each summer and focuses on the following productions: *Measure for Measure* (2003), *Henry IV, Part I* (2004), *Romeo and Juliet* (2005), *Hamlet* (2006), *King Lear* (2007), *Othello* (2008), and *Henry V* (2009). This final series of interviews rounds out the book by providing the actors' insightful perspectives on the productions with which they were so intimately involved.

To my longtime colleagues at the USF, I owe a special debt of gratitude, not only Fred Adams but also R. Scott Phillips, the executive director; David Ivers and Brian Vaughn, the new artistic directors; Doug Cook, Cameron Harvey, and Kathleen Conlin, former associate artistic directors; publications director Bruce C. Lee; art director Phil Hermansen; education director Michael Don Bahr; *Journal of the Wooden O* editor Diana Major Spencer and editorial board members Matthew Nickerson and Jes-

---

1. *The Arden Shakespeare*, ed. David Scott Kastan (London: Methuen, 2002).

sica Tvordi; and Charles Metten, the New American Playwrights Project director. Among the many fine directors with whom I have worked, I've been most influenced by Libby Appel, Robert Cohen, J. R. Sullivan, Russell Treyz, Eli Simon, Kent Thompson, Leslie Reidel, Jim O'Connor, Des McAnuff, Richard Risso, Howard Jensen, Scott Glasser, Pat Patton, Jim Edmondson, Michael Addison, Elizabeth Huddle, Henry Woronicz, Kate Buckley, John Neville-Andrews, David Ivers, Jesse Berger, Kirk Boyd, Jules Aaron, Blake Robison, Brad Carroll, Roger Bean, Joe Hanreddy, and B. J. Jones. Designers, fight directors, choreographers, and speech and voice coaches whom I count as close friends and colleagues include Donna Ruzika, Bill Forrester, Christine Frezza, Janet Swenson, David Kay Mickelsen, Bill Black, Troy Hemmerling, Chris Villa, Jeff Lieder, Joe Payne, Jo Winiarski, Jaymi Lee Smith, Stephen Boulmetis, Eric Stone, Robin McFarquhar, T. Anthony Marotta, Lonnie Alcaraz, Todd Ross, Gerald Rheault, Ben Hohman, Chris Pickart, Kirsten Sham, Phil Thompson, Jack Greenman, Lindsay Jones, and George Maxwell. And to the actors who have taught me so much about Shakespeare over the years, all I can say is thank you for sharing your talent and your passion with me. My sincere appreciation, finally, to Professors Robert Nelson and Lois Feuer and OSF Artistic Director Emerita Libby Appel for extremely helpful reviews of the manuscript; to University of Utah Press director and managing editor Glenda Cotter, assistant editor Stephanie Warnick, and acquisitions editor Peter DeLafosse, who believed in this project from the beginning; to Barbara Bannon for her copyediting expertise; to my wife, Kim Flachmann, and my dear friend Cheryl Smith for reading and critiquing earlier drafts of the manuscript; to my son, Christopher, and his wife, Abby, for their loving encouragement; and to my daughter, Laura, for all her help over the years with my Camp Shakespeare educational program at the Utah Shakespeare Festival.

Through the following essays, I'm delighted to share the joy, excitement, fascination, and immense energy I've discovered by helping to bring Shakespeare's plays to glorious and vibrant life onstage. Please join me in the design sessions, the rehearsal halls, and behind the scenes as I reveal some of the mystery of theatre.

The Birth of a Festival

The Utah Shakespeare Festival started with an investment of five cents. The year was 1961, when John F. Kennedy was president, the Dow Jones had soared above six hundred points for the first time, the median price of a new home was $12,500, the average annual income was $5,315, gasoline cost twenty-seven cents per gallon, *Mr. Ed* was the most popular show on television, and Chubby Checker's "The Twist" was blaring from all the jukeboxes. That same year, Fred Adams—a fresh-faced, thirty-year-old armed with an MFA from Brigham Young University—had just been hired as an assistant professor of theatre at the College of Southern Utah (later renamed Southern Utah University). He drove into Cedar City in his new '55 Ford T-Bird with his fiancée, Barbara Gaddie, where he began teaching while she took a position with the Iron County School District as an audiologist and speech therapist.

Once a week Fred and Barbara got together at the Fluffy Bundle Laundromat, where they washed their clothes and made plans for the future. They knew they wanted to settle in Cedar City, which they saw as a wonderful place to raise children, but they had goals far beyond teaching and speech therapy. Fred had long wanted to begin a professional theatre program. In fact, one of his graduate-school projects in a class called "Problems of the Producing Director" had focused on constructing a hypothetical Shakespeare festival in Logan, Utah, near his hometown of Montpelier. Fred was also enthralled with the success of the Oregon Shakespeare Festival in Ashland, which was a model for satisfying his dreams.

Consequently, on a charmed day in November, when snow was falling softly outside, Fred and Barbara put a nickel in the dryer and began

1. Building the first stage, 1962. Photo by Boyd D. Redington. Published with permission of the Utah Shakespeare Festival.

tossing around ideas about founding a Shakespeare festival while their clothes tumbled happily in the nearby Maytag. Fred took notes on a yellow legal pad, which he later transcribed into a blueprint for the new theatre. Such was the modest beginning of the Utah Shakespeare Festival (USF), which fifty glorious years later has become a Tony Award–winning organization with an annual budget of more than six million dollars; a seasonal staff of 420 directors, designers, actors, technicians, and other theatrical personnel; a year-round staff of twenty-seven; and an ambitious summer and fall production schedule of nine plays and two green shows seen by more than 150,000 spectators yearly in three venues: the 819-seat outdoor Adams Memorial Theatre, the 769-seat indoor Randall L. Jones Theatre, and the 900-seat indoor Auditorium Theatre.

This journey from a five-cent investment to a six-million-dollar theatre began with a series of excursions to Shakespeare festivals throughout the United States and Canada, where Fred talked with all the major regional theatre entrepreneurs of his time and sought their advice on the best way to build his festival. Fred's mother, Louise Crookshank Adams, had been yearning to go on a trip, so she hopped into her brand-new Chevy Bel Air and, in June 1961, set out cross country with Fred, Barbara, and two close friends who later got married, Julie Ann Farrer and Howard Jensen. Fred was equipped with a list of questions for his artistic-director counterparts, beginning with two principal ones: If you had to do it all over again, (1) what would you avoid, and (2) what would you definitely do? Interestingly enough, all the answers were different and therefore helpful to Fred and Barbara in unique ways.

Craig Noel at San Diego's Old Globe counseled Fred to "build a theatre that would last well into the future." The Globe's facility had been erected during the 1935 California Pacific International Exposition and wasn't serving him terribly well. As Fred remembered the conversation, Noel told him not to "lock yourself into a physical plant that doesn't lend itself to your mission." He also advised the group to avoid "big-name" actors: "I've been burned by Hollywood personalities over the years," he lamented. "Once you start bringing in stars, then you have to provide a bigger one next year and a better one the year after that."

In Ashland they met with Angus Bowmer, who strongly advised them to produce Shakespeare's plays with historical accuracy and without "conceptual gimmicks," which were nothing more, in his opinion, than "directorial masturbation." Bowmer's lone regret, he confessed, was severing ties with the local junior college (now Southern Oregon University). Tyrone Guthrie in Stratford, Ontario, urged the delegation to become the official state theatre of Utah and be as fiscally conservative as possible when budgeting the shows. Michael Langham in Stratford, Connecticut, was on the verge of bankruptcy when Fred and his party arrived, so money was on his mind. "Don't get into bed with the unions," he pleaded, and "sell as much wine and as many sandwiches as possible. We make most of our profit on concessions."

The parallels between Ashland and Cedar City were especially intriguing to Fred and Barbara. Both were small towns equidistant from major metropolitan areas (Portland and San Francisco for Ashland, Las Vegas and Salt Lake for Cedar City). Other similarities were the nearby ski resorts and a small local college in each town. The one advantage Cedar City had over Ashland, however, was the proximity of a major freeway, although that prospect had been in jeopardy until the last possible moment. Interstate 15 was for a brief and terrifying time slated to lie fifteen miles west of town, closer to the Utah/Nevada border, which would have isolated Cedar City from the rest of the state. When it was eventually rerouted nearer to the city, this simple act of geographic gerrymandering changed the economics of southern Utah forever.

When Fred and his group returned to Cedar City later that month, they had a plan for their 1962 summer season, a projected budget of a thousand dollars, and a slate of three shows: *Hamlet, The Merchant of Venice,* and *The Taming of the Shrew.* From earlier productions at the college, they had enough costumes for one and a half plays, so they decided to build the rest. They had already constructed the tiring house, so all they needed was a platform on which to stage the performances, some risers to support folding chairs for the audience, a few pallets, and money for scenic properties, benches, tables, and tools. Since volunteers were going to do all the work, and the theatre wasn't paying any salaries, they figured a thousand dollars would easily cover the rest of their costs.

The following summer, Fred directed all three shows, which ran for the first two weekends of July on Thursday, Friday, and Saturday evenings. During the four-week rehearsal period, each day started at 8:00 a.m. with an hour building scenery or sewing costumes. *Shrew* rehearsed from 9:00 a.m. to noon, at which time mothers brought over a pot of stew, soup, chili, or lasagna for lunch. That was followed by a four-hour afternoon rehearsal of *Merchant,* a free dinner at the student cafeteria, and a four-hour rehearsal of *Hamlet* ending at 11:00 p.m. One local resident, Ruth Hunter (whose husband owned the Hunter Cowan Store and Northeast Furniture), was concerned that the "children" weren't getting enough to eat, so she contributed a hundred dollars for food and continued to do that each year for the rest of her life.

Despite all this support and energy, the new festival had two difficult problems to overcome for its initial season: finding actors and raising money. Fred scoured his theatre classes and enlisted a number of students eager to be in the plays. Then he got some townsfolk as extras to play the gravediggers, the Player Queen, and two of the court ladies (both, as he recalls, were tellers at the local bank). His principal recruiting took place, however, during the winter before the festival's first season, when the college was staging *The Taming of the Shrew.* Fred went in desperation to his friend the football coach and said, "Goonie, I've got to have some men."

The coach told him to come to practice the next day, when he announced, "Guys, Freddie needs some actors! Any of you willing to be in a play?" A few hands went up, and then a few more, and pretty soon Fred had all the actors he needed for the shows. One of the young men, a tight end named Norm Childs, ended up playing Petruchio, marrying his Kate, and becoming quite a theatre aficionado. Another member of the team, Russ McGinn, decided to major in theatre, became a professional actor, and was later elected president of the western division of the Screen Actors Guild. "We started a few careers that summer," Fred confided.

That took care of the actors; finding the money was tougher. Knowing he needed a thousand dollars—quite a sum in those days—Fred canvassed Cedar City's civic organizations looking for a group to underwrite the shows, but he was turned down by the Chamber of Commerce (whose members actually laughed at him), the City Council ("Why would anyone pay money to see a Shakespeare play?" someone asked), and the Rotary, Kiwanis, and Elks Clubs—where his plea for financial backing, according to Fred, went over like a "pregnant pole-vaulter." Thankfully one of his students, Norma Jean Benson, saved the theatre. Her brother, Ken Benson, was president of the local Lions Club, and Fred quickly wheedled an invitation to address the group. "How much money will you need," one of the Lions inquired, to which Fred replied, "We're not asking for money; we only want you to underwrite us. I think we'll make it all back in ticket sales." The Lions roared their unanimous approval, and Fred had his thousand-dollar guarantee. True to his word, the season netted just over thirty-two hundred dollars, so he never had to use the Lions' generous offer. As Fred remembers it, the tickets cost five dollars each (with lower prices for children); based on two hundred seats each night for six performances, that gave him enough profit to fund the first season and salt away more than two thousand dollars for the second. The festival was on its way!

Additional help during this first year came from an unexpected source. Fred had initially asked Royden C. Braithwaite, president of the College of Southern Utah, for financial assistance, but the school was still a small two-year branch of the University of Utah and had little discretionary money. As Fred recalls, "President Braithwaite was a dear man, a real visionary, who said, 'I can't give you any funding, but I'll do what I can to help.'" His first act of generosity was allowing Fred and his actors to use the married students' dorms, called the Lambing Sheds, which were empty for the summer. He also volunteered the services of George Barrus and Bessie Dover from the college's marketing department, who gladly put together articles and posters advertising the festival, including a four-page brochure that the actors distributed throughout Cedar City and at Zion and Bryce Canyon National Parks. "We had no mailing list at the time," Fred admits, "so we had to hand out our brochures on the street."

One especially happy coincidence was the fact that Bessie's husband, Kent Dover, was in charge of the Arden and Meadow Gold Dairies, which distributed milk, cream, butter, and other products all the way from Mesa, Arizona, to Provo, Utah, an unusually wide service area. In those days, the dairy's cardboard milk cartons were imprinted on one side with the Arden and Meadow Gold logo, and the rest of the container was blank. Kent promptly had a description of the plays and their performance dates printed on the other side, which meant that the festival got wonderful PR on every breakfast table within a three-state area.

Fred was also contacted at the time by Harold Lundstrom, an "absolute fanatic" about Shakespeare who was the music critic for Salt Lake City's *Deseret News*, a church-affiliated newspaper with a huge readership. After inviting Fred up for an interview, Lundstrom put him in touch with Jackie Nokes, who had a CBS syndicated children's television show called *Miss Julie* on KSL-Channel Five and an anchor position on a noon news program named *City Beat*. Fred did three interviews with Lundstrom and Nokes the first season, which helped tremendously in spreading the word in the Salt Lake City area. Later in the season, Lundstrom came down and reviewed all three plays for his newspaper, which he continued to do for many more years. He also wrote special-interest stories about people involved with the festival. "He was a tough reviewer," Fred explains. "He pointed out our warts when we had them, and he was glowing about the things we did right. He gave us our first statewide recognition, which was immensely helpful during the early years of our development."

Another advantage Fred had was the proximity of the national parks. "We would send Greenshow dancers down to Zion, where they handed out brochures during the evening meals a few days before the festival began," he says. "There wasn't much to do at night in the parks those days, so we made sure the folks had an invitation to our plays." Fred's wife, Barbara, put together a madrigal group, which included Lorene and Frank Adams, Larry and Anne Jones, Jamie Fillmore, Burnett Baldwin, and others, that not only sang during the Greenshow but also marched in Cedar City's Fourth of July Parade every year with a Shakespeare banner and went into Hugh's Café (now the Market Grill), Sullivan's Café, and other local restaurants asking permission to sing to the patrons. "They went from table to table," Fred remembers, "singing 'Greensleeves' and 'Summer Is A-Coming In,' and the people just loved it; they ate it up! By the time they got back to the festival, our box office had received a call from someone wanting to know what time each day the Shakespeare group sang in the restaurants."

Lavede Whetten, a member of the Physical Education Department at the college and wife of the Cedar City mayor, recruited dancers for the Greenshow and taught them Renaissance maypole and ribbon dances, which were accompanied by the madrigal singers and a recorder group organized by Barbara Adams and Ena Heap. During subsequent seasons, the group put up window displays in the stores and had merchants hang banners advertising the festival. "That was the extent of our first-year marketing effort," explains Fred. "Everything just fell into place after that!"

Two other early supporters were Maurice and Catherine Crichton. "Maurice was an old Royal Air Force pilot," Fred explains, "who had been for many years stationed in India with his wife." After retiring from the military, the couple immigrated to America and ended up in Cedar City, where they were very happy. As expatriates, they adored Shakespeare, and with the help of another supporter, Gus Gooding, they founded the Utah Shakespeare Festival Guild, which was originally organized to provide funding for the plays.

As the festival matured, so, too, did the relationship between Fred and Barbara, who wed in May 1963. Sadly, after forty-six years of marriage, Barbara died in 2009. Their dream begun at the Fluffy Bundle Laundromat lives on, however, as a tribute to their foresight and creativity and the support of many thousands of people who have helped convert their brave vision into reality over the past fifty years. As a result, Fred's initial investment of five cents continues to pay immense dividends in the artis-

2. Winning the Tony Award, 2000. *Left to right:* R. Scott Phillips, Sue Cox, Douglas N. Cook, Fred C. Adams, and Cameron Harvey receiving the Tony at Radio City Music Hall. Published with permission of the Utah Shakespeare Festival.

tic, economic, and cultural life of southern Utah and the entire nation as the USF begins its journey into the next half century.

Author's note: This article is based on three two-hour interviews during the summer of 2009 with my dear friend and longtime colleague Fred Adams, founder of the festival and for more than four decades its executive and artistic director. During our discussions about the USF's early years, Fred easily remembered names, dates, and stories from nearly fifty years earlier as if the events had happened only yesterday. He has also read and approved this article. I am extremely grateful to Fred for allowing me to chronicle the early years of the festival.

ଔ I ଔ

Dramaturgy

DREAM MAKING IN CEDAR CITY

A Midsummer Night's Dream at the 1986
Utah Shakespeare Festival

A good theatrical production is somewhat akin to an iceberg: the tip of its onstage performance is supported by a vast amount of preparatory work unseen by the general public. Though few people have the opportunity to experience this process at close range, during the spring and summer of 1986, I had the good fortune to be in the midst of a group of designers, composers, stage technicians, and research consultants who helped Libby Appel direct *A Midsummer Night's Dream* for the Utah Shakespeare Festival's Silver Anniversary season. Our collaboration actually began in October 1985, more than nine months before the play's opening night in Cedar City.

Libby and I had known each other long before she came to the California Institute of the Arts as dean and artistic director of the School of Theatre. We first met in 1978 at the now-defunct California Shakespearean Festival in Visalia, where I was director of education and she was head of the conservatory program that trained young actors associated with the festival. Since that time, we've written two books together and worked side by side on a number of other theatre projects, but I had never before assisted her on a full-blown production of a Shakespearean play. For this reason, I was pleased when she called to ask if I would join her *Dream* production staff as *dramaturg*—a scholar who helps the director, designers, and actors investigate the script of a play.

Prior to our initial meeting, Libby made a thirty-minute audiotape of her thoughts, concentrating especially on a Jungian approach that highlighted the comedy's movement from the stark rationality of the city into the nightmarish, pulsating excitement of the woods. Her theory was that characters like Theseus and Oberon are actually "shadow selves" of the same person. The Athenian Duke represents "cool reason" while the Fairy King, his counterpart in the dream world, stands for passion and emotion. By the same token, Titania is the darker side of Hippolyta, Puck of Philostrate, and the fairies of the rude mechanicals (Bottom, Quince, and the other hard-handed working men of Athens).

Although Peter Brook had famously pioneered this doubling concept in his 1970 production of the play, Libby intended to flesh out the primal connections linking these doppelganger characters through a more systematic treatment of costuming, set design, lighting, stage choreography, and other theatrical elements. At the outset of the comedy, she reasoned, no harmony exists between ruler and subjects, father and child, husband and wife, lovers and friends. Only by journeying into this "dream landscape" (or through the unconscious, as Jung would say) can these characters merge with the other halves of their personalities. Moving well beyond a Freudian, sexual approach to the play, Libby's concept promised to examine the mythic, collective consciousness that unites all of us in a search for resolution, love, and happiness.

This tape—copies of which were sent to me, scenic designer Ron Ranson, and costume designer Claremarie Verheyen—served as the basis for all our early work on the play. It became clear to me from the very beginning that Libby was not merely imposing a foreign construct onto Shakespeare, but rather had made a genuine theatrical discovery by coupling Brook's earlier approach with her own inner search for meaning, using Jung as one of its guides.

While Ron and Claremarie were preparing their first design sketches, I put together a research packet for Libby containing annotated excerpts from Freud, Jung, David Young's *Something of Great Constancy*, C. L. Barber's *Shakespeare's Festive Comedies,* and a number of prominent articles on *Dream* that I hoped might spark creative ideas. I also included more than thirty reviews from *Shakespeare Quarterly* that contained detailed notes on concept, staging, costumes, and other important elements of previous professional productions in America and abroad. In addition, I spent a good deal of time studying the Arden edition of the play, looking up obscure words and phrases in the *Oxford English Dictionary,* and comparing the 1623 first-folio text with its literary antecedent, the 1600 first quarto, to establish a definitive script for our production.

Barber's book proved particularly helpful to us since it argues that the "festive" nature of Shakespeare's play produces a form of "comic exorcism" in which the audience members, like the characters, are "released" from their safe, rational, everyday existence and transported to a dream world of imagination, magic, and creativity that helps them see their lives more clearly. In Hippolyta's words, the enchanted experience in the woods grows to "something of great constancy" (5.1.26) for not only the characters but the spectators as well. We found further support for our interpretation of the play in Young's insistence that the kingdom of Theseus is bounded by time ("four happy days . . .") while Oberon's fairy realm is mythic and timeless. One of the principal rhythms of the comedy, therefore, is this movement in and out of time, which sets up a number of other polarities in the play: day/night, reason/imagination, sun/moon, love/law, dreaming/waking, dark/light, woods/city, madness/sanity, and illusion/reality. At the center of all this is the distinction between the fairy world and the mortal world, upon which we intended to build our production.

The challenge, of course, was in making the word flesh. Libby and I met once in mid-November to discuss the research packet I had sent her and survey the play's predominant themes and images for their possible impact on costumes, set, and staging. We began the meeting by discussing the motif of rebirth and fertility in the text, a topic that set off a chain reaction of ideas from Libby involving the use of fruits, vegetables, and water as stage decoration. She also felt, and I agreed, that we needed to pursue power and its misuse in the play—certainly with the characters of Theseus, Egeus, and Oberon but perhaps also with Puck, Bottom, Quince, and the young lovers. The exact shape of these images would have to be worked out later with the various designers, but we wanted the production somehow to incorporate this important dramatic theme. This led us into the concept of courtship and marriage, prompting Libby to inquire about the possibility of having Oberon and Titania bless the newlyweds and also the audience with some type of "fairy dust" at the play's conclusion—exactly the way we ended the production.

Another of our insights concerned the repetition in the play, particularly in relation to the four different character groups: Theseus and Hippolyta, the young lovers, the fairies, and the rude mechanicals. Libby suggested that this symmetry in plot design invited some occasional "mirroring" of costumes, blocking, lighting, and other theatrical devices—an approach that became quite useful during the play's rehearsal period as we sought to strengthen the Jungian connections that linked different characters and scenes. As we discussed such other central themes as metamorphosis, holidays, magic, love, lunacy, dreaming, and imagination, the concept behind our production slowly began to crystallize.

Our November conference served as the prelude to a subsequent gathering at Libby's house in early January that included Ron and Claremarie, who brought the designs they had been working on for the past two months. For me this occasion—when the production team assembles for the first time, and everyone can see the flashes of creativity that will eventually give their play its unique look onstage—is always one of the most exciting moments in theatre. Based on Libby's suggestions concerning the importance of time in the comedy, Ron's preliminary set design featured a preoccupation with Renaissance cosmography: an armillary series of sundials, moon dials, and astrolabes set on poles of varying lengths that first represented Theseus's garden and then, spinning slowly in the darkness and sprinkling light into the open-air theatre, became a fairyland of magic and illusion. A huge, golden moon on the upper stage waxed full or waned to crescent depending on the dramatic occasion. We all immediately dubbed the set design "Tudor high-tech."

Claremarie's period costuming featured the royal couple in regal golds and purples while their shadow selves, Oberon and Titania, were dressed in parallel garments tinted shimmering silvers and blues. Pyramus and Thisbe, who portrayed a comic "nightmare" extension of the dream—a further layering of the unconscious—were dressed to mimic the major characters. For example, Flute/Thisbe reflected Titania, who mirrored Hippolyta; likewise, Bottom/Pyramus echoed Oberon, who was the shadow side of Theseus. Disdaining a more traditional approach to Bottom's appearance as an ass, Libby recalled her earlier concept of a forest filled with vegetation and asked Claremarie to design a head of organic fruits and vegetables that echoed the style of sixteenth-century Italian painter Giuseppe Arcimboldo.

After this daylong meeting in January, we all returned to our respective cities energized by Libby's overall concept for the play. The designers were asked to revise their initial sketches based on the changes Libby had requested, and I began preparing for future discussions on the text of the play. Our next session was on February 7, during which the designers presented their complete plans for the production. Ron brought a scale model of the Utah theatre, with miniature armillary spheres flanking the main stage, a luminous moon above, and a small, star-shaped water fountain at stage center. Similarly Claremarie's costume renderings were fully detailed, stressing the intimate connection between sleeping and waking, the fairy world and the mortal world. Her color palette began with darker tones in the city, shifted to a dreamlike silver and white in the forest, then burst into brightly colored hues in act 5 with the play's movement toward spring, marriage, happiness, and rebirth. Also attending this meeting was Liz Stillwell, the lighting designer, who began her lighting plot based on the work of the set and costume designers.

On March 1, Libby and assistant director Paige Newmark came to my home in Bakersfield for two twelve-hour days devoted solely to the script of the play. We went over the text line by line, word by word, and punctuation mark by punctuation mark, all the while searching for image patterns, implicit stage directions, topical allusions, and other clues to help prepare Libby for the rehearsal process ahead. We selected most of the cuts that tailored the script to our specific production, and we chose several lines from the stormy quarrel between Oberon and Titania in act 2, scene 1 that eventually were used to establish an atmosphere of anger and suspicion at the beginning of the play.

Since Libby had requested additional research on a number of diverse topics, I was prepared with books and articles on everything from the phases of the moon to Greek mythology. Paige began the meeting by inquiring about the Elizabethan conception of the size and shape of fairies, suggesting that Oberon, Titania, and Puck seemed larger than life and therefore more physically powerful than the mortals. That assertion clearly ran counter to several references in the play to diminutive fairies creeping into acorn cups and wearing bats' wings for coats, so we resolved the confusion by consulting Katherine Briggs's *The Anatomy of Puck: An Examination of Fairy Beliefs among Shakespeare's Contemporaries and Successors*.

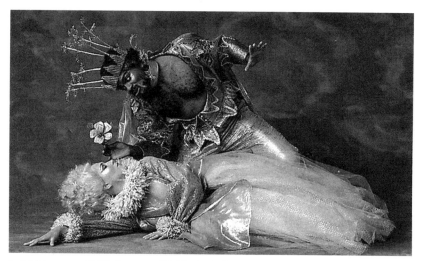

3. *A Midsummer Night's Dream*, 1986. Monica Bell as Titania and LeWan Alexander as Oberon. Photo by Boyd D. Redington and Michael Schoenfeld. Published with permission of the Utah Shakespeare Festival.

According to Briggs, Renaissance folklore envisioned four different types of fairies: hobgoblins (like Robin Goodfellow), trooping fairies (the aristocracy), water spirits (including mermaids), and hags (giants and monsters). Oberon and Titania, we decided, were trooping fairies; as such, they were larger than mortals, capable of shape shifting (changing form or becoming invisible), and well known for rewarding good deeds and punishing injuries. Time spent with them passed at a different rate than with mortals—which helped us understand Bottom's acute disorientation when his ass's head is removed. These particular fairies also loved to dance, play music, give presents, and bless houses; occasionally they stole babies and replaced them with changelings. Puck, a hobgoblin, was smaller and more mischievous by nature, delighting in practical jokes of the type described in act 2, scene 1. The other fairies in the play seemed to be water spirits of some kind, who were indeed tiny enough to inhabit acorn cups.

Our research on fairies—which also included Robert Reed's *The Occult on the Tudor and Stuart Stage,* Reginald Scot's *The Discoverie of Witchcraft,* and the anonymous *Huon of Bordeux*—clarified much of the supernatural interaction in the play. Instead of presenting themselves as minor elfin deities, Oberon and Titania became huge elemental spirits whose quarrel over the changeling child (a prized possession in fairyland) had caused major storms, death, and destruction in the world of the play. Titania's love for Theseus (which we found detailed in Thomas North's translation of Plutarch's *Lives of the Noble Grecians and Romans,* Ovid's *Metamorphoses,* and Chaucer's *The Knight's Tale*) provided ample reason for Oberon's jealousy and eventually assisted the actors playing these parts in understanding the depth of the dissension between these two characters.

Each decision at this stage of shaping the production had a domino effect. For example, since we now perceived Oberon and Titania as extremely regal, powerful figures, we knew their blocking had to be generally slower and more stately than that of the other fairies, their speech needed to be more authoritative, and their entrances and exits had to be accompanied by such stage effects as thunder, lightning, fog, or music. The other fairies, in contrast, were smaller and less important and could therefore move and speak more rapidly in their roles as servants and retainers.

Our research and discussion during this March meeting yielded a number of other insights. For instance, Libby wanted to know exactly what weavers and joiners did—a question that uncovered a wide range of expertise in these Renaissance artisans, running the gamut from simple laborers doing mundane work to skilled craftsmen producing exquisitely woven tapestries and well-wrought furniture. Since I had always envisioned Bottom and his cohorts in much the same way that I see the amiable, if bumbling, plumber who comes to fix our kitchen sink, I was suddenly intrigued with the possibility that the rude mechanicals might be portrayed as accomplished artisans, rather than semiskilled, inept tradesmen. Libby chose to move in this direction, eventually creating onstage characters who were more believable because they were not the usual dumb country bumpkins but honest, hard-working, skilled artists whose earnest effort to put on the play of *Pyramus and Thisbe* was absurdly out of their sphere of competence. We also learned during this investigation that Delsarte's book of theatrical poses supplied a sufficient number of contorted body postures for Bottom to adopt in the role of Pyramus, that Greek weddings always took place under a new moon (the crescent "silver bow" described by Hippolyta in act 1, scene 1, which determined both the shape and size of Ron Ranson's moon on the upper stage), and that Apuleius's *The Golden Ass* (a second-century Latin source for Shakespeare's love affair between a beautiful woman and a man transformed into an ass) prescribed a great deal of physical intimacy between Bottom and Titania.

In establishing a definitive script of the play—the graphic symbols on the page that would guide the actors—we still had several problems to solve. Shakespeare's comedy was written sometime between 1594 and 1595, yet it was not entered into the Stationers' Register until October 1600. Three distinct early editions claim some authenticity: the first quarto (Q1) of 1600, which was probably set from the author's working manuscript; the second quarto (Q2) of 1619 (falsely dated 1600); and the first folio of 1623, which was taken from Q2 and embellished with minor changes from a prompt copy. Since Q1 seems closest to Shakespeare's original in chronology and intent, it usually serves as the *copy text* for modern editions of the play. Scholars draw a useful distinction between *substantive* and *accidental* readings in such a text: between the words themselves and the spelling and punctuation that frame them. In questions involving substantive variants among different editions, the copy text generally takes precedence. However, since the accidentals were undoubtedly set by young, inexperienced typesetters, matters of spelling and punctuation carry less authority than the substantive readings and are open to much more conjecture in an acting edition.

Because of this priority on substantive readings in Q1, we seldom deviated from the Folger text (which is based upon Q1 and served as our acting script). One emendation we did make illustrates the complexity of this type of problem. In act 2, scene 1, during her long description of the terrible weather caused by her quarrel with Oberon, Titania explains, "The human mortals want their winter here: No night is now with hymn or carol blest" (101–2). Though all three early editions read "winter heere," the line simply does not make sense. Why would the mortals, beset with foul weather, "want their winter *here*"? Would they not already have enough winter to contend with in these unseasonable springtime storms? Thomas Hanmer's eighteenth-century emendation to "winter cheer" seemed preferable because of its implication that the humans lack the carols and other festivities (their winter cheer) that normally accompany a frigid Christmas season.

In our textual meetings and my conferences with the actors during rehearsal, I treated the script's accidental variants in an opposite fashion. Instead of closing down the text by resolving the distinctions among variant readings, I worked to open it up by encouraging Libby, Paige, and the actors to experiment with several different approaches to the punctuation. One of our happiest discoveries concerned the extent to which Q1's use of commas, especially in the Rude Mechanicals' scenes, offers helpful advice about the placement of pauses in delivering various lines. For example, in act 1, scene 2 of the Folger edition, Quince's second speech is punctuated in a fairly sparse and routine manner: "Here is the scrowle of every mans name, which is thought fit through al Athens, to play in our Enterlude before the Duke, and the Duchess, on his wedding day at night" (4–7). From the Q1 punctuation, however, emerges a much more interesting portrait of a man who seems shy and hesitant (or perhaps fussy and officious), pausing every few seconds to collect his thoughts: "Here is the scrowle of every mans name, which is thought fit, through al Athens, to play in our Enterlude, before the Duke, and the Dutchess, on his wedding day at night." Libby eventually opted for a fussy and officious Quince, principally because the comic talents of Tom Ford, the actor playing the part, lent themselves to that interpretation.

Overall I found the process of reevaluating the punctuation quite rewarding. For a diligent actor researching the part, such textual evidence often provides important insights into syntactic idiosyncrasies that betray a character's innate behavior and personality. At the very least, a close perusal of folio and quarto punctuation usually challenges actors to rethink lines that have become dull and conventional through the weight of tradition. Some directors even withhold punctuation marks entirely from their actors, forcing them to create a fresh, original interpretation from the words alone.

After our two-day conference in Bakersfield, Libby attended a design conference in Utah at the end of March; from that point on, the production took shape quite rapidly. On June 7, the entire company of 136 people arrived in Cedar City, 25 of whom were actors who had been selected earlier from three thousand applicants and more than five hundred auditions. Rehearsals started on June 12 and continued until opening night on July 10, a frantic and invigorating four-week period during which the cast members were assigned parts in each of the three plays, all the costumes and sets were built, the music was composed, and rehearsals were conducted. I was in residence with the company for three weeks, helping the actors explore their scripts for meaning, explaining obscure words and phrases, encouraging them to experiment with different kinds of punctuation, researching the answers to questions and problems that arose during rehearsals, and doing some textual consulting on the festival's other two productions, *Julius Caesar* and *Love's Labor's Lost*.

Perhaps the most rewarding experience of working with *Dream* was seeing the snug fit between the dramatic concept Libby had articulated and the various actors she chose to play the central roles. LeWan Alexander, a tall, imposing man with a wide vocal range, was a strong and regal Oberon while his consort, Titania, played by Monica Bell, made good use of her operatic singing voice, her skill in dance and movement, and her commanding stage presence. Steve Wilson's Puck was energetic and acrobatic, though his mobility was constantly at odds with the rather starchy costume provided him by Claremarie. I don't think we ever solved that problem entirely.

In the mortal world, Peter Bradbury's Theseus and Elizabeth Terry's Hippolyta presented further difficulties. The major stumbling block was that these characters are quite poorly developed by Shakespeare, which caused consternation as the actors attempted to create a consistent approach to their roles. Libby advised Bradbury to envision Theseus primarily as a powerful tyrant who had recently conquered Hippolyta—a focus that eventually elicited a credible performance from the young actor. Terry sought to develop the fact that her character was an alien in Athens—an outsider in this patriarchal society—by adopting a foreign accent for the first two weeks of rehearsal. After that time, she gave up the accent but maintained a sense of aloofness and dignity that was quite effective.

The chemistry among the young lovers—Barbara Bragg, Corliss Preston, Matt Davis, and Mark Corkins—worked extremely well, which is always one of the crucial elements in a production of this play. Likewise, the rude mechanicals were a cohesive group: they even formed their own bowling team during the long Utah summer. Irwin Appel (Libby's son) as Bottom was particularly adept at shifting dramatic gears from weaver to ass to Pyramus during the course of the play, changing his voice and body movement to flesh out each separate role.

A Midsummer Night's Dream played through August 30 on two stages and was seen by more than twenty thousand spectators (98 percent of capacity). As I watched the production on opening night, I marveled anew at the beauty and breadth of Shakespeare's vision. I marveled, too, at Jung's insights and Libby's intuitive process that had found a common ground where Shakespeare and Jung could coexist, each illuminating the other.

The Merchant of Ashland

The Merchant of Venice at the 1991
Oregon Shakespeare Festival

Libby Appel's 1991 modern-dress production of *The Merchant of Venice* in Ashland, Oregon, opened with the stunning image of commodities traders yelling at each other across the floor of the Venice stock exchange. This noisy theatrical confrontation seemed pale in comparison, however, to the angry real-life drama unleashed by audience response to this extremely controversial production. During its eight-month run from February 22 to October 27, its 104 performances were seen by 59,802 theatregoers, more than 96 percent capacity of the indoor Angus Bowmer Theatre. The play also generated more than one hundred reviews, articles, and letters to the editor in a number of prominent West Coast newspapers and occasioned shouting matches among patrons, heated discussions at festival seminars and workshops, mass mailings of Anti-Defamation League pamphlets to members of the design team and acting company, a withdrawal of donations to the festival, and a demand by local Jewish groups to censor or change certain elements of the production.

Of the many incidents surrounding the play during that long and difficult season, one particularly illustrates the depth of emotion felt by the small, but very vocal, percentage of the audience that generated much of the discontent: in April, when director Appel returned to the festival to participate in a symposium on the show, a man walked up to her during a break in the proceedings and said, "When I saw your production, I just wanted to spit on you"—an obvious reference to one particularly painful moment in the play when Shylock's Christian tormentors spat on him.

An in-depth examination of the reasons why this show caused such intense criticism—and why it sparked, in return, such equally fervent support—may be useful because it provides a perfect opportunity to consider a number of important questions that always seem to swirl around this provocative play: To what extent does updating *Merchant* make the experience of watching it more painful for Jewish viewers? Does the play help spread anti-Semitism or warn against its evils? Who decides what is a valid response to a text that clearly wants to ruffle a few religious feathers? Should the audience be inoculated in any way prior to seeing such productions by preplay discussions or special handouts that place Shakespeare's treatment of Jews within its proper historical context? And at what point do such politically correct attempts to encourage ethnic and racial sensitivity in modern viewers change the dramatic experience from art to propaganda?

To respond to such questions using the Ashland production as a case study, we need to understand the sequence of events that led from the early concept meetings with the director and her designers to the actual production and the wildly divergent responses it elicited from different theatregoers. The concept of the show seemed innocent enough during the initial planning stages and subsequent rehearsal period. Appel, who is herself Jewish, was anxious to portray Shylock as a largely sympathetic character trapped within an alien, hostile world. In fact, during the early design meetings, some members of the production team expressed concern that the play might anger fundamentalist viewers because of its harsh indictment of Christian hypocrisy. The director's plan was to create a dramatic universe where, according to the program note, "virtually every character is guilty of sins against humanity. The play's examination of racial hatred and the frenzied pursuit of wealth indicts Christians and Jews alike, dividing them into ethnic and social camps distrustful of everyone different from themselves."

To stress the greed and opulence of Venice, scenic designer William Bloodgood blended antique and modern elements to create a set dominated by a huge replica of the winged lion in St. Mark's Square. Stone walls surrounding glass and brass grillwork gave the impression of a magnificent corporate lobby—a powerful and impressive arena for the commercial pursuits of the play. In Belmont a brown brocade half curtain sliced across the stage, neatly covering the ironic motto of Venice carved in the stone edifice: "Pax Tibi Marce Evangelista Meus" (Peace to you, Mark my evangelist). During the Morocco, Aragon, and Bassanio scenes in Belmont, the three caskets ascended magically through midstage traps in the floor, then silently disappeared after the choices had been made. Costuming by Deborah Dryden was in the style of 1990s Giorgio Armani: slick, sensual, and flowing with everyone in wide trousers, scarves, and well-moussed hair as if they had just stepped off the pages of a trendy Italian fashion magazine. In act 1, scene 2, Portia and Nerissa dissected the suitors' flaws while uniformed servants trouped past carrying department-store boxes filled with newly purchased hats and dresses. In contrast to such elaborate finery, Shylock was clad simply in a rumpled dark suit and a *yarmulke* while Tubal wore under his coat a *tzitzit:* a fringed, white prayer shawl. Additional design elements such as a New Age music score by Todd Barton and lighting by Robert Peterson (which included the blinding flash of paparazzi cameras as Shylock left the courtroom in disgrace) were carefully coordinated to give the production the look and feel of modern Venice.

Characterization matched design in its attempt to portray the Christian world as acquisitive, xenophobic, and obsessed with surface appearances. Liisa Ivary's Portia, for example, was generally aloof and distant to her suitors, loving to Bassanio, full of girlish chatter with Nerissa, rude to Jessica, and openly contemptuous of Shylock in the trial scene. Dion Luther's Bassanio was young, beautiful, and sexually ambivalent, which helped explain his attractiveness to Tony DeBruno's sad Antonio. Shylock, brilliantly underplayed by Ashland veteran Richard Elmore, was a tired and somewhat brittle Orthodox Jew, weighed down by his tribal burden of centuries of oppression. The quality of mercy *was* strained throughout the play as race confronted race and religion attacked religion. Only in the fifth act, when the production sought comic redemption in the reunion of the lovers and the "touches of sweet harmony" from the heavens, did God's infinite mercy allow these deeply flawed characters to hear for an instant the spiritual harmony within their souls urging them to aspire to more perfect lives. The most notable omission in the play was the character of Old Gobbo, whose part was cut along with approximately two hundred lines of verse and prose, especially in act 2, scene 2; act 3, scene 4; act 3, scene 5; and act 5, scene 1.

The controversy began immediately after the production's opening night. Initial newspaper reviews were largely positive, including praise from such diverse sources as the *San Francisco Chronicle, Sacramento Bee, San Jose Mercury News, Richmond Post, San Mateo Times, Bellingham Herald, Medford Mail Tribune,* and *Ashland Daily Tidings.* "I've never seen Shakespeare staged or spoken with such flair and acuity," wrote Gerald Nachman in the *Chronicle* (June 26, 1991); "honest...superb...breathtaking...[and] marvelous," said Janos Gereben in the *Richmond Post* (February 27, 1991); and *"The Merchant of Venice* is...a stunningly opulent" play that makes us "laugh in deadly earnest," according to Peter Haugen in the *Sacramento Bee* (March 3, 1991).

Several international Shakespeare scholars and theatre professionals were equally pleased. Coppelia Kahn, for example, author of a number of influential books and articles on Shakespeare, wrote Appel that the production

> seamlessly joined the contemporary setting to the Shakespeare text. It worked. The glamorous, shallow, chic Venetians you updated to Giorgio Armani matched the tense, self-contradictory characters I know. Shylock was dignified, unsentimentalized, poignant. And the Bassanio-Antonio relationship was perfectly phrased: the older man restraining his passion and resigned to losing his love, but trying to sink in hooks of gratitude nonetheless. The sets and costuming were smashing; never a distraction, always working with the text to make its meaning.

Similarly Royal Shakespeare Company actor and director Tony Church wrote Appel that he was "delighted" with her production:

> Your grasp of the imagery and, in particular, the world of Antonio and his "good friends," as you describe them, is wonderful. The genuine sophistication, the stylish designs, and the cool wit make Venice an exciting place. I have never seen the "Salads" [Salerio and Solanio] played better. Bill Bloodgood's set designs are the right designs for the play in any period—that is, very clever—and Deborah [Dryden]'s costumes get wittier and even

sharper in Belmont. At last, a Portia who is a real highlife heiress. I thought Liisa [Ivary] had exactly the right mixture of intellectual strength and personal vulnerability, and that young lad Dion [Luther] was quite the best Bassanio I've encountered—really pretty and really cool.

Despite such widespread acclaim, criticism dogged the production from the beginning. A few mainstream newspaper reviewers found minor problems with the show, in particular with the casting and characterization, but the bulk of the negative comments were written and/or orchestrated by a small group of local Jewish theatregoers led by David Zaslow, an Ashland teacher, author of children's books, and rabbinical intern. Though he admitted that "the production, in artistic terms, is brilliant," Zaslow made the following complaints in a number of newspaper reviews and guest editorials: the modern setting made the production especially painful to Jewish viewers because it brought the inherent racism of Shakespeare's less-enlightened age into the present and helped perpetuate, rather than diminish, current anti-Semitic stereotypes; the use of Hebrew religious symbols and garments such as yarmulkes, prayer shawls, and the Star of David was sacrilegious and insulting to Jewish viewers; Shylock's one great speech, the "hath not a Jew eyes" monologue in act 3, scene 1 was all but drowned out by the jeering Salerio and Solanio, preventing the audience from hearing the single-most-important plea for sympathy in the script; and the festival should have done a better job of preparing its audiences to see and respond to the production through handouts, preplay and postplay symposia, and other educational outreach.

At the conclusion of his April 1991 theatre review in the Ashland *Lithiagraph,* Zaslow asked festival artistic director Jerry Turner to make six specific changes in the show:

(1) Remove the *yarmulkes* from Shylock and Tubal; (2) dignify Shylock's main speech; (3) have a one-page educational handout available for elementary and secondary age children and their teachers who come to see the play; (4) print a simple and clear statement about the nature of stereotypes in the *Playbill;* (5) have post-play discussions after every performance as the Festival did

last year for *God's Country*; and (6) script a few lines to be spoken to the audience before the play to clarify the fact that Shylock does not represent modern Jews or Judaism as the play implies.[1]

Turner responded that he would not make any changes in the production itself, citing the principles of artistic integrity and freedom of expression inherent in theatre. In a guest-opinion column in the *Mail Tribune,* he explained that demanding changes in a production because of possible misunderstandings "not only smacks of censorship, it is censorship. If I thought," he continued,

> *The Merchant of Venice* was merely a hateful anti-Semitic tract, we would not produce it in a post-Holocaust world. But Libby Appel's production is not that; it is a sensitive and intelligent (albeit painful) interpretation of 400-year-old themes from a contemporary perspective. It may well be misunderstood by some viewers (though it is surprising how much criticism comes from people who haven't seen it), but that's a risk one takes in a lot of Shakespeare's plays.[2]

Turner did agree, however, to arrange postplay discussions following the performances and distribute to student audiences a seven-page article by publicity and publications associate Beth Bardossi that had originally appeared in *Illuminations,* one of the festival magazines. "Maybe we have become overly sensitive to this issue," Bardossi explained in her essay. "Given the treatment of Jews throughout history, however, it is difficult to ignore. What may have been acceptable as comedy to an Elizabethan audience is not necessarily acceptable as comedy today. The Holocaust and the resurgence of the white supremacist movement, particularly in the Pacific Northwest, create a new frame of reference for *The Merchant of Venice.*"[3]

Despite this concession by Turner, the controversy continued to grow. A battle for "ownership" of the play commenced that pitted the festival,

1. David Zaslow, letter to the editor, *Lithiagraph*, April 1991.
2. Jerry Turner, letter to the editor, *Medford Mail Tribune*, May 7, 1991.
3. Beth Bardossi, *Illuminations*, summer 1991.

the director, and the actors against a small segment of the community who felt a proprietary right and responsibility to effect changes in a production that trespassed against their ethical and religious values. Zaslow published four other articles on the production, all of which were either reprints or revisions of the original *Lithiagraph* review; these appeared in the *Jewish Journal* (April 26, 1991), *Ashland Daily Tidings* (May 22, 1991), *Seattle Jewish Transcript* (June 28, 1991), and *San Francisco Jewish Bulletin* (July 12, 1991).

The debate was also picked up by a number of larger newspapers and journals that examined the issue in some detail: the *Los Angeles Times*, *Christian Science Monitor*, and *Theatre Week* (which titled its piece "P.C. or Not P.C.?"). In addition, the New York office of the Anti-Defamation League sent several members of the design team and acting company offprints of an article by Morris Schappes entitled "Shylock and Anti-Semitism," which argued that *"The Merchant of Venice* is anti-Semitic in its structure and backbone" and should never be produced.[4]

Guest-opinion columns also began to proliferate in local Oregon newspapers. Medford resident Victor Abel, for example, charged in a *Mail Tribune* article that Appel's production "reinforces the blatant, anti-Semitic lies of Shakespeare's day and proposes them as a fact of modern times. We are aghast at the effect this may be having on the thousands of school children attending special showings of the play."[5] Willamette University Professor Todd Silverstein referred to the play in a *Daily Tidings* editorial as "a gloriously racist spectacle…appreciated by a secretly anti-Semitic audience. If this play were as contemptuous of Blacks as it is of Jews," he asked rhetorically, "do you think a White theatre company would be performing it in this day and age?… So it seems that Jews are fair game but Blacks are not."[6] Abel wrote another critique in the *Daily Tidings* that excoriated the director for alleged ethnic caricatures: "Ms. Appel, we have questions for you. Since you claim to have been seeking authenticity in a modern setting; since you set the Jew as if from New York; why didn't you set the Venetians in the same milieu? How else are

---

4. Morris Schappes, "Shylock and Anti-Semitism," *Jewish Current,* June 1962.
5. Victor Abel, letter to the editor, *Medford Mail Tribune,* April 7, 1991.
6. Todd Silverstein, letter to the editor, *Ashland Daily Tidings,* May 30, 1991.

we supposed to know they are Italians? Can't you hear it? 'Hey, gombar, what's-a new on-a dah Rialto?'"[7]

Among the many articles and letters responding to such attacks on the play, two are particularly interesting. The first, by *San Francisco Chronicle* columnist Gerald Nachman, argued that Zaslow's original review

> insults the intelligence of any playgoer fortunate enough to see this remarkably lucid and, most of all, even-handed treatment of Shylock. Zaslow's complaints parrot the usual, and tired, cant that the play is anti-Semitic, when in fact it's not the play that's anti-Semitic, or Shakespeare, but the characters in the play.... What makes the play great, and this production especially powerful (enough to disturb the narrow sensibilities of Jews like Zaslow more interested in public relations than the roots of prejudice and counter-prejudice by anti-gentile Jews), is that it goes easy on nobody.

Nachman charged that Zaslow's attitude was "patronizing," as if "Jews need to be protected from the play, and as if non-Jews should not be allowed to see it for fear they're not smart enough to figure it out and to realize it isn't about Jews, it's about one Jew." To counter Zaslow's contention that Appel's production inflicted "gratuitous pain" upon its viewers, Nachman responded that "theatre isn't about promoting self-esteem, or presenting positive images and role models. It's about human beings and why they are what they are.... Moreover, the point [of the play] is to *cause* pain, even if it disturbs the wholesome view of 16th-century Roman society that Zaslow would prefer to see presented [italics in original]."[8]

A second article taking issue with criticisms of the production was written by Rabbi Dan Isaac of Temple Emek Shalom in Ashland—the synagogue where David Zaslow was a rabbinical intern. In his essay, Isaac refers to Appel's production as "cool and distancing, more in the mode of

7. Victor Abel, letter to the editor, *Ashland Daily Tidings*, June 3, 1991.

8. Gerald Nachman, letter to the editor, *Northern California Jewish Bulletin*, July 19, 1991.

Brecht than traditional Shakespeare. As a result, Shylock...is stripped of the qualities that would render him sympathetic. And it is precisely this that has caused pain and aroused the ire of some of the more vocal members of the Jewish community." Although he affirmed Zaslow's right to express his discontent, Isaac stopped well short of approving any censorship of the production:

> When David Zaslow states that "it is the modern director's duty to bring out Shylock's noblest qualities, and to play down the problems inherent in the script," I fear we are perilously close to the objectionable situation of one special interest group dictating doctrines of correctness for the public arena of artistic representation. To demand a change in the production is as much a move toward censorship as calling for a change in the text. Only if a text and production were likely to incite violent behavior would such demands be legitimate. The beauty and difficulty of living as an American in a democracy is that occasionally people are going to say things we desperately do not want to hear. The beauty and difficulty of this current production of *The Merchant of Venice* is that it abrasively confronts and forces us to consider the significance and sociodynamics of prejudicial stereotyping.[9]

One final event rounded out the chronology of controversy associated with Ashland's production of *Merchant.* In mid-June, Jerry Turner retired as longtime artistic director of the festival; his successor, actor and director Henry Woronicz, was immediately asked by Zaslow's group to provide audiences with some explanation of the disparity between contemporary anti-Semitism and the treatment of Jews during Shakespeare's time. In an understandable effort to satisfy those offended by the production, Woronicz took several quotations about Renaissance Judaism from a handout provided by the Anti-Defamation League and the American Jewish Committee, had them enlarged to poster size, and then placed them in the theatre lobby for audiences to view prior to the performances. The opening paragraph of the display read as follows:

9. Rabbi Dan Isaac, letter to the editor, *Medford Mail Tribune,* May 9, 1991.

The history of cultural domination the world over—one culture dictating "rights" for another—has produced serious and eternal scars in the evolution of our society. Nowhere in literature is this more self-evident than in Shakespeare's *The Merchant of Venice*. Unfortunately, the character of Shylock as written bears the marks of stereotypical villainy; therefore, when produced on stage, it is important to broaden and deepen this perspective to something more realistic and recognizable. A clear historical perspective shows why the role of Shylock was written stereotypically and why it is essential in a more enlightened time to provide a deeper portrayal of the character on stage.

When the actors discovered the poster, however, they immediately petitioned Woronicz as a group to have it removed, arguing that the display trespassed unfairly on the audience's preplay consciousness and undercut one of the production's principal points: anti-Semitism is, unfortunately, still alive and well in the twentieth century just as it was during the Renaissance. Woronicz agreed with the actors: art was becoming propaganda. The poster, which had been up for only one performance, was promptly taken down.

What conclusions can we draw, then, from this summary of events concerning Ashland's 1991 production of *Merchant*, and how does the controversy help us answer the types of questions raised at the outset of this article? To begin with, no one could doubt the sincerity and passion with which both sides advanced their arguments. Articulate spokespersons from both camps proved that productions investigating the boundaries of ethnic sensitivity are likely to erupt at any time into heated debates about the limits of artistic freedom versus the rights of audience members who feel insulted or aggrieved. Despite occasional low blows aimed at "publicity seeking Jews" and "self-hating Jews," the dialogue maintained a fairly respectful level throughout the summer.

Judging from the intensity of complaints about the production, it seems clear that updating the script to modern Venice *did* make the experience of seeing the show more painful for many Jewish viewers—but only because anti-Semitism is still painfully prevalent in today's world. If it were not, the production would not have been so difficult for some audience members to endure. Imagine, for example, a modernized version of a Renaissance play about the evils of astrology. Since we are not so addicted to stargazing as our sixteenth-century counterparts, such an updated production would seem merely quaint and anachronistic.

Not so with *The Merchant of Venice,* however. At the beginning of the rehearsal period in mid-January, SCUD missiles were raining down on Israel, which provided a sure sign that high-tech anti-Semitism still flourished. We need no Roderigo Lopez (the Portuguese Jewish physician executed for allegedly plotting to kill Queen Elizabeth in 1594) to remind us that Judaism is under attack in the modern world, especially after the well-documented horrors of the Holocaust. In fact, the chronological correspondence between the Middle-East war and the litany of complaints over the Ashland production help affirm the interesting theory that criticism of twentieth-century productions of *Merchant* has been most virulent when Israel was under attack by its enemies.

In retrospect could the festival have done anything to help diffuse the unhappiness generated by this production? Two principal actions were possible, though each presented difficulties. The first, suggested by several critics of the show, was that the festival should have consulted with local Jewish leaders prior to the beginning of rehearsals. Although such a gesture might have calmed some of the anguish and apprehension that often accompany productions of the play, it would have created additional problems. Who should speak for the Jewish community, for example, and how widespread should that community be? Would it be limited to the Ashland area? All of Oregon? The western United States? America in general? Besides, when two leaders such as Rabbi Isaac and David Zaslow from the same synagogue clearly disagree, who should be trusted? If such prerehearsal meetings were held, what should be the exact role of the Jewish leaders? Conferences intended merely as an opportunity to ventilate opinions would offer false hope that people outside the theatre actually have input into the creative process. And if these comments did have demonstrable influence over the concept of the production, isn't this de facto censorship? Imagine a prerehearsal conference during which Zaslow might have argued that the Ashland production should not be updated, not use any Jewish religious symbols, and not portray Shylock in an unsympathetic manner. Such demands would have clearly infringed upon the autonomy and artistic integrity of the director and the producing theatre.

The second concession the festival could have made to Zaslow and other critics would have been to accede to one or more of their demands, such as dignifying Shylock's "hath not a Jew eyes" speech or removing some of the Jewish symbols in the production, like yarmulkes and prayer shawls. Turner, Isaac, and Nachman are surely right in their assertions, however, that such changes would have constituted a surrender to censorship. A brief examination of Shylock's speech helps clarify the point. During rehearsals Appel and Elmore became convinced that these famous lines—which are often played as a plea for sympathy and ethnic sensitivity—are in fact a vicious and cold-blooded justification of revenge: "And if you wrong us, shall we not revenge? If we are like you in the rest, we will resemble you in that" (3.1.68–70). For critics of the production to reject that interpretation is a good example of the *expectational fallacy:* they expected the scene to be played a certain "correct" way and then disagreed because the interpretation did not fulfill their expectation. Appel's decision to have Salerio, Solanio, and the rest of the Christians jeer Shylock during his speech was absolutely in keeping with her concept of the production, which focused on the sins of all the characters. No one was portrayed in a sympathetic manner. Shylock was driven to commit an act of revenge because of the way his Christian persecutors treated him. To deliver the speech any other way would, therefore, have been a serious affront to the director's interpretation of the script.

The same reasoning justifies the desecration of religious symbols in the play. To help sever her familial and ethnic connection with her father, for example, Jessica wrapped the stolen jewels and coins in his prayer shawl before she gave them to Lorenzo—a vivid rejection of Judaism calculated to destroy her past and ingratiate herself with her new husband and his Christian friends.

Ultimately, the play was allowed to stand on its own—unchanged, uncensored, and unaccompanied by prefatory explanations of any kind. What emerged, as a result, was a superb production that illustrated—if anyone needed further proof—that *The Merchant of Venice* is a living dramatic document still subject to the vicissitudes of growth and reassessment attendant on all great art. The themes and images that make it painful to watch also confer greatness on it. The controversy surrounding the production was, therefore, proof of the play's vitality. Ironically, Zaslow helped ensure that the play will continue to be one of Shakespeare's most frequently produced. Controversy sells, and theatrical controversy sold in this case at 96 percent of capacity. The debate also confirmed the universal truth that theatre is not responsible for fulfilling the political, social, or moral agenda of any single group of people. Nor should artistic decisions be made according to whose ox is being gored at any particular time.

The most we can ask of plays like *Merchant* is that they move us, challenge us, and stimulate our deepest emotions. If the production accomplishes that, it has done its job. As Franz Kafka argued in another context, "I think we ought to read only the kind of books that wound and stab us. If the book we're reading doesn't wake us up with a blow on the head, what are we reading it for?"[10] The same can be said, of course, about plays.

Shakespeare would, no doubt, have been pleased by the debate. He would also have been glad that David Zaslow, like all others who published opinions on the production, played his part in the eternal dance of theatre—the critical give and take that helps bring meaning to our shared dramatic experiences. This dance should also, if we are fortunate, warn us against such social evils as religious hypocrisy and persecution, rather than furthering their pernicious effects. Actors act, and audiences respond: the ritual is ancient and productive. In the final analysis, many people in Ashland became sellers of merchandise during the spring and summer of 1991: Turner and Woronicz sold the festival and protected it from its detractors; Appel and her actors sold their vision of this exciting script; and Zaslow and others both defended and sold their own concept of Judaism. Everyone involved with the controversy became a merchant to some extent, which would have pleased Shakespeare most of all.

10. Franz Kafka to Oskar Pollak, January 27, 1904.

Rehearsing the Audience

The 1989 Utah Shakespeare Festival

Those of us who have worked at the Utah Shakespeare Festival for many seasons are always delighted to welcome newcomers to Cedar City, where approximately 35 percent of our audience members see their first festival plays each year and 25 percent experience their first live, professional Shakespearean production of any kind. I'd like to offer these new spectators a few tips to help increase your appreciation of this summer's productions. If you follow these suggestions, your "rehearsal" time can be just as important and effective as ours in preparing for the plays.

A DISCLAIMER

My first bit of advice is to ignore the rest of my advice. No one has yet defined the "right" way to watch a play, and I won't be foolish enough to attempt it here. No production worth its theatrical salt requires prior knowledge by the audience. Many directors, in fact, prefer their spectators to arrive at the theatre in a state of cultural innocence so the performance will have an entirely fresh and spontaneous effect. The counterargument, of course, is that the more you know about the play you are going to see, the better equipped you will be to appreciate its deeper mysteries.

WARM-UP EXERCISES

The simplest and often most effective way of rehearsing for the play is to read it before you see it. Does this strategy eliminate the suspense? Of course. But it also reveals subtle nuances in the text that would have been lost if you had not known the plot beforehand. If you can't make time to read the play prior to seeing it, you may want to look over the plot synopsis provided in the program. In addition, just as an athlete warms up before competition, you can discuss with a friend or relative some of the major themes in the theatrical event you are about to witness. In *Macbeth*, for example, some of the central issues are ambition, power, fate, free will, and prophecy; in *The Winter's Tale*, they include jealousy, renewal, forgiveness, and love; and in *The Tempest,* anger, revenge, blessing, magic, and reconciliation. After rehearsing (literally "rehearing") such topics, you will be in much better shape for the dramatic experience ahead.

SET DESIGN

Another technique to sharpen and refine your dramatic sensibilities is to focus on specific theatrical elements in each production. In terms of set design, ask yourself what sort of world these characters inhabit. Why, for example, does a huge crown dominate the scenic design of *Macbeth?* Why the asymmetrical display of broken armor? How does designer Ron Ranson signal evil and intrigue through his use of shape, size, texture, and color onstage? In *The Winter's Tale,* how does he distinguish between the hard, angular, male-dominated world of Sicilia and the softer, vibrant, feminine locale of Bohemia? And how does Tom Benson's set for *The Tempest* reflect the magic, energy, clarity, and power of Prospero's special island?

COSTUMING

Similarly consider the way costuming imparts meaning to the various plays by looking especially for color, shape, texture, and design. Although actors wear costumes, characters wear clothes; consequently, we can make some fairly accurate assumptions about the people in these plays from the clothing they select. In *The Winter's Tale,* for instance, costume designer Beth Novak makes a radical shift from dark, Rembrandt-inspired costumes in Sicilia to the earlier and more colorful Bruegelian fashions of Bohemia. To what extent does this geographical dichotomy match Ranson's parallel change in set design? How do the witches dress in *Macbeth?* And what effect does their supernatural attire (or lack thereof) have on Macbeth's responsibility for his fatal actions? In *The Tempest,* what kinds of clothes do Ariel, Caliban, Prospero, and Miranda wear?

LIGHTING

The best and most effective work by lighting, sound, and music designers calls little attention to itself but, rather, seems natural and appropriate within its own dramatic world. If you look carefully, however, you can learn a great deal about the plays from these important technical elements. Proper lighting lets you know where you are onstage—the season, the time of day, the temperature, and whether you are indoors or outdoors. It also focuses attention and creates dramatic mood through subtle variations in color, intensity, and direction. Be aware of the way lighting designer Liz Stillwell uses follow spots to single out certain characters in the opening scenes of *The Winter's Tale* and employs gobo effects to make springtime, leafy patterns onstage later in the same play. How does she create the early storm in *The Tempest?* And the gloomy mood of *Macbeth?*

SOUND AND MUSIC

Festival composer Christine Frezza and sound designer Stephen Shaffer have been busy for several months preparing the aural environment you will experience onstage this summer. *The Winter's Tale,* for example, has fourteen musical pieces and four entire songs while *The Tempest* features more than fifty distinct sound cues. These moments of music and sound alternately set the mood of a particular scene, underscore important words and phrases, tell us the time of day, and distinguish major characters (who are often accompanied by unique melodies). Occasionally music is the voice of a character who does not speak, like Hermione in the jail scene or Leontes in his study in *The Winter's Tale.* Music also puts Miranda to sleep, awakens Hermione's statue, heightens tension prior to the murder of Duncan, and performs a myriad of other important functions in these plays.

TRUSTING THE SCRIPT

Most importantly, don't be afraid of Shakespeare. Well-crafted productions like the ones you are about to see make the plays clear. If you miss a few words or phrases, be patient; the language of the stage explains all important details soon enough. Since plays both "speak" and "show," we can understand them in a variety of complementary ways: intellectually, emotionally, visually, viscerally, and imaginatively. We may not, however, understand absolutely everything. The best productions, like life itself, maintain a certain mystery. As opposed to television, which never dares confuse us, Shakespeare's dramas often leave us in suspense about certain salient details. We will never know, for example, why Macduff leaves his wife and children, why Duncan is so trusting, why Leontes suspects his wife's fidelity, why Prospero forgives his enemies. Great art is inexhaustible and impenetrable like the witches' prophesies.

A FINAL THOUGHT

In conclusion don't expect literal correspondence between the stage world and the real one. The shipwreck in *The Tempest* does not look exactly like a shipwreck; hopefully no one is actually killed in the battle scenes of *Macbeth*. This distinction between art and life is intentional and crucial to the dramatic experience. In return for your ticket price, the theatre sells you the chance to dream for a few hours—a rare luxury in a world that grows more literal minded and simplistic every day. Those of us who direct and design and act these plays need you, therefore, to make them complete. Your imagination must help create the ghosts, apparitions, lovers, bears, and goddesses in your heart and mind. For this reason, the theatre exists only at that one special moment in time when your rehearsal meets our rehearsal, when your imagination and preparation join ours to bring these plays to life.

Designing the Script

The 1990 Utah Shakespeare Festival

I think I've got the most exciting job at the festival, though few people know what I do. In the program I'm listed as dramaturg, which is a title little understood beyond the immediate world of professional theatre. Even my own mother has trouble explaining to her friends exactly what services I perform. So, for my mom and anyone else who is interested, here is a description of what a dramaturg does to help create the productions you are about to see.

My primary responsibility is to aid the directors, designers, and actors in understanding the language of the play they are producing. If costume designers design costumes and set designers design sets, then I assist in designing the script of the play: the words, the stage directions, the punctuation, the cutting and shaping of the scenes, and everything else associated with deciphering, evaluating, and explaining the black marks on the white page that we refer to as Shakespeare's plays.

My work begins early in the process of shaping the productions. Although different directors use me in different ways, a general chronological outline of my various duties looks something like this. Approximately nine months prior to the start of each season, I am one of the first members of the artistic team with whom the director talks. Usually we have a few lengthy phone calls (or at least a flurry of letters or e-mails) concerning the overall concept for the production. At this stage, I am a sounding board and also a quality-control officer. If I think the idea for the play clashes seriously with the text's inherent integrity, I have a duty to speak up.

During this early stage of developing the production, I am also responsible for finding and sending the directors research materials on any aspect of the text that needs further investigation. This information can range, for example, from books and articles on Scottish history for a production of *Macbeth* to drawings of arcane seventeenth-century French medical instruments for *The Imaginary Invalid*. I once dramaturged a production at the La Jolla Playhouse where an actress had to impersonate British Prime Minister Margaret Thatcher doing a striptease. Part of my research for that show consisted of locating old TV news videotapes of Thatcher and finding a real-life striptease artist, who came to the theatre for a week and gave the actress bump-and-grind lessons. My doctoral training never prepared me for that kind of assignment!

During January and February, I continue supplying research materials to the directors, and I make photocopies of the earliest-existing sixteenth- and seventeenth-century editions of the plays. I either suggest cuts to the directors or respond when they send me their edited copies of the scripts. At this stage, I also recommend which modern edition of the plays the actors should use. I may begin writing program notes, and I consult with the various designers about the textual accuracy of such decisions as whether the moon in *A Midsummer Night's Dream* should be full or a crescent, whether Cassio in *Othello* should have a beard (remember Iago's claim that he saw Cassio "wipe his beard" with Desdemona's handkerchief?), and whether the severed hands and heads in *Titus Andronicus* must actually appear onstage.

After the March production conference in Cedar City, when plans for the plays are confirmed and the summer production schedule is set, I go over the script of each play in great detail, making careful notes about the meanings of words, versification, scansion, rhyme, meter, staging possibilities, textual variants among different editions, and other discoveries that will help me explore the script with the actors in May and June when rehearsals begin. I do this work with the actors individually or in small groups, striving always to help them understand clearly what their characters are saying and equip them with a knowledge of the primary interpretive options available in each line of dialogue. If I do this phase of my job properly, the actors' subsequent work with the director should go smoothly because we have built the foundation of the production on a solid and thorough understanding of Shakespeare's language. If the script is the very center—the heart of any production of Shakespeare—it must be interpreted clearly and consistently and with the highest regard for textual accuracy. My job at the festival is to help see that this happens. So, Mom, if you're listening, what could be more exciting than that?

Cymbeline IN THE WOODEN O

The 2002 Utah Shakespeare Festival

As company dramaturg at the Utah Shakespeare Festival for the past nineteen years, I have had the privilege of serving on design teams for more than sixty professional Shakespearean productions, but none more exciting than our 2002 production of *Cymbeline,* one of the bard's most difficult and challenging plays. Replete with at least fifty characters, an episodic, sprawling narrative, and a denouement featuring twenty-four separate plot revelations in the final breathless scene, the play demands much in its transition from page to stage. In the following article, I take the reader behind the scenes in our work on this fascinating show, moving chronologically from the earliest stages of the process to design meetings, casting, rehearsals, and, finally, opening night.

Approximately two years prior to the beginning of rehearsals, the play was selected by the festival's team of producers: Fred Adams (founder and executive producer), Douglas Cook and Cameron Harvey (producing artistic directors), and Scott Phillips (executive director). Adding special poignancy to the season, Doug Cook retired this year after nearly four decades at the festival and was replaced by Associate Artistic Directors Jim Sullivan and Kathleen Conlin (who has also done a fine job as our casting director for several years). The play was then sequenced in with two other Shakespearean productions in the outdoor Adams Theatre—*Othello* and *As You Like It*—and three plays in the indoor Randall L. Jones Theatre—*Harvey, Hay Fever,* and *Man of La Mancha.* Production schedules were roughed out, publicity and fund-raising began, and the script started its inexorable progress toward performance.

4. *Cymbeline,* 2002. Michael David Edwards as Iachimo and Susan Shunk as Imogen. Photo by Karl Hugh. Published with permission of the Utah Shakespeare Festival.

In July 2001, verbal commitments were made with the director of the play, New Yorker Russell Treyz, whose brilliant talents had been displayed previously at the festival in *King John* (1998), *A Midsummer Night's Dream* (1999), and *The Pirates of Penzance* (2001), and would soon be seen in *Around the World in Eighty Days* (fall 2001). By October 1, the director, designers, and lead staff members were contracted, including veterans Bill Forrester (scenic design), Janice Benning (costumes), Donna Ruzika (lighting), Christine Frezza (composer), Amanda French (hair and makeup), Robin McFarquhar (fight director), Karen Wegner (production stage manager), and myself (dramaturg). Since most of us have been involved with many different productions at the festival, we work together smoothly, each equipped with a well-defined role, abundant artistic energy, and genuine respect for other members of the design team.

The actual creative process began when Russ sent us his director's notes in early November, which expressed his vision for the play, broke the script into different scenic locations, discussed characterization, and suggested a starting point for eventual decisions about set design, costumes, lighting, music, and all the other important theatrical elements. For example, Russ explained in these early design notes that

> Cymbeline seems to jump between four different worlds: the fairy tale society of Cymbeline's court, the Renaissance excess of Philario's court, the ancient Roman civilization of Caius Lucius and his legions, and the primitive society of Belarius and his two sons. I would like to create our own world that encompasses all of these worlds.... Instead of basing the design on particular periods and styles, I'd like to invent our own storybook location for the play. Cymbeline's court is elegant and simple; Philario's is decadent; Rome is more formal and military; and Belarius inhabits the natural world.... I would like to keep the setting to a minimum. I'll need some levels and seating areas to break up the stage, but overall I'd like to depend on the costumes and props to indicate the shift of locale rather than any major changing of scenery.

Equipped with these suggestions, each of the designers worked for the next two months on creating a plan for the production that would flesh out his or her area of responsibility. For instance, Bill Forrester constructed a scale model of the set along with several computerized scenic designs while Janice Benning gathered costume ideas from many different sources and created sample sketches of the main characters that included fabric swatches, trim, and hair/makeup ideas. During the same time period, I put together a big research book on the play that featured material on ancient Britain, reviews of previous productions, and other pertinent information to share with the director, designers, and (eventually) the actors at the beginning of rehearsals. Russ and I also began the task of cutting the script to the two-and-one-half-hour running time requested by the producers.

In early January, approximately six months before the play opened in Cedar City, all the directors, designers, and key festival personnel were flown to Los Angeles, where, at the Doubletree Hotel near LAX, we put together all six professional productions, three Greenshows, and a Royal Feaste in four whirlwind days of intense and exciting meetings. We began our *Cymbeline* sessions sharing all the work we had done in the past two

months, including Bill's proposed set designs, Janice's costume renderings, Donna's initial thoughts about lighting, and Christine's early suggestions about music and sound effects. We also talked about how to deal
with problem areas in the text, such as the headless corpse, the eagle, the
appearance of Jupiter, the ghosts, the battle scenes, and getting Iachimo's
chest on and offstage. The tables around which we worked were littered
with photographs, pieces of fabric, scale models of the set, and books
such as Terri Hardin's *The Pre-Raphaelites,* M. P. Vernevil's *Behind Golden
Screens: Treasures from the Tokyo Fuji Art Museum*, Miranda Green's *Celtic
Art* (including gorgeous pictures of Wales), and designer Issey Miyake's
Making Things. Finally, we did a scene-by-scene analysis of the script, during which design-team members began narrowing down choices in each
conceptual area of the production.

Decisions at this stage ricocheted into many different design areas.
Based on Russ's original concept notes, we opted for simplicity of design with Asian and Celtic overtones. A single "mythic" set would be
used with red curtains around the inner below to represent Philario's
residence; a throne, banners, and the slip stage for Britain; costumes and
music to suggest Rome; and translucent Oriental shoji panels illuminated
by strip lights for Wales. Because of the space required for the lighting instruments, we wouldn't be able to use staircases; as a result, we knew we
would need ramps and voms to bring characters on and offstage, which
meant that the aisles of the theatre would have to be lit. Since the 8:00 p.m.
curtain time is still broad daylight in the outdoor theatre, we transposed
two scenes in the script so we would be in Wales after dark, and the back-
lit scrims would then be visible to the audience.

Costumes began to take on an Arthurian motif with lots of animal
skins and human flesh in Wales, reds and golds in Italy, and rich, satu-
rated colors in Cymbeline's court. Christine's preliminary musical plot
included concert harp and viola for Britain; snare drum, wood block, and
cymbals for Rome; and primitive wind instruments for Wales. We also
decided that Guiderius and Arviragus would sing and the parts of Posthumus and Cloten would be doubled, which meant that Kathleen Conlin
would have to consider this when she cast the roles.

Following the January conference, all members of the design team
continued working on their respective areas. The set was further refined
and modified, and scale architectural drawings were produced; more

precise costume sketches were created, which included swatches of the specific fabrics; the lighting design was developed; music was composed; and I finished the cuts, sent the edited script to the festival, began writing song lyrics, and worked on the program notes. In the meantime, Kathleen auditioned more than six hundred actors in six different cities, craftspeople were hired, and publicity specialists and box-office personnel began selling tickets. The festival machine was ratcheting up toward full intensity.

Our next big group meeting was in Cedar City on March 14–17, when—surrounded by new-fallen snow—we expanded to a much wider circle of designers and technicians, including those responsible for hair and makeup, stage fighting, choreography, sound design, music, props, electrics, set construction, costume crafts, publicity, graphic design, and a host of other specialties. Bill Forrester shared his newly revised set design, Janice Benning showed her latest costume renderings and her drawing of Jupiter's eagle, and a preliminary cost analysis of materials and labor was begun. At this same meeting, all scenery, costume, and prop lists were finalized; music and sound cues were due; and a careful scene-by-scene review of the script took place to make certain we had prepared for all possible problems inherent in the production. We also determined which scenes and characters would be photographed for the souvenir program, decided which scenic elements would be moved indoors in the event of rain, and finalized rehearsal schedules.

On May 6, seven weeks before opening, all the actors convened for the first read-through, which is always a joyous time of seeing old friends and making new ones. Following several days of table work, during which the actors and director explored the script in great detail, everyone moved to the Adams stage for outdoor blocking rehearsals. Each show rehearsed for sixteen hours per week for seven weeks, although—discounting previews and dress rehearsals—the actors only had approximately one hundred hours to prepare for each production. During the same time, actors memorized their lines, were fitted for costumes, had voice and dramaturgical sessions, began the hair and makeup process, and participated in photo calls, media interviews, and dance and fight rehearsals. Simultaneously the sets were built, props were constructed and placed in their cabinet, wigs were prepared, and costumes were completed.

After all this frantic preparation, *Cymbeline* opened on June 25 to packed houses, appreciative audiences, and admiring reviews. It played twice a week on Tuesdays and Fridays from opening until August 30 and was seen by more than twenty-two thousand spectators—96 percent of capacity. Blessed by the regenerative love between Imogen and Posthumus, the primitive goodness of Wales, the benign magic of Jupiter, and months of hard work by hundreds of talented people, our production was extremely successful. And just when we had begun to savor that delicious feeling of a job well done, the process started all over again with a new season and six new plays!

The Kindest Cut of All

Editing Shakespeare's Scripts for Performance

So you're the guy who cut my favorite line in Macbeth.

Where was Old Gobbo? He's the best character in the show.

I paid my fifty-eight dollars; I want to see the whole *play!*
Are you going to cut the price of my ticket like you cut the script?

During my twenty-two-year career as company dramaturg at the Utah Shakespeare Festival (USF), I've heard a number of similar comments about my role in editing scripts for performance (though this is only a small part of my job). Few of these aggrieved patrons are placated by the suggestion that the many variant early quarto and folio editions of Shakespeare's plays hint tantalizingly that the author edited his own scripts for productions at different times and in different venues. Nor are they persuaded that the Prologue's reference in *Romeo and Juliet* (a play that runs well over four hours in a contemporary uncut production) to "the two hours' traffic of our stage" (12) is anything less than dramatic hyperbole. "Everyone knows," they argue, "that Elizabethan actors spoke much faster than modern ones do." Risking fanny fatigue à la *The Life and Adventures of Nicholas Nickleby*, they want the whole play and nothing but the play, even if Gertrude drinks her poison considerably after the midnight chimes.

One of life's great ironies is that I am entirely sympathetic to these arguments. To paraphrase Morocco in *The Merchant of Venice*, I hope audiences will "mislike me not" for my profession. As befits someone who started out as an English professor and then segued into the world of professional theatre, I cherish every word in the plays. In fact, theatregoers should be deliriously happy that someone like me is helping to cut the scripts since every word or phrase I delete is like ripping out a small piece of my still-beating heart.

I learned early in my theatrical apprenticeship, however, that the languid pace of reading Shakespeare's plays in the comfort of your own study or teaching the whole play to a group of undergraduate students must of necessity give way to the Realpolitik of the theatrical profession, where many different factors dictate the permissible length of a Shakespearean production. Since almost all theatres cut most of their Shakespearean plays, the question is not whether to slice and dice but how to make the best textual recipe possible while performing this necessary task. Consequently, I'd like to list the "top ten" determining factors in hopes of illuminating the exceptionally complex and often angst-ridden process of editing Shakespeare's plays for production. I also hope the following confessional essay about editorial practices at the USF inspires a dialogue among dramaturgs and literary managers at other theatres, where procedures may differ significantly from ours.

ABIDING BY TIME RESTRICTIONS

First (no surprise here), the length of our productions in Utah is initially dictated by our producers' desire to keep the plays between two and a half to three hours' running time (including one fifteen-minute intermission), which they have long felt is a comfortable length of time for audience members to remain in their seats. At the rate of a thousand lines of poetry per hour of stage time, this means that a play like *Hamlet*, sporting nearly 3,780 lines, must be cut by some 1,000 to fit into our procrustean theatrical bed. In fact, Fred Adams, our founder, and R. Scott Phillips, our executive director, start fidgeting if the shows run more than two and three-quarter hours. As a result, we have a mandate that the curtain must come down metaphorically by 11:00 p.m., based on a starting time of 8:00 in the evening.

Though this is relatively easy with shorter plays like *The Comedy of Errors* or *The Tempest*, it can be extremely difficult with one like *King Lear* or *Othello,* where audience members know the lines so well that they often mouth the words along with the actors. Several years ago, in fact, during the prince's crucial act 3, scene 1 soliloquy in *Hamlet* at the USF, the actor playing the title role followed the words "to be" with a long theatrical pause, during which a patron in the front row helpfully added "or not to be" in a rather loud stage whisper, which prompted audience laughter, rather than dramatic empathy. Additional factors like stage fights, music, songs, or scenic transitions often complicate the thousand lines per hour formula, though we've found the estimate useful in making rough initial cuts.

FACILITATING THE DIRECTOR'S CONCEPT

In addition, any editorial changes often reflect the director's attempt to shape the script to fit his or her vision of the production, which usually blossoms through weeding, pruning, and other horticultural adjustments to the play's verbal garden. Most of the cuts are forged through a dialogue among the director, dramaturg, and actors. Sometimes the director sends potential cuts to me first, and I respond, and sometimes the process works in reverse. It's always a sustained and spirited "conversation" at our theatre, however, which ends in a viable script intended for performance by specific actors for a known audience. I dramaturged, for example, a wonderful version of *The Winter's Tale* at Ashland in 1990 in which director Libby Appel envisioned Paulina, played by Mimi Carr, as a shaman whose magical control over the world of the play culminated in the brilliant statue scene at the conclusion. Had we not cut some lines and rearranged several of the speeches to highlight Paulina's central role in the show, I doubt the play would have worked so well. The three weeks we spent sending emendations back and forth through the mail paid handsome dividends in the eventual production.

The same has been true for several versions of *A Midsummer Night's Dream* I've dramaturged where the directors wanted to double the roles of Theseus/Oberon, Hippolyta/Titania, and Philostrate/Puck, which always necessitates some textual gymnastics. Sometimes the shaping is more controversial, as it was in a production of *The Merchant of Venice* I worked on at another theatre where the director cut Shylock's "fawning publican" speech (1.3.37–48) entirely to make the character more sympathetic to the audience, or more recently in Henry Woronicz's lovely production of *The Taming of the Shrew* at the USF in 2004, where the lines in the famous act 5, scene 2 "submission speech" (136–79) were alternately shared by Kate and Petruchio, crafting a conclusion much more amenable to modern postfeminist sensibilities. Most of the theatres where I've worked have permitted some cutting and rearranging of lines if the editing serves the overall design of the production without unduly compromising the integrity of the text. It's always a judgment call, however.

DELETING OBSCURE REFERENCES

Since only the most devoted antiquarians can blissfully sit through uncut catalogues of arcane references and historical trivia in challenging plays like *Troilus and Cressida, Love's Labor's Lost*, and *Henry VIII*, most theatres trim or somehow clarify obscure lines to maintain audience attention. At a certain point, directors inevitably ask themselves if the gestural histrionics required to clarify an incomprehensible sixteenth-century joke are worth the stage time involved. The whole "sheep/ship" business between Proteus and Speed in act 1, scene 1 (71–101) of *Two Gentlemen of Verona* is a good example of dialogue that may have been knee-slappingly funny in 1594, but modern actors have to use enough hand signals to land a 747 to get the idea across. The same theory applies to deleting references that may make some theatregoers uncomfortable. In Flute's allusion to "eke most lovely Jew" in act 3, scene 1 (90) of *A Midsummer Night's Dream,* for instance, the word "Jew" is undoubtedly a nonsensical repetition of the first syllable of "juvenal" earlier in the line, but you'd need a dramaturg in the wings shouting clarification to illuminate that subtle etymological point. Since it appears to be a gratuitous ethnic non sequitur, most productions cut or emend the line to sidestep confusion and avoid offending patrons.

Admittedly some directors like to focus on the more unintelligible moments in a script. For example, as the innovative modern director Peter Sellars once explained in a *Time* magazine interview, "When I direct Shakespeare, the first thing I do is go to the text for cuts. I go through to find the passages that are real heavy, that really are not needed, places where language has become obscure, the places where there is a bizarre detour. And then I take those moments, those elements, and I make them the centerpiece, the core of the production."[11] The rest of us, however, do just the opposite: we delete arcane, incomprehensible, or potentially offensive lines from a script, streamlining and clarifying the play for its audiences.

OMITTING DISPUTED LINES

The same is true of variant readings in the early quarto and folio editions of the plays, where the suspected lack of authorial authenticity often dooms a line or phrase to the cutting-room floor. Is Hamlet's flesh too, too "solid," "sallied," or "sullied"? It depends on whether you're relying on the folio, the quarto, or a nineteenth-century conjectural emendation by Horace Howard Furness. Which early edition of *Othello* is closest to Shakespeare's original manuscript: the 1621 first quarto or the 1623 first folio? And what do we do with the 160 lines that appear in the folio but not in the quarto? Should we include them in an acting edition? What about a play like *Timon of Athens,* the folio text of which seems to have been based on an early, unedited draft of the author's foul papers [handwritten early versions]? To what extent do we spruce up Shakespeare's scripts if he obviously didn't have the time or energy to do so himself? Such questions soon get us enmeshed in discussions of early printing-house practices, compositors' routines, Stationers' Register records, Elizabethan handwriting, joint authorship, and other bibliographical quibbles usually reserved for doctoral classes in the study of Shakespeare. Yet some knowledge of these complexities is necessary for anyone foolhardy enough to perform verbal surgery on Shakespeare's scripts.

CONSOLIDATING ROLES

Whether Old Gobbo actually appears in a production of *The Merchant of Venice* depends on many factors, including whether the script needs additional cuts to conform to a preordained running time, the director wants more or less comic relief in the show, and/or you've got a dynamite actor playing the part. Some or all of such roles undoubtedly get cut unless the production has the luxury of including all the dialogue from its so-called minor characters. Sadly it's the clowns who bite the dust most often, oc-

11. Richard Zoglin, "Shylock on the Beach, *Time*, October 31, 1994, 78.

casionally including, for example, some of Lavatch's more opaque lines in *All's Well That Ends Well*, a smattering of the Fool's dialogue in *King Lear*, Sly in the induction to *The Taming of the Shrew*, and much of the Froth/Elbow business in *Measure for Measure*. Sometimes several smaller parts are consolidated to save time, making one substantial role for an actor out of several lesser ones. How many gentlemen do we really need in *Lear*? And how many named citizens are required to swell the crowd in *Coriolanus* or *Timon of Athens*?

Such deletions, conflations, and doubling serve both temporal and economic ends. Combining several characters into one often saves time through script cuts, unnecessary costume changes, and a streamlined rehearsal schedule while the tactic also helps the festival conserve precious financial resources by eliminating the need for additional salaried actors to play the discarded roles. Most of the directors I've worked with over the years, however, prefer internal cuts to deleting entire characters or scenes; that solution makes the editing appear more seamless and doesn't deprive any actors of their well-deserved roles.

SENDING CUTS OUT EARLY

At the USF and most other regional theatres, scripts are mailed or e-mailed to the actors well before rehearsals begin. The first and most obvious reason is to allow acting company members more time to learn their lines before rehearsal. A second, equally important motive is to maintain actor confidence. There's nothing worse than playing the Second Gentleman, participating in the first read-through with your entire role intact, and then discovering at the second rehearsal that your part has been gutted of more than half its lines. Since most actors would interpret this as lack of confidence in their ability to perform the part, we try diligently to get cuts to the actors as early as possible. That way they take the deletions less personally, seeing them instead in the larger context of the director's approach to the show, mandated time constraints, budgetary realities, and other theatrical considerations that have little to do with their innate skills. All theatres make additional cuts during the rehearsal process, of course, though these generally reflect anxieties about running time, jokes that continue to fall flat (no matter how often they are retuned), last-minute personnel adjustments, crucial stage business, costume changes, fight and dance choreography, and other factors endemic to the living, breathing, evolving process of theatre.

EXPLOITING ACTOR STRENGTHS

The number of lines cut from an actor's role usually, of course, reveals the respect theatres have for that artist, who can often be extremely well known (and therefore a strong box-office draw), a longtime audience favorite at the festival, immensely talented, or all of the above. Hal Gould (*Rhoda, Golden Girls, The Sting, Love and Death*) played King Lear at the USF in 1992 and Prospero in 1995, and I don't believe we cut a single line of his in either show. The same is true when you've got Brian Vaughn playing Hamlet, Leslie Brott and Michael Connolly[12] acting Kate and Petruchio, Jamie Newcomb as Coriolanus, David Ivers as Benedick, or any other well-known and gifted performer in a major role. You want your featured actors to shine as brightly as possible.

The corollary is seldom true, however. Just because a theatre has lesser-known actors in smaller roles, their lines are not necessarily more vulnerable to cutting because of their pecking order in the company. The smaller roles may be in jeopardy due to their diminished importance in the play but not because of the gifted actors who play them.

TRADING LINES

Some cuts operate on the barter system. A common occurrence during rehearsal is for an actor to approach the director and intone some variant of the following familiar plea: "I've been looking over the cuts in my part, and I really need to have these six lines back to flesh out my character fully. The role just doesn't make sense without these lines." To this request, directors invariably reply, "Sure, I'll be glad to give those lines back to you. But to keep the running time where we need it to be, which six lines will you give me in return?" Such sobering discussions often encourage an actor to rethink his or her dramatic priorities while still respecting the theatre's right to bring in the production within its desired time limit. Ide-

12. Michael Connolly is referred to as Kieran Connolly in play programs and photographs because that is his professional stage name.

ally each actor would be able to say all the lines assigned to his character in the acting edition chosen for the production. But is this always desirable or prudent?

I've personally had some wonderful experiences working with entire uncut scripts in Shakespearean productions. For example, Des McAnuff's modernized production of *Romeo and Juliet* at the La Jolla Playhouse in 1983, featuring John Vickery and Amanda Plummer, used the entire folio edition of the play, including the dialogue among the musicians at the end of act 4, scene 5, which most productions omit. Although the performance was four and a half hours long, it was breathtakingly exciting. As I watched the musicians sit on the bed of the (supposedly) dead Juliet, I realized with great clarity why the episode is in the play: it provides a fictitious mourning scene to prepare the audience for the much-more-poignant actual death of the heroine three scenes later. Sadly, however, most full-text productions of Shakespeare please the scholar more than the average theatregoer, substituting a languorous museum piece for a fast-moving, vibrant, well-edited theatrical experience.

CUTTING OR EMENDING FAMOUS SPEECHES

Another important variable in determining which lines or speeches are subject to the ax is, of course, how familiar the play is to the audience. From the sublime to the ridiculous, we would certainly never edit out Hamlet's famous "how all occasions do inform against me / And spur my dull revenge" speech (4.4.32–66), or Macbeth's "tomorrow, and tomorrow, and tomorrow" soliloquy (5.5.19–28), or any other well-known, favorite lines. What would a Rolling Stones concert be without "Sympathy for the Devil"? If Caesar doesn't ask, "Et tu, Brute?" (3.1.77) we'd all demand our money back.

But what about some of the more obscure lines from *Henry VIII, The Two Noble Kinsmen,* or *King John?* Will anyone ever miss them? That's a question devoutly to be asked. This may be an odd way to run a railroad, but I suspect most directors and dramaturgs agree that the more obscure a line or speech is, the more vulnerable it is to excision. When you're scanning for lines to cut so you can abbreviate the play's running time, you look frantically for repetitions, non sequiturs, archaic or obsolete words and phrases, jokes that don't work, ornamental rhetorical flourishes, and, yes, lines that most people won't miss when they're gone. You need to keep the storyline intact, of course. That's job one. But when the production opens in a week and you still have to prune fifteen minutes, a surprising number of options miraculously appear.

No one likes these last-minute cuts—least of all the actors, who now have to delete from their memory banks lines and blocking they have painstakingly conned. This is another reason why we try hard to have almost all the cuts in place prior to the first rehearsal at the USF. Sometimes, however, our running-time estimates are just plain wrong, and we need last-minute textual emendations to save the production. That's when obscurity is our best friend.

Concluding this brief summary of the way we cut Shakespeare's scripts for performance, I'd like to mention a few problems we don't have to deal with at the USF, although other theatres routinely cope with them. The first has to do with the resources of the theatre. We're very fortunate to have two superb principal-performance spaces. Our outdoor Adams Theatre, built in 1977, is a beautiful, 819-seat, open-air venue with a thrust stage, a balcony and an inner below, ramps at stage left and right, a large trap, and a very serviceable slip stage. Patterned after early drawings of sixteenth-century theatres, it is considered so authentic that the BBC filmed a monumental documentary series here several years ago and compared it favorably to Shakespeare's Globe Theatre. Our 1989 indoor Randall Theatre is a state-of-the-art, 769-seat facility with a proscenium stage that can easily be equipped with a balcony and an inner below if the script and the director's approach call for them. In short, we're blessed with excellent venues where we can present Shakespeare's plays, as are many other wonderful theatres like the ones in Ashland; Stratford, Ontario; and the newly rebuilt Globe on the South Bank of the Thames in London.

Occasionally, however, theatres without such traditional architectural resources may have to cut, edit, or otherwise reconfigure the language of the plays to accommodate the limitations of their spaces. If you don't have an inner above, for instance, you have to find imaginative ways to do the balcony scenes in *Romeo and Juliet*, the scaling of the fortress walls at Harfleur in *Henry V*, Arthur's leap to his death in *King John*, and the famous tomb scene in *Antony and Cleopatra*. Without an inner below, presenting the world of the tavern in *Henry IV, Part I* and many other scenes that require preset furniture and props hidden behind a curtain on a slip stage is challenging indeed. Lacking a trap, you have to find a different way to do the dungeon episodes in *Measure for Measure,* the witches' cauldron in *Macbeth,* the parade of the seven deadly sins in *Doctor Faustus,* and many other crucial scenes where the action originates "below." In addition, cutting and rearranging is often required for small-cast productions of Shakespeare's plays (*Julius Caesar* presented by six actors, for example), which we have seldom done at the USF. Whatever the difficulties, however, creative directors, designers, and actors always find a way to perform the plays, even if they have to edit Shakespeare's language to make it happen!

To cut or not to cut: that *is* the question. And the answer, as the foregoing examples reveal, is often yes if we want to shape the plays to the tastes of contemporary audiences, newly designed theatres, and festival financial resources. Does Shakespeare suffer in the process? Perhaps. But the textual sacrifices we make in bringing the plays to life four centuries after the author's death are more than compensated for by the millions of appreciative theatregoers who applaud brilliant productions around the globe each year. If we're going to edit the scripts, we need to do it with all the compassion, sensitivity, reverence, and respect necessary to keep Shakespeare's artistic vision fresh and vibrant for the modern world. As Cassius metatheatrically asks of the conspirators in *Julius Caesar,* "How many ages hence / Shall this our lofty scene be acted over / In states unborn and accents yet unknown" (3.1.112–14). I doubt that Shakespeare had Cedar City, Utah, in mind when he wrote these lines, but their prophetic fury invites each of us to develop new and inventive ways to render his plays completely accessible to today's audiences. When a little editing is required to make that happen, we always look for "the kindest cut of all."

ஊ॥ஐ

The Comedies

The Errors of Comedy

The Comedy of Errors at the 1987 Utah Shakespeare Festival

Well-known physician and author Lewis Thomas has written an essay entitled "To Err Is Human" in which he argues that our innate propensity to make errors not only helps define us as human beings but also systematically improves our lives. Unlike cats, dogs, and other animals that appear infallible, our human species is genetically programmed to make mistakes, doomed forever to be bumbling, maladroit caricatures of our own self-images. At the same time, however, these errors often lead us to startling discoveries about ourselves and the world around us. By way of further explanation, Thomas asserts that a good laboratory must run flawlessly like a computer; but if it's a fortunate laboratory, someone will make a lucky mistake at the proper time: "the wrong buffer, something in one of the blanks, a decimal misplaced in the reading counts, the warm room off by a degree and a half, a mouse out of his box, or just a misreading of the day's protocol." And if it's a big enough mistake, "we could find ourselves on a new level, stunned, out in the clear, ready to move again,"[1] perhaps discovering the cure for a catastrophic illness, the secrets hidden in the brain, or the recipe for a happier, healthier life.

The great spate of mistakes in Shakespeare's *The Comedy of Errors* exhibits this same duality described by Dr. Thomas. First of all, the errors mark the characters as human beings who are all the more laughable because we, as audience, identify with their comic vulnerability. One of his

1. Lewis Thomas, "To Err Is Human," *New England Journal of Medicine* 294 (January 8, 1976): 99–100.

earliest efforts, Shakespeare's play is heavily indebted to classical drama, most particularly to two Latin works by Plautus that rely on error as a structuring principle: *The Menaechmi,* a farce revolving about the mistaken identity of twins, and *Amphitruo,* where a husband and his witty servant are excluded from their home while a stranger in disguise usurps the master's role. Shakespeare's adaptation of these Plautine sources compounds the comic possibilities by featuring two sets of long-lost twins who stumble through the play's dramatic landscape in search of their siblings, their parents, and romantic happiness. Most immediately apparent, therefore, is the effect these errors have on our sense of humor: the mistakes of the play are uniquely human, uniting all of us in the amusing search for identity in a complex and confusing world.

In a deeper and more significant sense, however, the errors of this comedy are also regenerative, placing the characters on a new level of existence that helps them restructure their fragmented lives and find the lost

5. *The Comedy of Errors*, 1987. Steve Wilson as Dromio of Syracuse. Photo by Boyd D. Redington and John Snyder. Published with permission of the Utah Shakespeare Festival.

halves of their split personalities. As if by miracle, the mistaken identities so prevalent in the play turn separation to reunion, suffering to salvation, and death to rebirth. In fact, all the comedy's important themes—illusion, madness, witchcraft, fortune, inversion of the natural order, romance, and the harmonizing influence of love—are part of a restorative movement toward happiness and fulfillment. Without the benefit of error, for example, the twins would stay separated, Egeon would die, Emilia would remain an abbess, Adriana would still be an unhappy wife, and Luciana would never find her sweetheart. Error improves the lives of everyone in the play—even the unfortunate Doctor Pinch, who is, no doubt, somewhat edified by having his beard singed off and his face doused with "great pails of puddled mire" (5.1.173).

Viewed in this way, Shakespeare's play is a paradigm for the mature comedies to come—*The Two Gentlemen of Verona, The Taming of the Shrew, A Midsummer Night's Dream, Much Ado about Nothing, As You Like It,* and *Twelfth Night*—all of which provide important dramatic evidence that error can be both delightful and instructive. This is so for not only the characters of such plays, of course, but also their audiences: a well-wrought theatrical experience can break through the numbing routines of everyday existence that sometimes hide from us important insights about our lives. Through these errors of comedy, we are invited to witness our human reflections onstage, our other selves, at once humorous and profound, distorted by comic form and the passage of time, yet true to life nonetheless.

"TOUCHES OF SWEET HARMONY"

The Merchant of Venice at the 1991
Oregon Shakespeare Festival

I am writing this program note in Ashland on the evening of January 16, 1991, during the initial bombing of Baghdad, painfully aware that each word falling on the printed page is echoed far across the globe by the explosive sounds of warfare. Unfortunately, little has changed from Shakespeare's time, though now we proclaim our hatred and xenophobia with F-14s and SCUD missiles, rather than more modest Renaissance instruments of oppression. Our world is greedy still, reaching for oil and land and power on a global scale.

Shakespeare knew this darker side of human nature and presented it unflinchingly in *The Merchant of Venice.* Although at first the text appears to focus principally on persecution of the Jewish moneylender Shylock, we have discovered in our rehearsals that virtually every character is guilty of sins against humanity. The play's examination of racial hatred and the frenzied pursuit of wealth indicts Christians and Jews alike, dividing them into ethnic and social camps distrustful of all those different from themselves.

Despite Portia's high-sounding rhetoric, mercy *is* strained throughout the play as race confronts race and religion attacks religion, creating stunning disparities within the characters. The widely respected Antonio, for example, seems to change disposition completely when he rails at Shylock and calls him "dog." Though she is undeniably intelligent and cultured, Portia mocks the races and nationalities of her various suitors, then cruelly strips the Jew of his money, humanity, and faith in the crowded courtroom. Lovely Jessica steals an immense amount of gold from her father and squanders it recklessly. And even the good-hearted Launcelot Gobbo decides to leave the Jew's service because his master is "a kind of devil" (2.2.25). Like the death's head hidden within the gold casket, hatred and prejudice are never far beneath the play's highly polished surface: each character's virtues are commingled with equal shares of reprehensible behavior. Perhaps the only real hero is Portia's father, whose stratagem of the lottery teaches us to look beyond surface appearances to find the truth within.

This mixture of good and evil elements is mirrored in the action of the play, which alternates between the two extremes of "hazard" and "tarry," creating a tension that structures most of the crucial dramatic moments. In act 1, scene 3, for example, Bassanio tries to rush Shylock into making a decision about the loan of three thousand ducats while the Jew slows the progress of the scene with Old Testament references and complaints about racial prejudice. Similarly in act 3, scene 2, Portia asks Bassanio to wait a few more days before venturing for his prize ("I could teach you / How to choose right" [10–11]), though her impatient suitor wants to try his fortune immediately. And in the trial scene (act 4, scene 1), Shylock doggedly pursues vengeance against Antonio while Portia delays the action with legal maneuvering. As the central image of the caskets suggests, this is a hazardous world of gamblers and risk takers unwilling to tarry, a fast-paced, glamorous parable about characters who live on the edge of life and death, wealth and poverty, yet are bored with money too easily won, too carelessly possessed. Such abundant material possessions, we soon learn, may bring momentary pleasure but will never satisfy the soul. By the end of the trial scene, therefore, we are left with the deeply disturbing portrait of a morally bankrupt society.

Fortunately Shakespeare's fifth act reaches for comic redemption through the music of the spheres, God's mercy, and the regenerative optimism of happy marriage. As Jessica and Lorenzo await Portia's return to Belmont, they listen to the "touches of sweet harmony" (5.1.57) that surround them—on earth and in the heavens. The rings Portia and Nerissa have cleverly begged from their husbands expand to concentric spheres of the Ptolemaic universe, which make celestial music by their cosmic friction. Through the eerie stillness of the night, the images of mythic lovers, and the patterns of bright golden stars on the "floor of heaven"

(5.1.58) God's infinite mercy begins to resolve all contradictions in the human spirit. Because of His love, these flawed characters are blessed and ennobled beyond their poor deserving. As Lorenzo explains to his new bride, the same harmony created in heaven also dwells within them, "But whilst this muddy vesture of decay/Doth grossly close it in, we cannot hear it" (5.1.64–65).

Although none of these characters merit divine mercy, God's great gift is to let them hear for an instant the compelling spiritual harmony within their souls, inviting them—as well as their audience—to aspire to more perfect lives free of the racism, greed, and anger that afflict us all.

The Forest of Arden

As You Like It at the 1992 Oregon Shakespeare Festival

In *As You Like It,* as in many of Shakespeare's other comedies, geography helps determine the destiny of the major characters. Such plays commonly begin in a harsh, repressive, urban environment, then move to a fertile, green world filled with magical or liberating influences, and finally return to the first location, which becomes a better place because of the characters' sojourn in the other world. This journey from society to wilderness to improved society refines and focuses the larger, more comprehensive shift from bad to good fortune that universally defines plays as comedies and confers happiness and success on most of their major characters.

The green world or wilderness in *As You Like It* is, of course, the famous Forest of Arden, a dramatic milieu that offers audiences some fascinating clues about Shakespeare's vision of the forces of nature that turn our lives toward good fortune and comic fulfillment through regeneration and renewal. The play presents three distinct dimensions of the forest—literal, mythological, and literary—each of which stands in sharp contrast to the decadent setting of Duke Frederick and his "envious court."

On the literal level, the Forest of Arden was a wilderness area in Warwickshire, near Shakespeare's home in Stratford-upon-Avon, which the author no doubt visited many times in his youth in search of its most celebrated inhabitant, the legendary Robin Hood. This forest and its environs provided ample role models for such colorful country characters as Silvius, Corin, William, Phebe, and Audrey, who populate the imaginary woods of Shakespeare's play. It might also have inspired one of the comedy's most important recurring motifs: life in such a natural wilderness is often harsh and difficult, yet the experience furnishes Duke Senior and his banished nobles with precisely the right blend of wisdom and suffering necessary to reform the kingdom when they return to it. Similarly the honest sexuality of Arden allows the infatuation between Rosalind and Orlando to blossom into mutual love. In Shakespeare's ironic universe, true civilization and contentment exist in the forest, rather than in the corrupt and vulgar court.

The mythological Forest of Arden—sometimes at odds and sometimes in concert with its literal counterpart—reaches back to the golden age of Greece and Rome, which the Renaissance perceived as a time of innocence, harmony, and great abundance of natural resources. This early mythos prefigures and anticipates the biblical Garden of Eden, which was a perfect world before the fall of man, complete unto itself, encoded through divine allegory with God's truth reflected in every breath of wind and blade of grass: "Tongues in trees, books in the running brooks, / Sermons in stones, and good in everything" (2.1.16–17). Through firsthand access to this demiparadise of Arden, Duke Senior and his men gain Edenic strength and wisdom; Rosalind and Orlando discover the heavenly beauty of love; and even Touchstone and Jaques, awkward transplants in this prelapsarian world, come face-to-face with their social and moral imperfections.

If Arden is both natural forest and mythological paradise, it also owes allegiance to the literary concept of Arcadia—a pastoral tradition with a rich and self-conscious heritage stretching back through Spenser's *Shepherds Calendar* and Sidney's *Arcadia* to the Greek romances and *Eclogues* of Virgil. In this imaginary rustic world, shepherds watch their flocks, sing of love, and live in perfect harmony with God and nature. Shakespeare's idyllic pastoral setting begins to deconstruct, however, when its courtly visitors are confronted by such decidedly imperfect challenges as bitterly cold weather, a scarcity of food, and dull, uncouth country bumpkins. These antipastoral elements challenge the artifice of Arden and force Duke Senior, Rosalind, Orlando, and others to see through the corresponding artificiality of their previous existence. As a result, the Duke learns the limitations of his unrelievedly cheerful view of life while Rosalind and Orlando discard their unrealistic Petrarchan love cures and amorous verses in favor of a more mature, honest, and mutual appreciation of true love.

Each of these three images of Arden, therefore, leads the principal characters toward comic fulfillment in its own way. Through the artistic vision of director James Edmondson and scenic designer Michael Smith, the sylvan world of the Ashland production is layered with ladders and different elevations so that upward progress on the physical level helps chronicle the personal and spiritual journey the characters make as they search for their proper identities and learn to love each other and themselves.

The movement toward self-definition within the play reveals one final symbolic function of the Forest of Arden: the audience, like the dramatic characters, inevitably moves toward happiness as it is transported from its modern reality into the wilderness of the play. This geographic displacement into the forest of the human heart heals us through comic catharsis and releases us from the artificiality of our world by revealing and examining the artifice of Shakespeare's theatrical universe. When the play is over, however, and we return to our own lives, we still carry with us these images of Arden, which sustain and lead us toward our own happy endings.

"Swear by Your Double Self"

Bassanio's Impersonation of Morocco and Aragon
in *The Merchant of Venice* at the 1992
Utah Shakespeare Festival

The ingenious idea of having Bassanio masquerade as both Morocco and
Aragon, Portia's two humorous suitors in *The Merchant of Venice*, has surfaced occasionally during the long and often controversial production
history of the play, though to my knowledge, no major regional or national theatre had actually attempted the doubling until director Eli Simon's
very successful 1992 summer production at the Utah Shakespeare Festival.[2] As dramaturg for the show, I was responsible for helping the director create his vision of the play, which included collaborating on all textual cuts, additions, and alterations necessary to make the doubling work
smoothly and effectively. Since we had no prior productions to guide us,
I kept careful notes on the problems we encountered and the solutions we
devised—with the hope that such information might be useful to members of the literary and theatrical communities who were intrigued by the
idea, yet wondered how it would work onstage.

This essay focuses principally on three issues closely associated with
the decision to have Bassanio play the parts of all three suitors: (1) the

---

2. Sir Lawrence Olivier apparently wanted Bassanio to play all three suitors for
the 1973 televised version of his 1970 National Theatre production, but director
Jonathan Miller urged him to abandon the concept. June Schlueter, "The Casket
Plot in Merchant," in *Shakespeare on Television: An Anthology of Essays and Reviews*,
ed. J. C. Bulman and H. R. Coursen (Hanover: University Press of New England,
1988), 173.

preliminary planning, including the necessary initial step of obtaining permission from USF's producers and then cutting and shaping the script to accommodate the doubling; (2) the way the doubling occurred onstage with reference to specific scenic moments, costume changes, props, and other theatrical choices; and (3) the primary ways in which the doubling influenced the overall production with particular emphasis on audience response, characterization, thematic impact, linguistic nuance, and the problems created by the entire process.

CONVINCING THE PRODUCERS AND SHAPING THE SCRIPT

Eli and I knew we wanted to double the roles as early as our initial meeting on the production in November 1991, though two immediate problems faced us: How would we convince the USF's producers to take a chance on such a radical idea? And how could we rearrange the text to allow us to make the concept work? After spending four eight-hour sessions combing through the text of the play, we found answers to both these problems. Convincing the festival administrators,[3] in fact, was much easier than either of us had anticipated. Eli made a few preliminary phone calls, then sent a letter on February 20 to the producers listing six principal reasons why we felt the doubling would be effective: (1) the theme of disguising would fit in perfectly with the play's focus on the duplicitous nature of men and women (for example, Lancelot's "conscience-devil" speech, Shylock's "merry bond," and the riddle of the caskets); (2) Bassanio's disguise in Belmont would balance Portia's courtroom impersonation of the lawyer and Jessica's masquerade as Lorenzo's torchbearer; (3) Gratiano's accompanying Bassanio to Belmont (both in disguise) would give him increased access to Nerissa, which would help explain the otherwise-abrupt announcement of their engagement; (4) the characters of Morocco and Aragon are so broadly drawn that they could easily spring from Bassanio's romantic and lavish imagination; (5) just as Bassanio is doggedly determined to shoot arrows till he hits the right target (1.1.140–52), so, too, does he continually choose caskets until he wins the girl; and (6) the doubling would heighten the comic elements

---

3. Fred Adams, founder and executive producer; Douglas Cook and Cameron Harvey, producing artistic directors; and R. Scott Phillips, executive director.

in the text. During the subsequent design conference on March 13–15 in Cedar City, Utah, the producers gave permission to proceed with the idea with the proviso that Portia should not discover that Bassanio had duped her until sometime after he had chosen the leaden casket; in this way, she would maintain the integrity of her sworn vow to abide by the terms of her father's will.

While we were negotiating with the producers during January and February, Eli and I were also editing the script. Our first changes, which had more to do with streamlining the play than facilitating the doubling, were to omit the character of Old Gobbo and conflate and abbreviate the two Morocco scenes (act 2, scenes 1 and 7). As a result, the production would move immediately from Shylock's bond in act 1, scene 3 to Lancelot's soliloquy in act 2, scene 2; scenes 3–6 would follow, after which the two Morocco scenes would be fused together. Following the intermission, which would come after Bassanio's exit in act 3, scene 2, the scenes would run in their proper sequence until the end of the production.

Only a few textual changes were required to support the doubling. At the conclusion of act 2, scene 2, for example, we decided to have Bassanio and Gratiano foreshadow their decision to visit Belmont in disguise by dropping into a Moroccan accent with "for we have friends / That purpose merriment" (190–91), and, at the end of the elopement scene in act 2, scene 6, we added a lengthy Italian drinking song so the actor playing Gratiano could exit early, apply his blackface makeup, and then reappear as Morocco's servant in the next scene.

The first real textual change would come at the end of the Aragon scene in act 2, scene 9, when we needed to have Gratiano—then disguised as Aragon's doddering grandmother—leave the stage so he could reappear immediately as "the young Venetian" (87) who announces Bassanio's approach to Belmont. To arrange this exit, we planned to have Bassanio read the schedule of his fortunes, bemoan his bad luck ("Did I deserve no better than a fool's head?" [59]), and then turn to the still-disguised Gratiano, secretly shove a paper into his hand, and whisper, "Deliver you this letter. Go, make haste." The only other textual change we required to facilitate the doubling came at the very end of the play after Portia revealed that she knew Bassanio had impersonated Morocco and Aragon. In response to this confrontation with the truth, Bassanio would beg Portia to "pardon these faults" (instead of "pardon this fault" [5.1.247]), which was meant to excuse not only the surrender of his wedding ring to Portia in her disguise as the lawyer but also his own masquerade as the two suitors, which she had discovered earlier.

MAKING THE DOUBLING WORK ONSTAGE

Armed, therefore, with permission from the producers and all the necessary textual support, we then set out to discover ways to make the concept work with the company in Utah. We already had an excellent actor as Shylock, veteran Equity performer Bill Leach, who had been precast in the role. Our next job was to find a Portia, Bassanio, Nerissa, and Gratiano equal to the task. Thankfully, the mid-May auditions at the festival produced four wonderful choices—Deanne Lorette, Paul Boehmer, Jamie Jones, and Tony Ward—all either students or recent graduates of MFA theatre training programs at various universities. During the six-week rehearsal period that followed, our original plan for the doubling was fleshed out in the following manner. At the top of the Morocco scene, Bassanio and Gratiano dashed onto the upper stage still nervously adjusting their blackface makeup and exotic costumes. After secretly glancing at Portia and Nerissa on the main stage below, they strutted down the stairs accompanied by a flourish of Moroccan music. Although the audience could clearly tell the two were Bassanio and Gratiano in disguise, Portia and Nerissa could not. During the dialogue that followed, Bassanio drew a huge scimitar with which he frightened the ladies, and Gratiano struck a large gong whenever Bassanio said something noteworthy. On Bassanio's "some God direct my judgment" (2.7.13), Gratiano whipped out a prayer rug, consulted a compass to position it properly, and joined Bassanio in a jumble of deep kneeling bows and mumbled pig Latin. Later, after choosing the wrong casket, the two ran offstage screaming furiously—which prompted wild applause every night.

6. *The Merchant of Venice*, 1992. William Leach as Shylock. Photo by Sue Bennett, Rich Engleman, and John Running. Published with permission of the Utah Shakespeare Festival.

The Aragon scene, equally well received by audiences throughout the summer, began in a similar fashion with both characters on the upper stage adjusting their Spanish costumes. When they descended to the music of a flamenco guitar, Gratiano, who was dressed in a wide and cumbersome pannier, had to navigate the stairs sideways, much to the delight of the crowd. Bassanio spoke in a lisping Castilian accent and peered at the caskets through a small monocle. After opening the silver chest, he asked, "What's here? The portrait of a blinking idiot" (2.9.54), all the while blinking compulsively at the audience. He then dismissed Gratiano, picked up the fool's head, and read the inscription, which was written on a long, multicolored tongue that unfurled from the mouth of the head like a stock-market ticker tape. He delivered his last lines rapidly, then exited in an abrupt and unceremonious manner, after which a servant entered to announce the real Bassanio's approach.

The next bit of stage business to assist the doubling occurred at the end of act 3, scene 2 after Bassanio had chosen the correct casket and Lorenzo had brought news of Antonio's peril at the hands of Shylock. Throughout the scene, Gratiano had been carrying a large bag, which he placed next to a bench just before everyone left for Venice. Portia noticed it and attempted to call Bassanio back but to no avail. She and Nerissa opened the bag and discovered—as the audience gasped—two large scimitars and a turban. Moroccan music underscored the action while the two women stared at each other in horror, then looked at the audience with revenge in their eyes as the lights slowly faded to black. After the intermission and the jailer scene, Portia and Nerissa staged a mock fight with the scimitars while planning their trip to Venice, which clearly implied that part of their purpose in disguising themselves was to get even with Bassanio and Gratiano for tricking them.

The last reference to the doubling occurred at the conclusion of the play, when Portia was berating Bassanio for giving away her wedding ring to the doctor. After she had said, "Mark you but that!/In both my eyes he doubly sees himself:/In each eye, one" (5.1.243–45), Portia reached behind a fountain at stage center, pulled out a Moroccan scimitar, held it up in front of Bassanio, and admonished him to "swear by your double self,/And there's an oath of credit" (245–46). Following a stunned silence, Bassanio realized he had been discovered and stammered his apology: "Pardon these faults, and by my soul I swear/I never more will break an oath with thee" (247–48). The dialogue that followed confirmed that Portia and Nerissa had forgiven the men, not only for giving away their rings but also for disguising themselves in the earlier scenes at Belmont.

HOW THE DOUBLING AFFECTED THE PRODUCTION

Although Eli and I had worked hard to anticipate all the ways that the doubling would influence the production, we did not know how profound and fascinating the effect would be until the first time we saw the show in front of an audience. Our initial impressions were strengthened throughout the summer as we talked with actors, audience members, and various USF administrators, who were likewise intrigued with the impact of this decision on our interpretation of the text. What we had done, in semiotic terms, was to change an important *sign* in the show: Bassanio—the insipid, avaricious, romantic suitor—had become Bassanio—the clever, avaricious, romantic suitor. In other words, the doubling added depth and complexity to Bassanio's character without deleting the most important negative element: his greedy, fortune-hunting inclinations.

This revised encoding invited the audience to reconsider a number of important thematic concerns in the play: in particular, the motifs of disguise, deception, and appearance/reality, which in traditional productions relate principally to Portia as lawyer. Audience expectations about the play were challenged and revitalized by our drawing attention to Bassanio's status as actor and manipulator, which deconstructed the performances and helped reveal the extent to which several other characters—like Shylock, Portia, Antonio, Jessica, and Gobbo—behave in a theatrical and manipulative fashion. Since Portia and Bassanio were both clever, they seemed better suited for each other than in other productions. Portia still had the upper hand, however, since she and Nerissa were able to penetrate the men's disguises while Bassanio and Gratiano had to be told their wives had impersonated the courtroom lawyer and his clerk.

This newfound cleverness in Bassanio also helped audiences understand why Antonio and Portia both loved him so. This production made him more than simply an attractive young man with high hopes and a penchant for spending large sums of money. Bright and innovative, he aggressively pursued both Portia and her vast fortune. Furthermore, the doubling helped reveal how much Bassanio manipulated Antonio in the play. The younger man's "childhood proof" about lost arrows and squandered money (1.1.140–52) seemed in retrospect less innocent and ingenuous than cold and calculating. As a result, Bassanio manipulated Antonio and his fortune in much the same way he circumvented Portia's father's will. The doubling also helped justify the huge amount of money

Bassanio borrowed since he needed it to support the amorous activities of three wooers instead of one.

Bassanio's earlier appearances as Morocco and Aragon certainly eliminated suspense in act 3, scene 2 since he knew the proper casket through a process of elimination, but they also deepened the scene in three delightful and unexpected ways. First, because the audience knew Bassanio would choose correctly, the director did not need to have Portia cheat by somehow signaling lead as the correct choice (as many modern productions have done, sullying her character). Second, this lack of suspense allowed the audience to focus on the more meaningful extent to which Bassanio's deliberation speech (3.2.73–107) was a learning process that chronicled his growing maturity as a potential husband. His insight that "the world is still deceived with ornament" (74) helped complete his character arc from callow youth to mature husband, which is so essential to the text. And finally, Bassanio's growing awareness of the world around him was clarified through his appearances as Morocco and Aragon. When he adopted their personalities in the earlier scenes, he chose as they would have done: through arrogance, pride, and stupidity. As a result, he learned from his disguising, just as Antonio learns about persecution from being victimized by Shylock.

The doubling also prompted a number of other insights about the relationships among characters in the play. For example, the foppery of Morocco and Aragon seemed more in keeping with Portia's descriptions in act 1, scene 2 of her other absurd suitors (for example, Monsieur Le Bon and Falconbridge, the young baron of England); the only difference was that we don't actually see the suitors described earlier while we do get to meet Morocco and Aragon. Similarly the doubling expanded Bassanio's camaraderie with Gratiano, who became a clever actor in the Belmont charades and, consequently, a better match for the witty Nerissa. Because the women discovered the men's duplicity at the end of act 3, scene 2, the doubling helped motivate and explain Portia's ring stratagem. In our production, she had a real reason to trick Bassanio since he had duped her by disguising himself as Morocco and Aragon. As a result, the doubling raised the stakes in Portia's attempt to get back at Bassanio and take control of their marriage. It also sent the audience buzzing into the intermission because the usual tension about the way Antonio would escape Shylock's revenge was compounded by suspense over when and how

Portia would confront her husband about his earlier deceptions.

Finally, the doubling exposed some interesting verbal nuances in the script not usually available to an audience. In the Morocco scene, for example, Bassanio begs Portia to "mislike me not for my complexion" (2.1.1), which became heavily ironic as he stood there in blackface makeup. Similarly his "I would not change this hue, / Except to steal your thoughts, my gentle queen" (11–12) brought a ripple of audience laughter since he would obviously have to move through the characters of Morocco and Aragon before returning to his native hue as Bassanio when he chose the leaden casket. Morocco's confused claim to have fought on both sides of the Persian / Turkish wars (2.1.25–26) also made more sense as mistaken bravado by Bassanio than it ever does as Morocco's legitimate military vita.

In the Aragon scene, Bassanio's reference to being "new varnished" (2.9.49) seemed to be a sly reference to his disguise, as did his indictment of those who pretend to be "honorable without the stamp of merit" and others who "presume to wear an undeserved dignity" (38–40). The doubling also clarified Aragon's hasty dismissal of the golden casket (as Bassanio he already knew it was an incorrect choice) and justified the abrupt exits by both the foreign visitors after they had chosen wrongly (Bassanio had no reason to linger since he was anxious to be reincarnated as the following suitor).

Despite the many advantages in interpretation conferred by the doubling, the device created several difficult problems that we had to address. The most crucial—discovered early in the rehearsal period— was that we were allowing the humor in the Belmont casket scenes to become too broad, which encouraged so much laughter that the comedy overflowed into the Shylock plot and undercut its seriousness. As a result, we had to learn to resist much of the potent comic seductiveness provided by the doubling, which eventually gave the production a better generic balance between happiness and sadness, comedy and tragedy. In addition, although the doubling made Bassanio's character more interesting, it simultaneously weakened his integrity, which adversely affected the romantic plot. In terms of festival casting, the decision to have one actor play three parts also robbed two company members of small, but lovely, roles as Morocco and Aragon, which created some understandable (and ultimately unsolvable) antagonism toward the actor playing Bassanio.

A final problem occurred immediately before the intermission. In the script, Portia urges Bassanio to go with her to church and call her "wife" before he leaves for Venice. Following his exit, however, Portia found the bag with the Moroccan scimitars, after which the stage went dark. Would she still have married him prior to his departure if she had just discovered his duplicity in the casket scenes? In retrospect perhaps we should have cut a few additional lines to sidestep this problem.

CONCLUSIONS

All things considered, I'm glad we chose to use the doubling in this production. According to my unofficial survey, at least 80 percent of the audience members at the USF enjoyed our interpretation of the script. Some traditionalists complained that we had seriously distorted Shakespeare's intent by doubling roles that were never supposed to be doubled while other theatregoers objected to the adverse effect of Bassanio's duplicity on the romantic plot. Surprisingly we received more criticism about the romantic trickery in the play than about the production's anti-Semitism, which created the curious impression that religious bigotry is less reprehensible than amorous deception. All this controversy prompted a fascinating seasonlong dialogue—which surfaced through such USF educational programs as the morning literary seminars, the acting workshops, and Camp Shakespeare—concerning whether directors and other members of theatrical artistic teams should replicate authorial intent whenever they can infer it. My own opinion is that we can never know Shakespeare's intended meaning, and even if we could discover it through some power of divination, that knowledge should not limit our modern productions of his plays. As theatre artists, we are allowed—perhaps even mandated—by our profession to interpret, shape, and change these texts to help illuminate their meaning for contemporary audiences.

My experience with *Merchant* helped me see how theatre provides an intriguing Rorschach test for its audiences, separating those who want creativity and experimentation from others who are only comfortable with more conservative approaches. In my opinion, the first choice is almost always more satisfying for people who truly love theatre.

Festive Comedy

Twelfth Night at the 1995 Oregon Shakespeare Festival

The latest and most sophisticated of Shakespeare's "festive comedies," *Twelfth Night* owes much of its structure and thematic cohesion to the twelve-day holiday following Christmas. During this time, the traditionally stern Elizabethan code of conduct was inverted to allow excessive and licentious behavior presided over by the raucous Lord of Misrule. Related to the Feast of the Epiphany and the Feast of the Magi, the holiday also had its origin in the pre-Christian rite of Saturnalia in the ancient Roman world. Written sometime between 1599 and 1601, Shakespeare's comedy betrays its indebtedness to the Twelfth Night celebration through not only its characters and plot but also the way it has consistently charmed and delighted audiences over the past four centuries.

The names of the principal characters in *Twelfth Night* predict their dramatic destiny. Feste the clown, whose name clearly invokes the drama's festive origins, reigns over a world turned upside down—particularly when, as Sir Topas the curate, he imprisons, interrogates, and ultimately helps "cure" Malvolio, Olivia's pompous and puritanical steward. Through the play's holiday atmosphere, wisdom and folly change places: Feste's exuberant spirit triumphs over "Mal-volio," who "wishes evil" upon the other characters. Sir Toby Belch is a Renaissance Uncle Buck whose joie de vivre and wit elevate him to the position of the Lord of Misrule, who presides over Olivia's household and our hearts as well. Viola, whose name hints of music and flowers, conquers love through her disguise as Cesario, just as her ancient namesake, Julius Caesar, triumphed over the Roman world. Even the lovesick Duke Orsino's name may owe some allegiance to a real-life Italian nobleman, Don Virginio Orsino, who apparently was a guest of honor at an early performance of the play in the court of Queen Elizabeth on Twelfth Night (January 6, 1601).

This joyful holiday mood, so apparent in the semiotics of names and characterization, is reinforced through Shakespeare's plot construction, especially in the narrative movement from union to wandering to reunion, which chronicles the shift from bad to good fortune that defines *Twelfth Night* as a comic play. Viola and her twin brother, Sebastian, are united through birth, yet separated at the outset of the play by a shipwreck, which allows each to wander through the kingdom of Illyria unencumbered by the "shadow self" of their split sexual personality. Freed from the restrictive conventions of female behavior, Viola matures through her experiences in the play as her holiday from gender and kinship permits her insight into the proper meaning and purpose of her life. When she and Sebastian reunite at the conclusion of the play, both have found themselves and discovered true love in the process: Viola with her amorous duke, and Sebastian with the Countess Olivia.

In a deeper and more satisfying way, however, the comedy betrays its festive nature by inviting audience members to take part in the regenerative ritual of a holiday experience. Just as Viola and Sebastian successfully reunite as brother and sister after their sojourn in Illyria, so, too, did Shakespeare's sixteenth-century audience members return refreshed and rejuvenated to the comfortable everyday routine of their jobs and lives following the exhilaration of the Twelfth Night holiday.

This same movement from play to work and imagination to reality is also available to modern audiences, whose participation in Shakespeare's festive comedy moves them from release to clarification during the action of the play. Sheltered from their daily problems during the performance, they emerge from the theatre with a clearer vision about their lives that matches the shift from bad to good fortune in Viola, Sebastian, and many of the comedy's other major characters.

Surrounded by real-life Puritans like Malvolio who wanted to close down the theatres, Shakespeare wrote *Twelfth Night* as an *ars poetica*, a play in defense of playwriting that illustrates all the excitement and creative energy available to people who choose to make theatre an important part of their lives. In this regard, the play itself becomes the holiday experienced by the audience: we have allowed Shakespeare's creative vision to shape our imaginations during the "two hours' traffic" of his stage, and we benefit greatly from the curative effects of participating in this dramatic experience. As a result, Viola's wandering becomes ours, and just as she finds fulfillment in her dramatic progress through the play, we as members of the audience discover our path to happiness through *Twelfth Night,* Shakespeare's most joyous festive comedy.

THE SINS OF THE FATHER

Parent-Child Relationships in *The Merchant of Venice*
at the 2000 Utah Shakespeare Festival

After the tragic death of his only son, Hamnet, in 1596, Shakespeare began an extensive theatrical study of the relationships between parents and children. Although *Hamlet, King Lear, The Winter's Tale,* and *The Tempest* are the most notable plays devoted to this theme, *The Merchant of Venice,* written less than a year after his son died, offers rich and varied insights into the issue of paternity in Shakespeare's plays.

The first and most obvious paternal relationship is between the Jewish moneylender, Shylock, and his daughter, Jessica. Devastated by the death of his wife, Leah, many years earlier, Shylock has kept the house in mourning out of respect for her, and this deification of her image creates distance between Shylock and his daughter, who can never understand the great love her parents shared and is still angry at her mother for deserting her.

Antonio, the merchant of the title, also fulfills a paternal role in the play through his foolishly indulgent friendship with Bassanio, who eventually wins the beautiful and affluent Portia by solving the riddle of the gold, silver, and leaden caskets. Acting as a father figure to the young man, Antonio borrows money from Shylock, pledging the infamous pound of flesh as security, so Bassanio can travel to Belmont to court his love. Antonio's great devotion to his friend, however, is in ironic contrast to the bigotry and prejudice he showers upon Shylock prior to signing their "merry" bond.

This same theme of father-child relationships resurfaces in the comic subplot of the play, as well, through the kinship that unites Old Gobbo and his son, Launcelot, who is first a servant to Shylock, then later to Bassanio. Old Gobbo's physical blindness echoes the spiritual myopia of the first two father figures in the play, Shylock and Antonio, and implies that clarity of vision is an important metaphorical ingredient in religious as well as paternal disputes. In addition, the genuine loving rapport between this aged father and his son exposes the inadequacy of the relationships between Shylock and Jessica and Antonio and Bassanio.

The fourth and final parent-child association in *The Merchant of Venice* features Portia, the wealthy heiress, and her deceased father, who set up the stratagem of the caskets prior to his death. A paternalistic and controlling figure in the play, Portia's father reaches out from the grave in his attempt to protect his daughter from her own innate xenophobia and the greed and duplicity of the world around her. By requiring her various suitors to seek the truth beneath the appearance of each of the caskets, he hopes that Portia's eventual spouse will perceive her interior personal value through the highly polished surface of wealth and privilege. In this fashion, he can bequeath her directly from father to husband as if she were inherited property handed down from one generation to the next, in much the same way that Shakespeare must have presided over the lives of his two surviving daughters.

Ironically, neither Portia nor Jessica has a living mother with whom to identify. Although the absence of female parents in the play may have much to do with the limited number of boy actors available to play the women's parts in Shakespeare's company, the lack of feminine role models in *The Merchant of Venice* requires Portia and Jessica almost instinctively to disguise themselves as males to find independence within their respective worlds. Abandoned by their parents, they can only discover romance by denying their proper gender and adopting the masculine identity of their dominant fathers. Viewed in this fashion, the two women usurp parental control to take charge of their lives.

Shakespeare's emphasis on the importance of parenting in the play pales in significance, however, when contrasted with the immense power of religion and ethnicity to corrupt humankind. Despite the best attempts of Shylock, Antonio, Old Gobbo, and Portia's father to inoculate their

7. *The Merchant of Venice*, 2000. *Left to right:* Richard Thomsen as Anthony, Kathleen McCall as Portia, and Anthony De Fonte as Shylock. Photo by Karl Hugh. Published with permission of the Utah Shakespeare Festival.

children against the evils that surround them, the indignities of racism and bigotry infect everyone in the play. In fact, the only hope for the future rests not in the parents but their children. Portia and Bassanio, who are less encrusted by the weight of social tradition than their father figures, have the opportunity to begin new lives by fusing the play's awkward geographical dichotomy. In their amorous union, Portia represents the female-dominated, magical, harmonious, nighttime world of Belmont while Bassanio symbolizes the male-dominated, mercantile, discordant, daytime world of Venice. Joined together in marriage, these two fragmented environments of the play evolve into a complete and well-balanced universe for the lovers to inhabit.

Likewise, Jessica and her lover, Lorenzo—two children of opposing religions—unite Judaism and Christianity through an interfaith marriage that achieves the social symmetry so alien to Shylock and Antonio, mortal enemies who are inextricably entwined in their hatred for each other. Listening to the "sweet harmony" of the spheres in act 5, scene 1, the two lovers help us forget for a precious moment the religious discord that mars both Shakespeare's world and our own, transporting us to a heavenly future where such prejudice will be merely a distant memory. However, Shakespeare seems to be saying that the journey will be a hard passage for such odd companions as Lorenzo and his "Jew's daughter," who is still struggling with unresolved issues concerning her parents and her religious loyalties.

Although the sins of the fathers are indeed visited upon their children, each generation marks an improvement over the ones before. Perhaps, as Shakespeare suggests, the child of such a union offers the best hope for success. This is the playwright's legacy of happiness for parents and their offspring—forbidden in his life due to the death of his son, yet proclaimed eternally through his theatrical genius.

THE TWO COMIC PLOTS OF VERONA

The Two Gentlemen of Verona at the 2001
Utah Shakespeare Festival

Pay attention now: which of the following makes *The Two Gentlemen of Verona* a comedy? Is it the goofy dog named Crab; the two slapstick servants, Launce and Speed; the bumbling, inept outlaws; the hilarious disguises; the intriguing mixture of friendship and love; or all of the above that defines this early play by Shakespeare as "a pleasant comedy"? If you answered all of the above, you would be only half right because determining the genre (or literary type) of a play depends less on individual comic circumstances and more on the overall design of the drama. Most people would agree, for example, that *King Lear* and *Romeo and Juliet* are tragedies despite the fact that both plays include comic characters and amusing situations. So if an occasional dog or joke doesn't make a play a comedy, what does?

As we all learned in Miss Hickey's ninth-grade English class, tragedies move from good fortune to bad while comedies progress from bad to good. All Shakespeare's comic plays, in fact, follow the same evolutionary pattern. If we look more closely at this theatrical paradigm, however, we can arrive at a much more sophisticated and satisfying definition of comedy that helps explain the inner workings of the genre and also its deeper dramatic purpose.

Shakespeare's comedies move in two distinct, intriguing patterns: either (1) from society to wilderness to improved society, or (2) from union to wandering to reunion. The first of these models—most clearly illustrated by such plays as *A Midsummer Night's Dream*, *As You Like It*, and *The*

Winter's Tale—takes its characters from an urban, civilized environment to the green world of a forest, then back to the original society, which becomes a better place because of the freedom and personal growth the characters experienced in the wilderness. In *A Midsummer Night's Dream*, for example, all four principal character groups—royalty, young lovers, fairies, and rude mechanicals—move from bad to good fortune because of a single, wonderful night in Shakespeare's enchanted woods.

In contrast, plays like *Twelfth Night, The Comedy of Errors,* and *All's Well That Ends Well* illustrate a movement from union to wandering to reunion. In *Twelfth Night,* for instance, Viola and her brother, Sebastian, are parted at the outset by shipwreck, wander separately throughout the play, and are then reunited in a climactic reconciliation scene that brings love and happiness to both. In similar fashion, the principal characters in many Shakespearean comedies gravitate toward wedlock at the conclusion, which certainly seems like good fortune to those of us with happy marriages.

An awareness of these important comic patterns also helps us understand the deeper, more significant manner in which watching a comedy transports us from our mundane, everyday world of bills to pay and kids to chauffeur into a theatrical dreamscape that restructures our imaginations and enables us to see our lives more clearly after the curtain falls. We are metaphorically united with our everyday lives, then separated from them so we can undergo the joyful journey of the comedy, and then united again with lives made richer, sweeter, and more meaningful by the dramatic progress of the play. Interpreted in this fashion, viewing a play like *The Two Gentlemen of Verona* is comic because it carries us toward good fortune and solved problems through the ancient and timeless ritual of responding to actors who appear before us on a stage.

Interestingly enough, *Two Gents* is unique within the genre because it fulfills both these comic patterns. The play begins in Verona, then moves rapidly to Milan, the "city of gold"—a highly sophisticated, urban environment from which the four lovers escape into a forest near Mantua, where all the conflicts are resolved and the sweethearts return to their proper mates. In a play where the names of characters such as Valentine, Proteus, and Julia predict their behavioral idiosyncrasies, we should not be surprised that a brave and resourceful young woman named Silvia represents the sylvan wilderness that helps shape the outcome of the play.

8. *The Two Gentlemen of Verona*, 2001. *Left to right*: Danforth Comins as Valentine and Christopher Marshall as Proteus. Photo by Karl Hugh. Published with permission of the Utah Shakespeare Festival.

Similarly, through its focus on the two title characters, Shakespeare's comedy portrays the union of Proteus and Valentine in Verona, their separate adventures wandering through Milan and the forest, and their reconciliation as dear friends at the conclusion of the play.

Shakespeare's combination of these two comic patterns is more understandable when we recall that he yoked together two different sources in constructing this play: (1) Jorge de Montemayor's *Diana,* a Spanish pastoral romance celebrating the virtue of love, which moves from society to wilderness to improved society; and (2) the story of Titus and Gisippus in Sir Thomas Elyot's *The Book Named the Governor,* which progresses from union to wandering to reunion in arguing that male friendship is a higher type of human behavior than erotic love. Although these two complimentary sources define the play as a double comedy that moves in intricate, overlapping patterns toward its optimistic conclusion, they also create dramatic tension by setting Valentine's love of Silvia into stark contrast with his platonic affection for his friend Proteus. Both plots join instantaneously in the forest when Valentine, reunited with Proteus, presents his lover to his friend: "That my love may appear plain and free," he offers, "all that was mine in Silvia I give thee" (5.4.82–83). Though the moment often elicits howls from the audience and a strong onstage reaction from Silvia, it seems appropriate in a play that somewhat awkwardly fuses two comic patterns and two literary sources.

Shakespeare's dual plots also allow the comedy to carry more than its normal share of important themes, including maturity and metamorphosis. This is a play featuring very young characters with few older people serving as positive role models. The four young lovers in particular must learn—through the progress of the play—how to function in an adult world. Appropriately the comedy ends with the dawn, the beginning of a new day in the lovers' journey into maturity. If, as Valentine argues, "love's a mighty lord" (2.4.136), so, too, the characters discover, is friendship. And finding a proper balance between the two extremes of love and friendship is an important lesson in becoming an adult—in Shakespeare's comic universe and ours as well.

"My Daughter, My Ducats"

Love and Money in *The Merchant of Venice* at the 2006
Utah Shakespeare Festival

More than in any other Shakespearean play, affection and avarice are uneasy bedfellows in *The Merchant of Venice* (1600). When Solanio mimics Shylock's anguished cries of "My daughter! O, my ducats! O, my daughter!" (15) in act 2, scene 8, his words suggest one of the principal motifs of this intriguing play: money may placate the flesh, but only love enriches and satisfies our souls. Part of a rich fabric of themes and images, this central truth is immediately apparent in the preoccupation with finance displayed throughout the play.

In the opening scene, for example, Bassanio describes Portia as "a lady richly left, / And she is fair" (1.1.160–61). Wealth first, then beauty seems to be his principal motivation. Similarly the Jewish moneylender Shylock admits in an aside in act 1, scene 3 that he hates Antonio because he is a Christian but more since "he lends out money gratis, and brings down / The rate of usance here with us in Venice" (41–42), an assertion suggesting that finance is stronger than both love and hate. Later in that same scene, Shylock distorts the biblical story of Jacob and Laban (Genesis 30) to justify the relatively new practice of charging interest on loans—a necessary evil for entrepreneurs like Antonio during this period of rapid mercantile expansion in Renaissance Italy. Although the roots of usury go back to the early Greeks, where money was described as "barren," the ancient word for "interest" (*tokos*) meant "child," which betrayed a deep ambivalence over the ethical and moral propriety of earning money without the slightest hint of physical labor. Nowhere is this paradox more clearly articulated than in the playwright's *Timon of Athens* (1606), where the title character's naïveté about the compounding of interest drives him to financial ruin.

Although Antonio and Portia give lip service to the commonplace adage that money can't buy happiness, both characters, like Bassanio, are obsessed with wealth. Antonio's avaricious pursuit of foreign markets stretches his fleet of ships to the breaking point while Portia, newly won in the casket stratagem, waxes arithmetic in her declaration to Bassanio that she wishes to be

> trebled twenty times myself,
> A thousand times more fair, ten thousand times
> More rich, that only to stand high in your account
> I might in virtues, beauties, livings, friends,
> Exceed account. (3.2.153–57)

Later, when she learns of Antonio's peril at the hands of Shylock, Portia blithely tells her new husband to double payment of the bond, then double that sum again, then "treble that, / Before a friend of this description / Shall lose a hair through Bassanio's fault" (3.2.300–302). As interest compounds in the play, so, too, does love. Unfortunately for the Christians, Shylock's affection is not so easily bought as Bassanio's. When offered twice the sum in court, the usurer claims that "if every ducat in six thousand ducats / Were in six parts, and every part a ducat, / I would not draw them; I would have my bond" (4.1.84–86).

As this cruel numbers game implies, the dramatic arc of Shylock's character has evolved greatly from the beginning of the play, where "monies" was his only "suit" (1.3.116). Devastated by his daughter's elopement with a Christian and her theft of so much of his wealth, Shylock begins to understand that human relationships are more precious and ephemeral than the pursuit of riches. When his friend Tubal tells him earlier that Jessica has traded his deceased wife's ring for a monkey, Shylock replies in anguish that he "would not have given it for a wilderness of monkeys" (3.1.113–14). In contrast, Bassanio and Gratiano cavalierly offer their wedding rings to the disguised Portia and Nerissa after Antonio's acquittal. No amount of money can bring back Shylock's wife and daughter, just as nothing but Antonio's death can compensate for years of anti-Semitic scorn and ridicule. In his Old Testament world of "an eye for an eye, and a tooth for a tooth," Shylock reasons that only the death of a Christian can make restitution for the loss of his Jewish child.

Shylock's attempt to cut out Antonio's heart nicely parallels Shakespeare's artistic effort to pluck hatred out of his Christian audience. Though cloaked in such admirable virtues as romantic love, devotion to close friends, and the attempt to move up the social and economic ladder, the Christians of Shakespeare's play—like Antonio's "goodly apple" (1.3.98)—are rotten at the core. When Portia returns home after her victory in the trial scene and compares the conquest of Shylock to "a good deed" shining brightly "in a naughty world" (5.1.91), her words prefigure the abhorrent ethnic cleansing that came later to Europe and the religious myopia so prevalent in today's society. The dearth of any normative role models in the play—save perhaps Portia's dead father—means that audiences always have difficulty identifying with characters whose bigotry and xenophobia consistently betray their lack of moral integrity.

This Christian hypocrisy is only apparent, however, if we, unlike most of Portia's suitors, accept Shakespeare's invitation to look beneath surface appearances and find a deeper reality in the world around us. Shakespeare's play—like a dramatic casket—hides many truths within its glittering exterior of loving Christians triumphing over a greedy Jewish moneylender: one is that Shylock is the only person in the play who truly progresses from his obsession with wealth to a more profound understanding of the importance of human relationships. Part of Shakespeare's genius is that he ironically chooses his antagonist—the evil, blocking character—as the sole exemplum of positive change within the play. Because all the other characters remain static in their pursuit of love and money, they must excise Shylock as an alien presence since he is a constant reminder of their avarice and cruelty toward those different from themselves. Like Roderigo Lopez, the Portuguese Jewish physician convicted of plotting to poison Queen Elizabeth just prior to the play's initial performance at the Globe Theatre, Shylock is a scapegoat whose defeat at the end of the play signals a return to social homogeneity and wedded bliss, in contrast to the discord and conflict so apparent earlier in the play.

If any hope exists for the Christians in the play and in Shakespeare's own society, it lies in the union of Jessica and Lorenzo, two characters from very different worlds, who—like the contrasting geographic locations of

9. *The Merchant of Venice*, 2006. *Left to right*: Elijah Alexander as Bassanio, Michael Sharon as Antonio, Sara Kathryn Bakker as Portia, and John Pribyl as Shylock. Photo by Karl Hugh. Published with permission of the Utah Shakespeare Festival.

Venice and Belmont—must come together for the play to end happily. As Lorenzo explains while tutoring his wife in the mysteries of Christian theology, God's "harmony" exists within our perfect souls, but we cannot hear it while the "muddy vesture" of our bodies "doth grossly close it in" (5.1.63–65). A multitude of stars—like a wilderness of monkeys—look down upon us as audience members, each promising that God's blessings will be showered on those who strive for more perfect lives: ones free of hatred, prejudice, and the lust for money. Only love, which sits at the center of the universe, ennobles us all, Christians and Jews alike.

"This is Illyria, Lady"

Twelfth Night at the 2007 Utah Shakespeare Festival

For Shakespeare's major characters, geography often drives destiny. In *A Midsummer Night's Dream* and *Cymbeline,* for example, the lovers' journey to the woods liberates them from patriarchal and societal restrictions so they can mature and prosper while Desdemona's sea voyage from the sophistication of Venice to the male-dominated, claustrophobic, and licentious world of Cyprus helps doom her precarious relationship with Othello. In the same manner, locating *Twelfth Night* in Illyria offers some crucial clues to an attentive audience about the dramatic world of this beloved comedy.

Oddly, modern scholarship has been little help in decoding the relevance of place to play as far as Illyria is concerned. Generally dismissed as a mythical or fantastical locale, its importance in *Twelfth Night* may be summarized in the words of Isaac Asimov, who echoes the opinion of many other critics when he says that "we need not be overconcerned with actual geography" in *Twelfth Night* since "Shakespeare's Illyria, like his seacoast of Bohemia in *The Winter's Tale* and his Forest of Arden in *As You Like It,* really exists nowhere but in the play."[4]

On the contrary, however, Shakespeare's choice of Illyria, an offbeat and infrequently visited milieu, as the setting for *Twelfth Night* eloquently reveals the playwright's purpose. Although Illyria was a real place during Shakespeare's time in the western part of the Balkan peninsula on

---

4. Isaac Asimov, *Asimov's Guide to Shakespeare,* vol. 1, *The Greek, Roman, and Italian Plays* (New York: Wings Books, 1970), 576.

the eastern shores of the Adriatic Sea—the location of present-day Yugoslavia—its allure can be summed up in a single word: pirates! Orsino refers contemptuously to Antonio as a "notable pirate" and a "salt-water thief" and asks, "What foolish boldness brought thee to their mercies / Whom thou, in terms so bloody and so dear, / Hast made thine enemies?" (5.1.57–60). The only other reference to Illyria in Shakespeare's plays occurs in *Henry VI, Part II*, where Suffolk rebukes the lieutenant as more threatening than "Bargulus, the strong Illyrian pirate" (4.1.108), confirming the association between piracy and Illyria in the minds of Shakespeare's audience.

This relationship between pirates and the Balkans dates back to at least 250 BC, when tribes like the Ardriaii and Antariates preyed on Greek colonists on the eastern coast of the Adriatic and around such neighboring islands as Pharos and Corfu. Impatient with this disruption in their trade routes, the Romans—during the Illyrian Wars of 229 and 219 BC—overran outlaw settlements in the Neretva Valley, captured Gentius (the last king of Illyria), and curtailed the piracy that had made the Adriatic unsafe. By Shakespeare's time, however, the Balkans had taken on the additional aura of an unconventional locale perched dangerously on the great divide between Christendom and Islam, where the infusion of many different tribes and cultures created a flavorful stew of Gypsies, mountaineers, prostitutes, and other socially marginalized creatures who dwelt alongside the truly devout followers of two wildly divergent religions. In fact, George Sandys, a well-known Renaissance author of travel literature, wrote the following colorful description of Illyrians during his voyage to the region in 1610, just nine years after *Twelfth Night* was first produced: "The men wear half-sleeved gowns of violet cloth with bonnets of the same. They nourish only a lock of hair on the crown of their heads, the rest all shaven. The women wear theirs not long and dye them black for the most part. Their chief city is Ragusa, heretofore Epidaurus, a commonwealth of itself, famous for merchandise and plenty of shipping."[5]

Into this exotic world of pirates, Gypsies, religious fanatics, and other semifictionalized inhabitants, Shakespeare deposits Viola, his recently shipwrecked heroine, whose disconnect between her abandoned condi-

---

5. George Sandys, *A Relation of a Journey Begun Anno Domini 1610* (London: W. Barrett, 1615), 2–3.

tion and the foreign universe she now inhabits liberates her from responsibility and facilitates the discovery of her true identity, unencumbered by social, moral, or gender restrictions. Although she initially adopts a male disguise for self-preservation, Viola soon discovers that men in the Renaissance were permitted much more flexibility in their social and moral behavior than their female counterparts. Impersonating a young man, she enjoys the luxury of getting to know Orsino as a friend and confidant as they slowly fall in love. The same regenerative liberty is apparent in Olivia's sudden infatuation with Cesario, which permits the heiress to shed her mourning pretense and experience the genuine, heartfelt passion that she later happily bestows on Sebastian.

Perhaps the most obvious embodiment of *Twelfth Night*'s Illyrian atmosphere is Feste the clown, whose inspired antics turn the world of the play upside down, especially in his impersonation of Sir Topas the curate, when wisdom and folly change places. The well-known motif of the "wise fool" implies that behaving foolishly—particularly within a region

10. *Twelfth Night*, 2007. *Left to right*: Donald Sage Mackay as Malvolio, Anne Newhall as Maria, and Carey Cannon as Olivia. Photo by Karl Hugh. Published with permission of the Utah Shakespeare Festival.

consecrated to piracy and Gypsy lore—is a wise course of action since it helps all the principal characters find themselves through the liberating effects of love, wine, music, mistaken identity, and the play's other tempting aphrodisiacs. Only Malvolio, the odd one out in this cast of libertines, fails to prosper through the Illyrian aspect of the play since he is a puritanical scapegoat who expunges the sins of the other characters through dramatic catharsis. Bloated with self-pride, he takes himself much too seriously in a world where the spirit of licentiousness rewards love over law, revelry over sententiousness, and license over the dull monotony of moralistic values.

Inspired by the miracle of theatre, we audience members also find our true selves through the exotic experience of the play. As we immerse ourselves in this alien world and allow Shakespeare's poetic brilliance to wash over us, we are cleansed and refreshed by the magical power of the stage. Like Arion—rescued on the dolphin's back because of the sweet music he played on his lyre (1.2.15)—we are buoyed up by the fortunes of the play's successful characters and ascend through the spiritual and aesthetic artistry of this joyful dramatic event. In theatre, as in life itself, strange new worlds like Shakespeare's Illyria rejuvenate and replenish us, scouring away what is old and tired and unproductive to restore our more-perfect selves.

Love's Labor's Won

Love's Labor's Lost at the 2005 Utah Shakespeare Festival

Although the performance history of *Love's Labor's Lost* had been largely moribund until a series of successful revivals in the twentieth century reawakened interest in the play, it is quite appealing, focusing principally on the doomed attempt by the king of Navarre and his companions—Berowne, Longaville, and Dumaine—to devote themselves to an ascetic three-year period of study, fasting, and abstinence from women. The fun begins, of course, when the lovely princess of France and her three beautiful companions arrive at court, weakening the brittle veneer of male resolve and proving conclusively—as our mothers, wives, and daughters have told us all along—that women will always be victorious in the battle of the sexes. Supporting this feminist parable is a delightful cast of characters, including the exuberant and pompous Spanish braggart Don Adriano de Armado, the pedantic schoolmaster Holofernes, the bumbling Constable Dull, a rustic clown named Costard, Moth the diminutive page, and the pious curate Nathaniel, all of whom bring the play to vibrant life onstage.

Despite these theatrical charms, however, some elements of the play may seem antiquated and even a bit precious to modern audiences unaccustomed to a style more allied to earlier theatrical conventions than later mature Shakespearean comedies like *Much Ado about Nothing, As You Like It,* and *Twelfth Night.* According to current scholarship, the play was written near the beginning of Shakespeare's career—perhaps as early as 1588—then later revised for production in 1596–97 and first published in a 1598 quarto, the title page of which states "newly corrected and augmented." As a result, the play has a Janus vantage point, simultaneously looking forward to the great comedies to come and backward to a number of prior literary stimuli that would have been infinitely more familiar to Elizabethan viewers than audiences of today.

Chief among these early influences was an immensely popular literary style called *euphuism*, taken from John Lyly's novel *Euphues: The Anatomy of Wit* (1579), which featured an overabundance of rhyme, alliteration, antithesis, simile, and examples drawn from classical languages and pseudonatural history. When, for instance, Don Armado writes this series of questions to his beloved country wench, Jaquenetta—"Shall I command thy love? I may. Shall I enforce thy love? I could. Shall I entreat thy love? I will. What shalt thou exchange for rags? Robes. For tittles? Titles. For thyself? Me." (4.1.80–83)—he is engaging in an affected linguistic paradigm that flourished from the 1580s through the 1590s and was ripe for parody by Shakespeare's time. Even for a modern devotee of linguistics, however, a little bit of euphuism goes a very long way. This evolutionary preoccupation with language and style, which is also apparent in such other early plays as *The Comedy of Errors, Titus Andronicus,* and *Romeo and Juliet,* marks *Love's Labor's Lost* as a fledgling effort by a young playwright still infatuated with the trendy success of previous authors.

Another early influence on the play was the Italian commedia dell'arte, a popular theatrical style featuring broad improvisation and well-known comic figures, such as the aged pantaloon or the buffoonish harlequin. In *Love's Labor's Lost,* these stock characters include Holofernes the pedant, Costard as the *zanni* rustic servant, Nathaniel the parasite, Armado as the *miles gloriosus* braggart soldier, and a profusion of stereotypical lovers whose Petrarchan sexual yearnings seem quaintly detached from their literary heritage. Part of Shakespeare's genius in the play, therefore, lies in his ability to excerpt these commedia character types from their native literary milieu and endow them with new life through the cleverness of his dramatic art.

Love's Labor's Lost also owes a debt to the topical satire so popular in the late 1580s and early 1590s, which in this play spotlights such well-known historical figures and events as Henry of Navarre (King Henry IV of France) and his lords Biron and DeMayenne, Sir Walter Raleigh, pamphleteers Thomas Nashe and Gabriel Harvey, the Earls of Northumberland and Essex, Italian scholar John Florio, the Dark Lady of Shakespeare's

11. *Love's Labor's Lost,* 2005. *Left to right*: Corliss Preston as Rosaline and Melinda Pfundstein as the princess of France. Photo by Karl Hugh. Published with permission of the Utah Shakespeare Festival.

sonnets, the frequent royal "progresses" made by Queen Elizabeth into the countryside, and contemporary Anglo-Russian relationships. Equally intriguing is Shakespeare's use of the older literary tradition of the *debate*, where two or more characters—like the owl and the cuckoo at the end of the play—personify different sides of a single controversial issue, and his similar resuscitation of the *masque*, seen in the presentation of the Nine Worthies in act 5, scene 2.

Much of the brilliance of *Love's Labor's Lost*, therefore, lies in its ability to glance back casually at these earlier literary traditions while still anticipating—via the relationship between Berowne and the Princess of France—the stylish and witty combat displayed by later pairs of Shakespearean lovers like Beatrice and Benedick in *Much Ado about Nothing* and Rosalind and Orlando in *As You Like It*. Likewise, the gloomy entrance of Marcadé at the end of the play—announcing the demise of the king of France—reaches back to the Dance of Death and mythological journeys to the underworld, yet simultaneously forecasts the dark fatalism of such imminent tragicomedies as *Measure for Measure, The Merchant of Venice,* and *Troilus and Cressida*.

If love's labor is indeed lost in this play, it is accompanied by the remnants of many other literary traditions that Shakespeare experimented with and then discarded in his journey toward theatrical maturity. Thus, the earlier influences on *Love's Labor's Lost*—such as Lyly's euphuism, the commedia dell'arte character types, the abundant topical references, and the motifs of the debate and the masque—all glitter like precious jewels in an archeological excavation soon buried by the newer layers of the author's later comedies. From our vantage point as spectators, though, the artistic labor of the lovers is indeed victorious as Shakespeare cleverly endows these early literary traditions with a tantalizing hint of the transcendent comic dramaturgy to come later in his career. As is always the case, the proof of such assertions exists in live performances of this lovely play, which should properly be called *Love's Labor's Won*.

The Taming of the Script

The Taming of the Shrew at the 2008
Utah Shakespeare Festival

Although most contemporary Shakespearean productions live in at least three different worlds, director Jane Page's delightful version of *The Taming of the Shrew* this summer seamlessly blends four unique times and places: the first three are 1593 London (when the play was first written), late sixteenth-century Italy (where the action was originally set), and 1947 post-World-War-II Italy (where this year's Utah Shakespeare Festival production takes place). As if such time travel weren't expansive enough, the show is being viewed by a modern audience in 2008 Cedar City, Utah, which adds another layer to the intriguing chronological puzzle.

The last time the festival produced *Shrew* was in 2004, when Leslie Brott and Michael Connolly duked it out in a wonderful period production on the outdoor Adams stage where the alleged taming seemed more benign than brutal due to its sixteenth-century setting. That was a time when men dominated women—the argument goes—so we shouldn't judge the play's sexual politics too harshly by today's liberated standards.

Regardless of the era when the play is set, however, the notion of a man such as Petruchio subduing a beautiful and high-spirited woman like Kate provides some interesting opportunities for American twenty-first-century directors, actors, and audiences. We have met this challenge by moving the production indoors and about 350 years forward into the future, where Petruchio is an Italian American GI courting Kate while romance basks in the radiance of an allied victory. How successfully does this time warp fashion the production for a modern audience? And what special qualities in the text are illuminated by its rebirth in postwar Italy? To answer these intriguing questions, we need to take a closer look at the way this particular script prospers within its updated setting.

First of all, by viewing the play through our new dramatic lens, we see a world happily suspended between Shakespeare's era and our own. The general rule with such a script—which Page has observed nicely—is to move it close enough to our own time to make it meaningful while positioning it far enough away to keep the taming from enflaming contemporary sensibilities. Observed from this vantage point, the year 1947—like the temperature of Baby Bear's porridge—seems just right!

Second, we can tolerate and even enjoy this slightly misogynistic theme if taming becomes a metaphor for falling in love: an alliance where each partner allows his or her wilder aspects to be subdued in the interest of future domestic bliss. This summer's production implies that Petruchio goes through the same cleansing process that Kate endures, where both are deprived of sleep, food, luxurious clothing, and other necessaries so that—newly purified by denial—they can become one flesh. If Petruchio's "falcon now is sharp and passing empty" (4.1.178)—if Kate is so hungry that, like a ravenous hawk, her breastbone protrudes from her chest—he shares those hunger pangs in the name of love.

Third, the 1947 setting gives the production a sentimental atmosphere appropriate for not only the script but also the euphoria following the end of World War II, which engendered hope, optimism, and the possibility of unexpected global alliances after the horrors of battle. Fighting ends in cooperation and newfound amity on the international level as well as in the daily affairs of men and women like Petruchio and Kate, who find themselves in love as did many American servicemen and their attractive imported Italian brides. Just as Shakespeare's original text juxtaposes a young man from Verona and a woman from Padua, so, too, does Page's updated version blend the twin cultures of Petruchio's American heritage and Kate's Italian upbringing to signal a resurgent world order where the cooperation of nations is represented by two people from different countries falling in love.

Finally, to help audiences make this transition from crisis to compromise, set designer Jo Winiarski envisioned Padua not as a ruined landscape but as what she called in production meetings a "lighthearted, bombed-out city," a "Technicolor version" of the aftermath of brutish

12. *The Taming of the Shrew*, 2008. Grant Goodman as Petruchio and Melinda Parrett as Katherine. Photo by Karl Hugh. Published with permission of the Utah Shakespeare Festival.

military engagement. If love is a kind of battle, then conflict often leads to concord, as Lucentio implies at the end of the play in a comment that yokes military and amorous squabbling while seeming to invite this summer's joyful military approach to the script: "At last, though long, our jarring notes agree, / And time it is, when raging war is done, / To smile at scapes and perils overblown (5.2.1–3).

One of the great pleasures of live theatre is that it allows us to travel to different times and places so we can understand our own world a little better. Like Tranio and Lucentio, who go to Padua to "institute / A course of learning and ingenuous studies" (1.1.8–9), so, too, are we as audience members tutored by our journey to mid-twentieth-century Padua, which imbues Shakespeare's delightful script with the enthusiasm and confidence of a postwar generation.

Viewed within this hazy glow of romantic, war-torn Italy, the USF's updated and inventive production of *The Taming of the Shrew* seems comfortable with its transition from Shakespeare's era to one much closer to our twenty-first-century lives. By setting the play in 1947 Italy, Page has tamed not only the central characters but also the text, which sheds much of the emotional baggage that has weighed it down during the last sixty years of feminist commentary and becomes once again a simple story about a man and woman who find a way to love each other despite the gender and geographic stereotypes that surround them.

Much Ado about Something

Much Ado about Nothing at the 2010
Utah Shakespeare Festival

The title of Shakespeare's *Much Ado about Nothing* (1598) is clearly ironic since the play deals with such significant topics as a young bride-to-be falsely accused of infidelity, her apparent death, and her joyful resurrection, coupled with an incendiary romance between two strong-willed individuals who are convinced—against their own sexual appetites—that they love each other. Typical of other mature comedies like *The Merchant of Venice* (1597), *As You Like It* (1598), and *Twelfth Night* (1600), *Much Ado* reveals at every turn the complexity in style, form, and content that audiences have come to expect from Shakespeare's later comedies, deepening our enjoyment when we watch a good production. Unlike such earlier efforts as the delightful, if somewhat monochromatic, *The Two Gentlemen of Verona* and *Love's Labor's Lost*, *Much Ado about Nothing* gives viewers more for their entertainment dollar than a few belly laughs and some interesting plot developments because it is comic in a much more profound sense.

Not surprisingly, the intricacy of the text is signaled as early as the title's pun on the word "nothing," which was pronounced much like "noting" during the Renaissance, conjuring up images of slander, overhearing, gossip, innuendo, musical notation, and sexuality that structure the play and give meaning to its plot. As anyone who has ever been the subject of gossip can attest, it is the "notings" that prompt all the "ado": for example, Antonio's servants mistakenly report that Don Pedro loves Hero (act 1, scene 2); Borachio revels to Don John that Hero is actually loved by Claudio (act 1, scene 3), who later hears from Don John that the prince is trying to steal her from him (act 2, scene 1); Benedick and Beatrice both overhear their friends discussing their alleged love (act 2, scene 3 and act 3, scene 1); Claudio is deluded by Margaret's impersonation of Hero on the night before his wedding (act 3, scene 2); and the Watch overhear Borachio confessing his villainy to Conrad (act 3, scene 3), which leads to Hero's redemption and the resulting happy ending.

The play's witty and ironic plot is supported by a depth in characterization seldom seen in Shakespeare's comedies. If the old cliché is true that tragedies rely on character development while comedies are more plot driven, the best plays—regardless of genre—provide a mixture of both. Such is certainly the case with *Much Ado,* where the conventional Petrarchan relationship between Hero and Claudio starkly contrasts with the incredibly human, volatile, and endearing love affair between Beatrice and Benedick, which teaches us that honest (if sometimes erratic) affection always outshines idealized love. Much like such blockbuster 1930s Hollywood romantic comedies as *Top Hat, His Girl Friday,* and *The Thin Man,* featuring Fred Astaire, Ginger Rogers, Cary Grant, Rosalind Russell, and other legendary actors, the mercurial love affair between Beatrice and Benedick sizzles with sexual energy, witty combat, and unrequited passion. These are real characters grappling with real amorous problems in the fictional context of a Shakespearean play, which makes them au courant for a postmodern world filled with sexual angst. They easily transport the play into the twenty-first century, where it is guaranteed to intrigue contemporary audiences.

Another index of authorial sophistication is the complexity of the play's themes, which range over a wide array of powerful and allusive issues. Chief among these is the maiden falsely accused, which leads to the motif of death and rebirth central to this play and such transcendent late romances as *Pericles, The Winter's Tale,* and *Cymbeline.* Similarly Shakespeare's movement from real to amorous war invokes the Renaissance motif of the *miles amores* (soldier of love), through which Claudio—like his later counterparts, Othello and Antony—demonstrates the oxymoronic impossibility of being a lover and a soldier at the same time. Additional themes and images include the growing realism of Shakespeare's villains (Don John as a precursor to Iago and Edmund), the use of sports and game playing as dramatic metaphors for love and the struggle for

13. *Much Ado about Nothing*, 2010. David Ivers as Benedick and Kymberly Mellen as Beatrice. Photo by Karl Hugh. Published with permission of the Utah Shakespeare Festival.

power, the animosity between brothers (see *As You Like It* and *King Lear*), the importance of language (Dogberry's malapropisms parody the linguistic expertise swirling around him), and the skillful and didactic use of dramatic irony, where only the audience knows the complete reality in the play at any given moment.

Even the staging of *Much Ado* profits from the play's maturity in conception and design. The two discovery scenes where first Benedick and then Beatrice are tricked into falling in love, for example, require incredible ingenuity on the part of the director and actors in finding spaces onstage where the lovers can hide as they overhear the conspirators' dialog. In addition, the two sequential gulling episodes must be different enough that viewers don't get bored watching these mirrored scenes. Beyond such formidable challenges, theatrical companies must find ways to encourage their audiences to forgive Claudio, who as one of Shakespeare's first seriously flawed young lovers must end the play worthy of the second chance that Hero offers him. And finally, the script provides theatrical companies with brilliant dramaturgical treasures like Beatrice's "kill Claudio" (4.1.288), where the author deftly fuses love and hate into a single, breathless beat change.

In the final analysis, *Much Ado about Nothing* is a superb example of Shakespeare's mature comic style, uniting, as it does, a complex plot, spectacular depth in characterization, a number of intellectually engaging themes and images, and staging possibilities that make extensive use of theatrical resources and the audience's imagination. Perhaps the play's greatest and most unexpected strength, however, is the way it employs the pure, simple, homespun virtues of the humble Dogberry and his Watch to uncover the diabolical plotting of Don John and his henchmen, which would surely have warmed the hearts of spectators during the Renaissance like it does today. As is so often the case in Shakespeare, the working-class characters—rather than the aristocrats—are the moral and ethical center of the play. For a comedy with such charming surprises, perilous circumstances, thematic intensity, romantic realism, and abundant laughter, surely *Much Ado about Something* seems a more appropriate title!

III

The Histories

Parrot, Parody, and Paronomasia

"Damnable Iteration" in *Henry IV, Part I* at the 2004
Utah Shakespeare Festival

The skies of *Henry IV, Part I* are aflutter with talking birds. In act 1, scene 3, for example, after the abrupt termination of his interview with the king, Hotspur angrily vows to train a starling to speak "nothing but 'Mortimer'" in harassment of "this vile politician Bolingbroke" (221–225, 241). Elsewhere in the same scene, Percy claims that the foppish lord who demanded his prisoners on the battlefield was little more than a "popinjay" (49) or a noisy parrot, while Kate later calls her choleric husband a "paraquito" (2.3.88) when he refuses to answer questions about his preparation for war. Likewise, Hal and Falstaff discuss cuckoos (which mimic cries of other birds) and sparrows (2.4.379–89), estridges and eagles bate the wind (4.1.97–99), and Worcester accuses the king of mistreating his family "as that ungentle gull the cuckoo's bird / Useth the sparrow" (5.1.60–61). Most memorable, perhaps, is Hal's metaphoric indictment of the intellectually challenged Francis, who has "fewer words than a parrot, and yet the son of a woman" (2.4.110–11). Like Hotspur, Francis has descended a full link on the great chain of being, with both men degenerating into bestial parodies of the divine potential encoded within their immortal souls.

These omnipresent chattering birds, mocking their surroundings with satiric glee, are emblematic of a play where echo, resonance, and mimicry reverberate throughout the dramatic landscape. Such repetition is not only evident in the language and action of the text, but it also reveals important truths about Shakespeare's experimentation with the relatively new genre of historical drama so popular in England at the time and helps explain why *Henry IV, Part I* is arguably Shakespeare's most admired, accessible, and satisfying history play.

An important early example of this repetition is apparent in the many parodic games Hal and Falstaff play in what we might call the "churls gone wild" sections of the play, which we can dub "name that proverb," where one contestant offers a sustained prose version of a famous saying or maxim while the other attempts to guess its better-known equivalent. In act 1, scene 2, for instance, after Falstaff's lengthy depiction of the "old lord of the Council," who railed at him unsuccessfully in the street, Hal correctly deduces that Falstaff is referring to the adage "wisdom cries out in the streets, and no man regards it" (1.2.94–100). When Falstaff subsequently praises his young companion's "damnable iteration" (101), he refers, of course, to Hal's skill at repeating phrases with a satiric twist—to damn or ridicule through comic repetition. Like the chattering birds elsewhere in the play, this "damnable iteration" is everywhere apparent, especially in the ubiquitous puns or paronomasia that add humor to the dialogue while simultaneously supporting the action of a play deeply indebted to parody.

A mere fifty lines into the text, for instance, the king mimics Westmoreland's report of "uneven and unwelcome news" with the "smooth and welcome news" brought by Sir Walter Blunt concerning Hotspur's victory (1.1.50, 66). Similarly Falstaff refashions the word "thieves" through such genteel euphemisms as "Diana's foresters," "gentlemen of the shade," and "minions of the moon" (1.2.28–29). Verbal echoes such as "were it not here apparent that thou art heir apparent" (1.2.64–65), the quibble on "obtaining of suits" (80), the incessant repetition of "when thou art king," and Hal's sun/son puns all characterize a relationship between the two friends that thrives on what Falstaff casually refers to as "unsavory similes" (89). Even the play's occasional couplets emphasize repetition and parody—particularly in such slant rhymes as "deaths"/"this" (3.2.158–160) and "horse"/"corpse" (4.1.122–123), where the second word of the couplet clearly mocks the first.

The remainder of the text, in fact, is laced with parody: Falstaff mimes a preacher (1.2.170–73); Hotspur imitates the foppish courtier in his speech before the king (1.3); the second carrier echoes Gadshill's request for a lantern (2.1.43–44); Falstaff copies the jargon of thieves (2.2.87–90); Hotspur ridicules the letter of the unsympathetic lord (2.3); Kate acts out

Hotspur's nightmare references to "sallies" and "retires" (2.3.50–58); Poins
and Hal mimic the innkeeper in calling for Francis the drawer (2.4.37–89);
Hal impersonates Hotspur and Kate in his "fie upon this quiet life, I want
work" speech (2.4.102–8); Falstaff repeats, then exaggerates, the number
of men whom he allegedly fought (2.4.182–213); Hal and Falstaff mirror
each other's invective-filled diatribes (2.4.237–44); Bardolph's "choler,
my lord, if rightly taken" is echoed by Hal's "no, if rightly taken, hal-
ter" (2.4.320–21); Falstaff reiterates his own praise in "sweet Jack Falstaff,
kind Jack Falstaff, true Jack Falstaff, valiant Jack Falstaff…and old Jack
Falstaff" (469–72); Glendower and Hotspur parody each other with "he
wisheth you in heaven…and you in hell" (3.1.9); Glendower brags that
he can "command the Devil" while Hotspur counsels him to "shame the
Devil / By telling truth" (3.1.53–55); Lady Mortimer's father repeats her
Welsh lament in perfect English (3.1.188–215); Kate admonishes Hotspur
to listen to "the lady sing in Welsh," and he counters that he would rather
hear "lady my brach howl in Irish" (3.1.229–30); Hotspur mimics Kate's
"not mine, in good sooth" with his own litany of tepid oaths (3.1.240–50);
the king reminds Hal of the time Richard II was mocked by "gibing boys"
(3.2.66); and Hal's pledge to his father that he "will die a hundred thousand deaths" reverberates two lines later when the king states, "A hundred thousand rebels die in this" (3.2.158–60).

These verbal parallels are echoed and underscored by situational
repetition, which is also abundant throughout the text and helps identify *Henry IV, Part I* as self-consciously parodic. Just as Hotspur's talking about a starling and Hal's reference to Francis as a dim-witted parrot
introduce the motif early in the play, another important image confirms
the repetition near the conclusion—the specter of counterfeit kings. After Douglas kills Sir Walter Blunt in act 5, scene 3, for example, Hotspur
explains that his victim was "semblably furnished like the King himself"
(21) but was not, in fact, the royal object of their search. "The King hath
many marching in his coats" (25), confesses Hotspur, to which Douglas
angrily replies, "I will kill all his coats! / I'll murder all his wardrobe, piece
by piece, / Until I meet the King" (26–28).

One scene later, when Douglas finally confronts Henry on the battlefield, he moans in exasperation, "Another king! They grow like Hydra's
heads" (5.4.24), which is itself a classical image of uncontrollable repetition. "What are thou," he continues, "that counterfeitest the person of a

king?" (5.4.24–27). Told he is speaking to the king himself, not another of his shadows (5.4.29), Douglas admits, "I fear thou art another counterfeit,/And yet, in faith, thou bearest thee like a king—/But mine I am sure thou art, whoe'er thou be,/And thus I win thee" (34–37).

This metaphor of counterfeiting, which further develops the motif of parody and repetition in the play, is introduced earlier by Falstaff when he counsels Hal never to "call a true piece of gold a counterfeit" (2.4.485–486) and repeated later with Sir John's description of his threadbare soldiers as "slaves" and "scarecrows" (4.2.24, 38). Although disguising commoners as kings was a well-known protective tactic in medieval warfare, the symbol of a counterfeit ruler in this play invites comparisons to Henry's alleged role as usurper and the royal aspirations of Hal and Hotspur, who both have designs on the throne. A counterfeit king—like a slave, a shadow, a scarecrow, an old knight (like Falstaff) who "bates" and "dwindles" (3.3.2), and a worthless golden coin—is a pale, devalued echo of its former self, maintaining the image of its predecessor but not the true value beneath its façade. It is a "damnable iteration" like the fuzzy, distorted, repetitive image of a third- or fourth-generation video copy, laughable in its pretensions and constantly mimicking the original on which it is based.

On another, more metatheatrical level, the counterfeiting in the text becomes more significant when we realize that Blunt's impersonation of the king mirrors the manner in which Shakespeare's actors simulate all the historical characters in the play. In fact, through the process of theatrical doubling so familiar to a Renaissance audience, *Henry IV, Part I* in performance constantly reminds attentive viewers that the same relatively small group of actors is continually entering and exiting the stage—replete with a variety of costumes, beards, and vocal accents—in a repetitive creative process that breathes life into well-known personages from the recesses of English history.

Framed between these images of talkative parrots, counterfeit kings, and recurrent actors are a number of additional parodic elements in the action and imagery of the play that complement its verbal references. Chief among these, of course, is the manner in which the comic subplot echoes the more substantive main story. While Hotspur and the Percy clan are planning their rebellion, for instance, Hal is doing battle with drawers at the Boar's Head, where he upbraids Poins in military jargon for having

14. *Henry IV, Part I*, 2004. *Left to right*: Charles Metten as Bardolph, Kieran Connolly as Sir John Falstaff, Kirsten Fitzgerald as Mistress Quickly, R. Brian Normoyle as Edward Poins, and Jonathan Brathwaite as Henry, Prince of Wales. Photo by Karl Hugh. Published with permission of the Utah Shakespeare Festival.

"lost much honor that thou wert not with me in this action" (2.4.20–21). Similarly the relaxed prose of the subplot mimics the stately verse of the main story until Hal—by accepting his responsibility as the future king of England—changes the rhythm of his destiny with the rhythm of his speech. His first-act soliloquy is an anticipatory pre-echo (or, in modern cinematic jargon, a prequel) of his reformation.

In short, the hero's ignoble behavior at the outset of the play acts as a dramatic mirror where the reformed prince in triumphant maturity can look back at his earlier frivolous self. Hal's prescience in this early soliloquy turns the entire play into a dramatic fulfillment of his vowed reformation in much the same fashion that Poins's prediction in act 1, scene 2 about the postrobbery behavior of Falstaff becomes corpulent flesh during the fat knight's epic defense of his honor in the tavern scene (act 2, scene 4). When Hal finally does break through "the foul and ugly mists / Of vapors that did seem to strangle him" (1.2.196–97), he fulfills the pledge in his act 1, scene 2 soliloquy and his interview with his father in act 3, scene 2, confirming the audience's faith in the veracity of his word and commemorating the virtue of a play that always seems to deliver what it has promised.

Additional parodic events in the play include Falstaff's ludicrous description of the robbery in act 2, scene 4, which simultaneously reprises his cowardice at the conclusion of act 2, scene 2, echoes the rebel plot to steal the throne, and is burlesqued by Sir John's accusation in act 3, scene 3 that his seal ring "worth forty mark" (80) has been stolen in the tavern. In this sequence, Falstaff steals from others and is then the victim of two subsequent comic robberies. Likewise, the linguistic clumsiness of Francis parodies the verbal expertise swirling around him; Hotspur's misguided and egocentric behavior is clearly a perversion of the well-known chivalric code of honor; and Falstaff, who is an exaggerated caricature because of his immense size and comic exuberance, descends to self-parody later when his subdued demeanor is a weak echo of his earlier robust self.

In addition, Hal and Hotspur—the twin doppelganger Harrys—are mirror images of each other as they move inexorably toward their final confrontation on the field of Shrewsbury, just as Falstaff and the king both serve as father figures to the young prince. Early in the play, when King Henry openly wishes that "some night-tripping fairy had exchanged / In cradle-clothes our children where they lay, / And called mine Percy, his Plantagenet" (1.1.85–88), he sets up a comparison where Hal is the "counterfeit" prince, while Hotspur is the "true piece of gold." In typical ironic fashion, however, the end of the play reverses this parodic relationship when Hal—in triumph over his fallen foe—ends the "double reign" of adversaries and contrasts his rise in power with Hotspur's "ill-weaved" and "shrunk" ambition (5.4.65, 87).

Most impressive, perhaps, is the anticipation of the real confrontation between Hal and his father in act 3, scene 2 via the mock interview featuring Hal and Falstaff in act 2, scene 4. The text provides, in fact, a double prefiguration of the later scene by first having Hal play himself opposite Falstaff's king, then reversing the roles so that Hal impersonates his father and Falstaff enacts the prince. Both play-acting episodes create a sense of déjà vu for audience members when they are finally treated to a solemn version of the two earlier humorous scenes, forecasting the play's eventual movement from comic to serious via the final defeat of the rebels and the restoration of royal order.

Thus, the text creates a Janus vantage point, where viewers watching the play-acting scene can look back in time to the real-life interview between Hal and his father that undoubtedly took place, as well as forward to the later theatrical encounter in Shakespeare's play. In addition, we learn a great deal about this dysfunctional father-son relationship through the earlier mirror scenes involving Hal and Falstaff. Not only do the two "actors" brilliantly anticipate the speech patterns of the prince and his father in act 2, scene 4, but the intensity of the king's anger at his son is expertly anticipated in the earlier scene. Further, Hal's "I do, I will" (527) provides a pseudocomic prediction of his eventual rejection of Falstaff at the conclusion of *Henry IV, Part II* in the same way that Falstaff's agonized "give me my horse, you rogues, give me my horse…" (2.2.28–29) can be read as a foreshadowing of King Richard III's "A horse! A horse! My kingdom for a horse" (5.4.7)—but that's a topic for another paper.

This vast network of verbal and situational parody and paralleling encourages us to consider other important ways that the rhetorical device of repetition serves the text. To do so, we need to step back from the play and evaluate its proper place in Shakespeare's *Henry IV* tetralogy and the larger span of the author's entire series of history plays. *Henry IV, Part I* is, of course, the second play in the four-part series dealing with the beginnings of the Wars of the Roses, which includes historical events ranging from the early 1390s to Richmond's victory over Richard III in 1485. The second tetralogy—the first three parts of *Henry VI* through *Richard III*—was written first, yet it surveys historical events following those of the *Richard II–Henry V* series. In this sense, the *Richard II* tetralogy is also a prequel—composed later, yet dealing with earlier historical material.

All theatrical versions of history are repetitive, of course, since the very nature of the genre relies heavily on an audience's prior knowledge of past events. In these two tetralogies, for example, Shakespeare was indebted to narratives derived from Holinshed, Daniel, Hall, Froissart, and other chroniclers of the time whose sole purpose was to record historical information for a reading public eager to learn more about its national identity. As a result, Shakespeare's plays echo and reshape his sources, which are themselves a compilation of historical moments that lie at least three removes from the plays that rehearse and popularize these factual events. When Shakespeare's characters speak of the "pattern" of history, then, as they do in *The Winter's Tale* (3.2.36) and elsewhere, the phrase suggests the commonplace adage that "history repeats itself," which enables the past—represented by these plays—to become our present via the miracle of theatre. Through the repetitive hearing and rehearing of these well-known stories—the "rehearsal" of history—we situate ourselves within a chronological continuum that teaches us our proper place in the universe and our complex relationship to the millions of lives that surround us.

Among these eight popular chronicle plays, therefore, Shakespeare's *Henry IV, Part I* may be considered the only true comedy since it contains rich and plentiful humor along with a plot structure that clearly moves from problem to solution and bad fortune to good. Perhaps the ultimate parodic element in the play, then, lies not in its repetitive language or dramatic situations but in Shakespeare's manipulation of the genre. In this crucial sense, the entire play is a parody of English history, putting a positive comic spin on well-known factual events. Somewhat akin to Polonius's "tragical-comical-historical-pastoral" subgenre in *Hamlet* (2.2.398), Shakespeare is refining the relatively new dramatic category of *historical comedy*, which was still in its infancy in the evolution of theatre. If history is a story told by the winners, then *Henry IV, Part I* may legitimately be viewed within the comic context of Hal's rise to power and eventual ascent to the throne. Although Hotspur is a worthy antagonist, he is defeated as much by the inexorable forces of history and the inevitable movement from feudalism to nationalism as by the deadly sword of Prince Hal.

As a result, Shakespeare has created what *New Yorker* movie critic Anthony Lane has, in another context, called "the comedy of apocalypse" by turning the horrors of war and death into a comic masterpiece.[1] History plays are usually parodic since playwrights are always under pressure to rearrange and massage past events to create an ending that congratulates the victors.

In a more meaningful way, however, *Henry IV, Part I* is comic because Prince Hal is an obvious paean to Elizabeth I. For an attentive Renaissance audience, England's "ideal king" is a precursor of England's "ideal queen" within the majestic and enduring symphony of time. Like Prince Hal, "who never promiseth but he means to pay" (5.4.43), the text of *Henry IV, Part I*—through its abundant mimicry, echoing, repetition,

---

1. Anthony Lane, "This Is Not a Movie," *The New Yorker*, September 24, 2001, 79.

and parody—confirms audience expectations at every turn, satisfying the dramatic appetite it has so cleverly created. Though Prince Hal dwells at the center of the play's "damnable iteration," this textual repetition is violated in a single, meaningful way when the son refuses to copy the actions of his father. To become a mirror for magistrates, Hal must of necessity articulate a different vision of kingship than the one presented by Henry IV, whose stain of usurpation and manifest behavioral flaws Hal must eschew before he can rightfully govern the kingdom. In this sense, the play is an intensely personal parable about a young man who breaks out of the repetitive and parodic world around him to find his own unique and ultimately comic path to the throne of England.

Historical Narratives

Richard II at the 1993 Utah Shakespeare Festival

Shakespeare's *Richard II* (1596) projects English history in much the same way a modern carnival mirror distorts and redefines the object it reflects. The goal of such revision is not to reproduce actual reality but to create an imaginative theatrical narrative that teaches us more than mere history ever can. As a result, an increased awareness of the manner in which a playwright has altered his historical sources can often point the way toward a deeper understanding of the themes and symbolic correspondences generated by the newly conceived dramatic story.

Shakespeare departed from his principal source, Raphael Holinshed's *Chronicles* (1587), by expanding and redefining the characters of John of Gaunt, the Duchess of York, and the Earl of Northumberland; by creating a largely fictitious role for Queen Isabel (who was a child of eleven at the time of Richard's deposition); by adding the famous garden scene; and, most importantly, by inventing out of whole cloth much of the sympathetic, poetic nature of King Richard. Samuel Daniel's *The First Four Books of the Civil Wars* (1595) may have suggested some of these refinements to the playwright, but most of them undoubtedly resulted from Shakespeare's instinctive desire to construct an improved historical reality that entertained and edified its Renaissance audience through intriguing characters, expanded roles for women, and clearly drawn antagonists whose bold and memorable personalities elevated the action to symbolic prominence.

The major themes and images of this freshly constructed narrative offer fascinating insights into the most important social and political con-

15. *Richard II*, 1993. Jack Wetherall as King Richard II and Karla Nielson as the queen. Photo by Sue Bennett, Rich Engleman, and John Running. Published with permission of the Utah Shakespeare Festival.

cerns of late-sixteenth-century England. Chief among these is the stark contrast between Richard the king and Bolingbroke the usurper. In the language of William Butler Yeats, Bolingbroke is the vessel of clay while Richard is the vessel of porcelain. Bolingbroke is durable, utilitarian, unattractive, necessary; he is the pragmatic, de facto ruler, the right man at the right moment in England's inevitable struggle for political stability. Richard—less efficient yet more compelling—seems exquisite, fragile, gorgeous, and impractical; the last of the medieval kings, he must of necessity yield to his rival—the rough and unpolished Henry Bolingbroke—who, as the first Renaissance king, consolidates political power by sharing it with his subjects.

Through Shakespeare's brilliant poetry, Richard also becomes an archetype of Christ, divinely anointed, whose loss of the kingship symbolizes a fall from "this other Eden, demi-Paradise" (2.1.42). Bolingbroke's victory, though necessary historically, is morally repugnant because he has unseated God's heavenly appointed representative on Earth. Not surprisingly, Richard advocates the divine right of kings, a widely accepted concept of political sovereignty intended to shield him from rebellion: "Not all the water in the rough rude sea," he argues, "can wash the balm off from an anointed king" (3.2.54–55). Bolingbroke also disrupts Richard's role as a "scourge of God" meant to punish England for its past sins and social excesses. According to this doctrine, a country was required by moral law to suffer the indignities of an inept ruler in "passive obedience." If God wished to punish a people, he might send them a king like Richard to test their true submission to His almighty will.

The paradox is instructive: Richard is a divinely appointed, yet incompetent, ruler whose very presence on the throne serves as a "mirror for magistrates"—an exemplum provided by God to tutor future monarchs in proper administrative conduct. Through Shakespeare, we study history to avoid the errors of the past. While Bolingbroke seizes all the political power, however, Richard usurps the theatrical power of the play. As audience, we condemn Richard as a king yet learn to revere him as a complex and fascinating human being whose fall from grace elevates him to tragic stature. Though Bolingbroke tends the garden of the kingdom, Richard nourishes our very souls with his clear-eyed self-perception and soaring verse.

This is, of course, the ultimate irony of Shakespeare's play. We stare into its dramatic mirror, expecting visions of Renaissance politics and history, yet what we see most vividly is our own reflection through the character of Richard: flawed, ambitious, sensitive, betrayed, and—above all else—triumphantly alive. As a result, the play is nothing less than an examination of human destiny presented through a shimmering glass that simultaneously reflects reality and falsehood, fact and fiction. And our master playwright so cleverly blends all these elements that, in the final analysis, the truth of history seems much less enduring and meaningful than the truth of art.

Richard III and the Theatricality of Evil

Richard III at the 2003 Utah Shakespeare Festival

During his 1483 coronation ceremony, Richard III invited a group of actors to perform in the church to commemorate his investiture. This tantalizing detail, willed to us by history, offers great insight into the motives and persona of Shakespeare's most celebrated monarch. Theatricality is at the heart of all Richard's actions in the play, extending from his initial soliloquy vowing to seize the throne, to his systematic manipulation and murder of most of the central characters, to his highly stylized dramatic monologues, and finally to the various convincing roles he adopts in the play—particularly his impersonation of the dying martyr/king, whose title is usurped by Richmond at Bosworth Field. A metatheatrical chameleon, Richard becomes Shakespeare's most-loved villain, an oxymoronic actor whose wit, charm, ambition, and immense courage turn this controversial play into an episodic historical narrative about the insidious alliance of politics and religion. Filled with breathless energy, the play compresses nearly ten years of real life into three hours of stage time, chronicling its pseudofactual events with all the subtlety of a speeding freight train.

To emphasize Richard's theatricality, director J. R. Sullivan has wisely set this season's Utah Shakespeare Festival production in a Gothic cathedral, which brilliantly establishes the scene for Lady Anne's funeral procession, the search for sanctuary by Elizabeth and the princes, and, of course, the coronation. The triptych arrangement of the stage likewise implies a debt to the mystery of the Holy Trinity in its division of the playing area into three visual panels or "sedes." This sacred setting also

16. *Richard III*, 2003. Henry Woronicz as Richard. Photo by Karl Hugh. Published with permission of the Utah Shakespeare Festival.

reflects Shakespeare's artistic debt to the morality play, which originated in medieval churches in the fourteenth and fifteenth centuries, giving devout parishioners their first taste of the fascinating vice characters whose theatrical descendants include not only Richard III but also such premiere Shakespearean villains as Iago in *Othello,* Edmund in *King Lear,* and Don John in *Much Ado about Nothing.* Through the immense ritualistic power of the morality motif, the characters in *Richard III* undergo a *psychomachia* or "soul struggle," where the forces of good and evil contend for moral control of an entire nation.

In this sense, *Richard III* is a modern historical morality play cunningly narrated by its central character. Like the medieval vice persona, Richard draws the audience into his machinations, making us complicit in his murderous plots. Knowing far too much about Richard's cruelty to remain innocent, we receive a voyeuristic thrill in seeing his victims get their just desserts, even as we applaud the artistry with which he choreographs each one's demise. This "knave in a nave" leaches energy from the other characters like a dramatic vampire, gaining power as his opponents fall.

Since this historical parable is told in a church, however, we are simultaneously intrigued and edified by the dramatic progress of the play. Richard is both villain and savior, devil and priest in this strange, but deeply moving, religious parable about the sin of ambition and the limits of political power. As he undertakes the deceitful actions that ultimately bring about his downfall, he concurrently attracts us toward and repels us from behaving in a similar fashion. If we are intrigued by his manipulation of evil, we are also repulsed by our own fascination with his diabolical charms. Everywhere we look, Richard sets up a mirror where we can see our own flaws writ large upon the stage before us.

Although Richard is the titular hero of the play, the sinner whose sufferings are at last absolved is England itself—the woeful nation fated to undergo torment at the hands of an unjust ruler. According to the doctrine of the divine right of kings, English monarchs were anointed and inspired by God. They ruled by celestial authority, which could never be challenged. Subjects beset by an evil king were required to endure him through "passive obedience" under the assumption that God, in his infinite wisdom, was punishing them for past crimes or purifying them in preparation for some future blessing. When Richmond defeats Richard at the conclusion of this play, therefore, not only is England cleansed historically of a terrible tyrant, but the soul of this great nation is purified and regenerated through God's blessed mercy.

That Richmond's victory happens in a church set within a theatre is ironically appropriate. *Richard III* offers many joys to attentive audiences, not the least of which is the opportunity for a spiritual conversion where the faith of the spectators is strengthened by the very theatricality of evil. As we are seduced by Richard's obscene lust for power, so, too, are we edified by his fall from grace. In the end, God's heavenly wisdom embraces us all, enclosing everything that lives in that great flood of time streaming from the Garden of Eden through our unique chronological moment. Great theatre is the divine conduit, the medium that helps us understand our place in the historical continuum spanning the gulf between Shakespeare's age and our own.

Poetic History

Henry IV, Part I at the 2004 Utah Shakespeare Festival

One of Shakespeare's best-loved and most exciting histories, *Henry IV Part I* (1597) is the second episode of a four-play tetralogy depicting the origin of the Wars of the Roses. Starting with *Richard II* and progressing through *Henry IV, Part I; Henry IV, Part II;* and *Henry V,* this dramatic saga chronicles the rise to power of Henry of Lancaster (1387–1422), who distinguished himself as Prince Hal of Wales in the Battle of Shrewsbury (1403), took over the throne as Henry V (1413), defeated the French at the Battle of Agincourt (1415), married Catherine of Valois (daughter of the French King Charles VI), and reigned as king of England and regent of France until his death in 1422.

Beneath this bland catalog of historical statistics lies a charming, morally instructive parable about the coming of age of an insightful and charismatic young man, the uses and abuses of friendship, the flowering of national pride, and the moral justification of war. Events of the play immediately follow the murder of King Richard II at the instigation of Hal's father, Henry IV, whose subsequent reign is marred by the guilt of regicide, rebellious nobles, and his son's riotous behavior with Sir John Falstaff in the working-class taverns of Eastcheap. In his eventual ascent to the throne at the end of *Henry IV, Part I,* Prince Hal must overcome not only the distrust of his father and the seductiveness of Falstaff but also the armies of three powerful rebels—the envious Hotspur and his Percy clan, the valiant Earl of Douglas in the north, and the "damned magician" Owen Glendower to the west in Wales.

17. *Henry IV, Part I*, 2004. *Left to right*: Charles Metten as Bardolph, Kirsten Fitzgerald as Mistress Quickly, and Kieran Connolly as Sir John Falstaff. Photo by Karl Hugh. Published with permission of the Utah Shakespeare Festival.

Underscoring this historical narrative are a number of important themes and images that distinguish *Henry IV, Part I* as one of the best and most compelling plays of its genre. Paramount among these is the way Shakespeare blends history, philosophy, and poetry to present a series of dramatic lessons about the ordination of "England's ideal king." Working principally from such sources as Raphael Holinshed's *Chronicles* (1587), Samuel Daniel's *The First Four Books of the Civil Wars* (1595), and an anonymous earlier play entitled *The Famous Victories of Henry V* (1587), Shakespeare shapes history to his purpose, making Hotspur younger to

match Prince Hal, inventing a climactic battle between the two antagonists, expanding Glendower's legendary skills in magic, converting the
historical John Oldcastle into a fascinating, though fictitious, Sir John Falstaff, and emphasizing the Machiavellian politics of the age. The result is
a dramatic primer that offers important revelations about the beginnings
of the Renaissance, the proper qualities of a hero, the attractiveness of
youthful abandon, the natural antagonism between fathers and sons, and
the moral justifications of war.

Shakespeare's great gift to us in this popular dramatization of English
history is his ability to personalize the past, to reduce this great swath of
time to a series of isolated and highly symbolic incidents such as the dal-
liance between Hal and Falstaff, the crucial interview between the king
and his son, the battle at Shrewsbury, and Hal's eventual ascension to the
throne of England—now governed not by a frivolous and irresponsible
youth but a mature, thoughtful, and majestic king. This is a world where
historical accuracy gives way to the brilliance of poetry, where Shakespeare's imaginative vision of English history is much more vivid and
expressive than the dull ramblings of chroniclers and historians. Poetry,
which is seldom indebted to factual accuracy, offers the most powerful
truth of all since its details may be arranged to support mythic insights
that clarify our divine presence in the universe.

Nowhere is the poetic nature of truth more apparent than in the text's
alternation between prose and verse, which lies at the heart of the play's
dramatic meaning. In the early scenes, Shakespeare cleverly divides the
dialogue of his characters between the measured speech of nobility and
the arrhythmic discourse of Prince Hal and his working-class companions. In other words, the king and his nobles speak in the traditional, ten-
syllable, "heartbeat" cadence called iambic pentameter while Hal, Falstaff, Poins, Bardolph, and the rest of the subplot characters converse in
prose. As Hal is drawn abruptly into the main plot during the interview
with his father in act 3, scene 2, his language shifts effortlessly from prose
to verse, adapting verbally to the changing royal responsibilities insti-
gated by a father's anger, a noble's rebellion, and a renewed acceptance of
his fate as the future king of England. Thus, the reality of Hal's existence
is captured in poetry, which ennobles, structures, and defines his role in
the play and in life. As he moves closer to the throne, the mandate of his
destiny changes with the rhythm of his speech.

Shakespeare's creation of the characters in this enchanting play—governed by history, yet made flesh by the imaginative power of poetry—is so vivid and compelling that audiences feel they have actually lived among Hal and his confederates for the "two hours' traffic of our stage."[2] By bringing dull, historical stereotypes to life, the playwright allows us to see these crucial events from the past personified by characters who are very much like us, equipped with the same hopes and fears that haunt us daily. Journeying into our past allows us to become more aware of our present. If all the world's a stage, then history is a play performed for a universe of spectators. As Shakespeare deliberately blurs the distinction between past and future, we, too, become characters in that great drama of life—growing and maturing like Prince Hal, misunderstanding our children like King Henry, rebelling like Hotspur, and seeking youth and companionship like Falstaff. As the credits roll in this theatrical newsreel, nothing changes but the names of the actors.

2. *Romeo and Juliet,* prologue, 12.

IV

The Tragedies

The Medieval Heritage of Iago

Othello at the 1988 Utah Shakespeare Festival

The summer of 1988 brings to the Utah Shakespeare Festival one of Shakespeare's most perplexing and fascinating creations: Iago from the tragedy of *Othello*. Although audiences and scholars have tried for almost four hundred years to probe the depths of his psyche, the "ancient" villain of this play remains maddeningly opaque, and his ferocious assault on the moral destiny of the other characters seems just as horrifying and senseless now as when he first appeared onstage in 1604.

To be sure, Iago provides reason enough for his actions—his lack of military promotion, his prejudice against Moors, Othello's alleged lust for Emilia, and Cassio's attraction to Desdemona—but these sporadic and insubstantial charges are largely insufficient to explain his great onslaught against the innocents of the play. Unlike Shylock—whose anger toward his Christian tormentors appears entirely justified by his dramatic predicament—Iago is a "demi-devil" whose pure devotion to evil for its own sake richly merits Coleridge's well-known description of "motiveless malignity."

Much of this abstract and inhuman nature that Iago displays may be traced back to the literary heritage of the vice character in late-medieval dramatic tradition. According to Bernard Spivack's *Shakespeare and the Allegory of Evil* and other seminal books and articles on the topic, the character of Iago has its ethical roots in such fourteenth- and fifteenth-century morality plays as *Mankind* and *The Castle of Perseverance,* which dramatize a *psychomachia* or "soul struggle," where the vice character contends against the forces of good for the spiritual salvation of an Everyman-type

18. *Othello*, 1988. LeWan Alexander as Othello and Monica Bell as Desdemona. Photo by Michael Schoenfeld. Published with permission of the Utah Shakespeare Festival.

central character. These early plays—wholly didactic in intent—were thinly disguised Christian allegories meant for the religious edification of their audiences.

As a descendant of the medieval vice character, Iago exhibits at least four principal qualities of this stock dramatic figure: superfluous and misleading motivations for his actions that do little to mask his inherently evil nature; self-congratulatory asides and soliloquies to the spectators, whom he takes into his confidence and makes terrified witnesses of his malevolent plots and schemes; the use of humor (often bawdy) to help disarm his unwitting victims; and, finally, an entirely amoral nature that distances him from the ethical responsibilities shared by his fellow dramatic citizens. Immensely popular onstage for more than two hundred years, the vice character resurfaces in such later Shakespearean figures as Falstaff, Richard III, Aaron the Moor, Don John, and, of course, Iago—all of whom seem slightly at odds with their transplantation from the pulpit of the morality play to the naturalistic cauldron of Shakespeare's more sophisticated theatrical style.

If Iago were simply a medieval vice character revisited, however, that anachronistic figure from the past would do little to explain his immense popularity with modern audiences. Fortunately Shakespeare has grafted all the familiar trappings of Renaissance humanity upon this antique figure from another world, creating in the process a hybrid character whose vivid flesh tones change him from a metaphorical abstraction to a human antagonist whose behavior is intriguing and repugnant at the same time.

Precast in the role for this summer's production, veteran USF actor Patrick Page will concentrate on finding the inherently human qualities that make his Iago lively and memorable for festival audiences. But always lurking beneath the surface—like some primordial image grinning at us through the centuries—is the medieval vice character, whose victims are no longer dull allegorical types within a morality play but living, breathing people like Othello and Desdemona, whose ruin by the forces of evil we mourn deeply.

Family Matters

Romeo and Juliet at the 1998 Utah Shakespeare Festival

Romeo and Juliet is, above all, a play about families. From the opening choral prologue that invites us to meet "two households, both alike in dignity" (prologue 1) to the bloody conclusion, where both clans flood into the tomb as witnesses to the lovers' tragic deaths, Shakespeare emphasizes the often-contorted and always-intense connection between individuals and the families to which they belong. In fact, one mark of the play's greatness lies in the way different characters respond to the family pressures that alternately define, nourish, and sometimes suffocate them.

As the word "households" implies, many of the relationships in the play are rooted in extended families. The Capulet clan, for example, consists not only of such immediate blood relations as the father, mother, and Juliet but also a wider circle that includes Tybalt, the nurse, Peter, Petruchio, and many other assorted relatives and retainers. Like servants who don the livery of their masters, these family members wear their affiliation on their sleeves for everyone to see, much as modern gang members sport colors to identify themselves. Similarly the Montagues, no less in "dignity," claim an extensive variety of members on their familial turf.

Although such family affiliation nurtures and protects, it also smothers, which means that hot bloods like Mercutio and Tybalt must continually push the envelope of social behavior to distinguish themselves as unique members of a common community. The feud persists, in part, because of the desire these younger men have to find identity through rebellion, repudiate the rival family, and differentiate themselves from the older and less aggressive members of their tribes.

Part of the tragedy of the play, therefore, is that Romeo and Juliet must transcend their kindred to consummate their love. So long as they are trapped within their respective families, their relationship has little chance of survival. For Juliet, being cloistered within the Capulet clan is like awakening in a tomb—a collective body of deceased relatives "whose foul mouth no healthsome air breathes in" (4.3.34). Surrounded by such stifling kinship, she will "die strangled" (35) unless rescued by her lover. Unfortunately, Juliet's principal attempt to escape her family through Friar Lawrence's sleeping potion is marred by a fatalistic lack of initiative that draws her deeper into the morbid embrace of her dead kinsmen; she basically does nothing and hopes that things will turn out well. In seeking life with Romeo away from the clutches of her parents, she finds only death within the family burial chamber.

In like fashion, Romeo also attempts to separate from his parents and friends. Romeo's father explains to Benvolio at the outset of the play that Romeo "private in his chamber pens himself, / Shuts up his windows, locks fair daylight out, / And makes himself an artificial night" (1.1.138–40). With Juliet in the famous balcony scene, Romeo willingly agrees to renounce his Montague family name "because it is an enemy to thee" (2.2.56). And in act 2, scene 4, he admits to giving Mercutio and his other friends "the slip" (51) when they pursued him after the party. All forces in the play, however, conspire to keep Romeo mired within his family. His attempts to be "new baptized" (2.2.50) are thwarted by Mercutio's death, the nurse's disloyalty, and the friar's "osier cage" of "baleful weeds" (2.3.7–8). Even the plague, which keeps Friar John from delivering his fateful letter because he is "sealed up" within an infected town (5.2.11), emblemizes the deadly and claustrophobic nature of family relationships in this play.

Similarly the desire of Juliet's father to entice the wealthy and well-connected Paris into the Capulet family is thwarted by his daughter, who—like an ill-trained hawk "mewed" in its cage (3.4.11)—refuses to snatch up this rich morsel to help sustain her family. Confronted by Juliet's apparent suicide in act 4, scene 5, Capulet thinks immediately of his own loss of progeny when he tells Paris that "Death is my son in law,

19. *Romeo and Juliet*, 1998. Brandy McClendon as Juliet. Photo by Karl Hugh. Published with permission of the Utah Shakespeare Festival.

death is my heir;/My daughter he hath wedded. I will die/And leave him all" (38–40). The loss of his only child foretells the eventual demise of the family line that defines his very existence. Juliet's eventual suicide in the tomb in act 5, scene 3 brings death, therefore, not only to herself but her entire future household.

Like Romeo and Juliet, we must all separate from our families as the children we used to be grow into the adults we must become. In this play, however, the sin of breaking away proves fatal because of the deadly context in which these young lovers exist. Beset by feud, plague, dysfunctional relatives, and a sense of isolation, Romeo and Juliet become "poor sacrifices" to the enmity of their elders (5.3.303) through their vain attempt to transcend family for love and kinship for self-identity. The loss of childhood becomes real, rather than symbolic, and the devastating effect of leaving the family emphasizes the brevity and fragility of young love just as it confirms the price of revenge in a world where forgiveness has never been a virtue. The deaths of Romeo and Juliet achieve, therefore, a tragic beauty that allows us to see the brilliance of their devotion to each other shining amidst the dark hatred of the family feud. Ironically, in separating from their families, they lose their lives at the exact moment when they find themselves.

Lear's Mythic Journey

King Lear at the 1992 Utah Shakespeare Festival

Once upon a time, an old king had three children; he unwisely divided his kingdom between his two ungrateful daughters, who eventually killed the third daughter and caused their father's death. Through this simple, almost mythic narrative, the parable of *King Lear* reaches through the centuries and invites modern audiences to consider a number of complex and intriguing themes that are just as provocative today as they were four hundred years ago when Shakespeare wrote his play (1605) and five hundred years before that when Geoffrey of Monmouth first recorded the ancient and well-known legend in his *Historia Regum Britanniae* (1136). Chief among these recurring motifs are the relationship between parents and children, the virtue of suffering, the need for reconciliation and forgiveness, the seductiveness of evil, the search for meaning and wisdom in life, the "second childhood" of old age, and the indifference of the gods to human misery.

Perhaps the play's most compelling theme, however, involves the symbolic journey its central character takes through the unfamiliar territory of the human heart. As in such medieval morality plays as *Everyman* and *Mankind,* where the protagonist's pilgrimage along the road to salvation is beset with many temptations, the aged king moves through the literary landscape of the play on three different allegorical levels—physical, psychological, and spiritual—which will all be displayed at the Utah Shakespeare Festival's production of *King Lear.*

On the physical level, Lear's progress through the play begins with his abdication of the throne in the first scene and accelerates when he

20. *King Lear*, 1992. *Left to right*: Don Donohue as the Fool and Harold Gould as King Lear. Photo by Sue Bennett, Rich Engleman, and John Running. Published with permission of the Utah Shakespeare Festival.

disowns his faithful daughter, Cordelia, and is then rejected by Goneril and Regan, the two ungrateful daughters to whom he unwisely gives his kingdom. Cast into the storm like a beggar, Lear wanders through the barren heath accompanied only by a fool, a madman, and a faithful friend. After railing angrily at the heavens over the cruelty of his children, the frail and exhausted king falls asleep. He awakens—restored not only to his right wits but also to the love of his devoted daughter, Cordelia, who has returned from France to save him from her evil sisters. This joyful reunion is short lived, however, since the two are soon captured by the sisters' army, and Cordelia dies before help arrives.

Although Lear's physical journey moves tragically from the loss of his kingdom to the loss of his life, his psychological progress charts a more-optimistic, upward path. Pampered and indulged for more than eighty years as a royal monarch, Lear has become separated from his own humanity. He behaves with imperial disdain toward his subjects, including his own daughters, whom he treats like servants. Insulated from the world around him, Lear is rudely awakened to its cruelty when he gives up his crown to Goneril and Regan, who then reject him because they no longer have reason to indulge the irritating behavior of an aged and useless father.

When Lear is cast into the storm, the tempest in the heavens echoes the one in his mind. In his isolation, confusion, and anger, he must learn again the way to be a human being; he must regain his lost ability to empathize with all living creatures, no matter how wretched and ignoble they seem. His psychological journey, therefore, takes him from a king to a man and ironically confers on him the self-knowledge and insight he previously lacked. The layers of courtly clothing he strips off in the wilderness represent decades of kingship encrusted with pride, self-indulgence, and arrogance that he must shed to emerge as an "unaccommodated man...a poor, bare, forked animal" who has come to terms with his own humanity (3.4.110–11).

This self-awareness gained through suffering enables Lear to reconcile with Cordelia—not as a king condescending to his subject but a father embracing his devoted daughter. Awakened from his restorative sleep, he looks deeply into her eyes and discovers his proper place in the world: "As I am a man, I think this lady / To be my child, Cordelia" (4.7.69–70). Lear's psychological journey in the play has finally made him worthy of Cordelia's unconditional love, which he could only experience and appreciate as a man, not a king. At the same time, this journey provides a dramatic surrogate to audience members: through Lear's redemption, we gain insight into our own moral condition. We suffer greatly with Lear, and when he begins to know himself, we are edified by our self-knowledge, which follows and parallels his.

On the third and final level, Lear's progress takes him on a spiritual journey through death and purgatory, which concludes in a heavenly reunion with the beatific Cordelia. When Lear gives up his throne at the outset of the play, he dies as a king so that he can be reborn as a man. His agony in the storm that follows this death is purgatorial because it punishes him for his sins and also purifies him for the eventual reunion with his daughter, whom he describes in celestial terms after awakening from his sleep: "You do me wrong to take me out o' th' grave. / Thou art a soul in bliss; but I am bound / Upon a wheel of fire, that mine own tears / Do scald like molten lead" (4.7.44–48). Lear's purgatorial torment—complete with imagined instruments of torture—thoroughly cleanses his spirit so that he can finally experience, at the very end of his life, the regenerative love of his angelic Cordelia.

Through tragic irony, this sweet and long-awaited moment of heavenly reconciliation is followed immediately by the cruel deaths of both Lear and Cordelia. Shakespeare has been careful, however, to counterbalance defeat in the physical realm with victory in the psychological and spiritual ones. Lear dies but only after he gains wisdom through suffering and heavenly compassion through the redemptive grace of Cordelia.

Our journey as spectators is just as regenerative as this old king's progress through the play. Most people go through life without ever knowing themselves or being assured of eternal bliss. As a result of following in Lear's footsteps, we may have moved a little closer to achieving these distant goals.

Biological Finance

Timon of Athens at the 1993 Utah Shakespeare Festival

Quick, what interest rates are you paying on your home loan and your credit-card purchases? How much money are you earning on your savings account? Like it or not, coping with such questions is an inescapable burden of living in our modern, credit-oriented society. Most of us are continually treading water in an economic whirlpool of plastic cards, Visa bills, car payments, and immense home mortgages.

To an audience so sophisticated in the uses and abuses of money, Shakespeare's *Timon of Athens* initially appears to be a rather simple parable about the destructive consequences of borrowing money you cannot repay. As recent scholarly research (especially articles by Michael Chorost, John Ruszkiewicz, and Coppelia Kahn) illustrates, however, the thematic concerns of the play are much deeper and more complex. At the heart of the matter is the intriguing concept of *biological finance.*

Timon, like tribal chieftains in many primitive societies, is an archetypal gift giver who bestows lavish presents on the members of his clan to dramatize and reinforce his superior social status. His gifts become, therefore, a constant proof of his dominant position among his friends. Such ostentatious generosity helps satisfy his emotional need to be loved and revered and, at the same time, creates indebtedness among the recipients that can never be repaid. Since he is essentially manipulating people into expressing exaggerated affection for him, no true camaraderie exists in this court that seems rich in love but is wealthy only in borrowed money. Unlike circular gift economies, where presents are reciprocally given and received, Timon perpetuates a linear form of generosity through which

21. *Timon of Athens*, 1993. *Left to right*: Sheridan Crist as Timon of Athens and Bradford Wallace as Apemantus. Photo by Sue Bennett, Rich Engleman, and John Running. Published with permission of the Utah Shakespeare Festival.

his largess flows solely from him to his beneficiaries. Such a one-sided economy creates power but only the illusion of friendship.

Finance merges with biology when Timon finally realizes that his habit of borrowing huge sums of money to support such extravagance has placed him deeply in debt. Unlike the precious jewels, paintings, statues, and other rich gifts he has given, the money he owes his various creditors has reproduced through the accumulation of interest. He now is in debt for not only the sums he has borrowed but also the exorbitant fees on the original loans.

The Renaissance was an age—unlike our own—that was uneasy with this concept of usury: many capitalists, like the character Antonio in *The Merchant of Venice,* desperately needed financial credit for business ventures, yet scorned the moneylenders for demanding interest on their loans. By setting his play in ancient Athens, Shakespeare invokes all the well-known Greek injunctions against what Aristotle called the "unnatural" practice of usury. Money was "barren": God did not intend it to increase as living creatures do; it was a method of buying goods, not a commodity in itself. Despite such warnings, rising commercialism and human avarice ensured that usury was a hotly debated ethical topic well into the seventeenth century. The constant tension between the old world and the new was further reflected in the fact that the Greek word for "interest" was *tokos,* which meant "offspring" or "child." Even as Greece's philosophers were condemning currency as sterile, its language was breathing life into the country's financial dealings and helping create the impression that money was organically and biologically alive since it could grow through the compounding of interest.

This same concept of the reproductive ability of money helps explain not only Timon's actions in the first half of the play, when the biology of finance and the ingratitude of false friends turn him from philanthrope to misanthrope, but also the second half, when he digs for roots in the wilderness and ironically discovers gold instead. Through the dark and brooding progress of the play, Timon finally uncovers the root of all evil, the *radix malorum*—greed—that destroys everything from human relationships to entire civilizations.

Shakespeare's dramatic lesson is instructive, whether his audience is the newly crowned king of England, James I, who was rapidly running up a million-pound debt through the corrupt Jacobean patronage system, or a poor slob in modern America trying to stay one step ahead of the credit crunch. The play speaks to us through the centuries about a world where money breeds easily while love and friendship are sterile. Unfortunately, Shakespeare's Athens looks very much like home.

The Scottish Play

Macbeth at the 1996 Utah Shakespeare Festival

Written early in the reign of James 1 (1603–25), Shakespeare's *Macbeth* is a typical Jacobean tragedy in many important respects. Referred to superstitiously by actors as "the Scottish play," the text commemorates James's national heritage by depicting events during the years 1040 to 1057 in his native Scotland. The play also celebrates the ruler's intense interest in witchcraft and magic, which was recorded in a book he wrote in 1597 entitled *Demonology*. Further topical allusions to the king include all the passages in the play mentioning sleeplessness because James was a well-known insomniac.

The most memorable references to Jacobean England in the play, however, are those that chronicle events of the notorious Gunpowder Plot—a conspiracy by Catholic sympathizers to blow up Parliament and all the heads of state within it on November 5, 1605, approximately one year before Shakespeare's play was written. On that date, Guy Fawkes and his band of Jesuit-sponsored papists smuggled an immense amount of gunpowder into a vault under Parliament, which would have killed everyone in the building in a fiery cataclysm had the king not detected the plot prior to its execution. According to a recent book by Garry Wills, *Witches and Jesuits,* James claimed to have discovered the plan by "inspiration" from God, who wished to save England from Rome's "Popish plot." Through popular mythology following the event, Jesuits were branded as equivocators who had tried to attack both England and the Reformation through a perverse use of not only gunpowder (often described as "the devil's invention") but also the nature of language, which they employed

22. *Macbeth*, 1996. Angela Iannone as Lady Macbeth and Robert Lee Martini as Macbeth. Photo by Wesley Bernard and Marielle Hui Wilkes. Published with permission of the Utah Shakespeare Festival.

in double and triple entendre to hide their fiendish intentions from the king and his court.

Not surprisingly, Shakespeare's play reflects these topical Jacobean events through its word choice, plot, and themes in an intriguing blend of Scottish history, contemporary political references, and authorial creativity. The language of the play, for example, includes a litany of references to the Gunpowder Plot that would have been familiar to all the king's loyal subjects in 1605. Such terms as "vault," "mine," "blow," "devils," "fuse," "powder," "confusion," "corpses," "spirits," and "combustion" set up a linguistic landscape where Macbeth and the witches kill a king and take over his throne in a mirror image of the aborted Popish plot during James's reign. Similarly the play's riddling prophesies mimic the ease with which Jesuits equivocated between truth and falsehood, good and evil. If "fair is foul, and foul is fair" (1.1.11), the deaths of King James and his entire Parliament would have seemed fair indeed to the Romish conspirators, though foul to anyone loyal to the Protestant cause.

In this summer's Utah Shakespeare Festival production of the play, director Robert Cohen has sought to capitalize on the Jacobean origins of *Macbeth* by placing its action in the early seventeenth century. Scenic designer Dan Robinson's elegant, refined set—dominated by the open timbers, painted ceilings, and grotesque Tarot images of affluent Scottish castles—creates a sophisticated dramatic universe where the evil of Macbeth stands in stark contrast to its opulent, polished surroundings. By focusing their production on the time the play was written, rather than the chronology of its eleventh-century source material, the director and his designers have shaped a world not unlike our own, where we are more susceptible to moral depravity because it lurks innocently behind the thin veneer of civilization. Macbeth and his lady are not barbarians living within a primitive, medieval era; instead, they are refined, successful aristocrats whose degenerate ambition seems savagely out of place in this Jacobean milieu.

Set within this updated, sophisticated seventeenth-century context, many of the play's principal themes take on fresh clarity. The tragedy's powerful oxymorons, for example, gain emphasis through the marked contrast between Macbeth's brutality and the cultured society that has nurtured it. In a world that is both fair and foul at the same time, a number of other important polarities stand out in stark opposition to each other—including dark/light, sin/grace, salvation/damnation, discord/concord, desire/performance, good/evil, angel/devil, and heaven/hell—all of which characterize a play that was suspended precariously between the extremes of the Middle Ages and the Renaissance.

Similarly Dean Mogle's exquisite, early Jacobean costume designs—including ruffs, high collars, and a slightly looser silhouette than previous Elizabethan styles—delineate a society where sumptuous and colorful courtly clothing masks the depravity within many of the principal characters. "Mock the time with fairest show," Macbeth warns his wife prior to the killing of Duncan; "false face must hide what the false heart doth know" (1.7.82–83).

A further important clothing motif is apparent in all the ill-fitting garment images in the play. By usurping a great king's throne, Macbeth has literally and figuratively stepped into clothes that are too big for him. As Angus says toward the end of the play, Macbeth feels his title "hang loose about him, like a giant's robe/Upon a dwarfish thief" (5.2.21–22). These and other prominent clothing images in the script achieve a new emphasis in the USF production's seventeenth-century costuming that would not have been so apparent in the more-traditional medieval setting for the play.

Other important themes likewise find a new definition within this production's more modern world. The sexual inversion, for instance, where Macbeth gradually assumes more womanly characteristics while his wife takes the dominant male role, seems somehow more appropriate in this postmedieval, prefeminist, updated society while all the references to fathers and sons transport us from the eleventh century to the Jacobean era through the witches' pageant of successive kings.

This same telescopic time travel is also evident in Macbeth's oft-stated desire to see into the future so he can control his own fate. In addition to his reliance on the witches' prophesies, Macbeth has a number of other moments in the play when he looks forward in time. Having been named thane of Cawdor in act 1, scene 3, for example, he exclaims in an aside about the kingship that "the greatest is behind" (117); and later, in act 5, scene 5, informed by Seyton that his wife is dead, he replies, "She should have died hereafter" (17). In fact, the entire "tomorrow, and tomorrow, and tomorrow" speech that follows (19–28) is an ironic realization that all his attempts to forecast and control the future have been in vain. Similar references to sickness and medicine, the divine right of kings, sexual energy, pregnancy, blood, death, omens, beast imagery, innocence, the corruptions of power, the loss of faith, and knowing one's place in society likewise gain renewed strength through Cohen's decision to update his production to Jacobean Scotland.

In the final analysis, this movement forward in time brings the play several steps closer to our own world, which makes Shakespeare's early seventeenth-century version of an eleventh-century historical story more accessible and meaningful than more traditional productions of the play. Macbeth and Lady Macbeth are like us in their ambition, love of power, and desire to manipulate their own future. Consequently updating the set and costumes invites us into a world very like our own, where evil is seductive and believable, yet reprehensible nonetheless.

The Art of Dying Well

Hamlet at the 1997 Utah Shakespeare Festival

Embedded deep within the well-known plot of *Hamlet* are a number of highly resonant themes and images relating to death and dying that were undoubtedly more accessible to Shakespeare's contemporaries than to today's audiences. If the exciting narrative of murder, revenge, ghosts, pirate ships, duels, romance, and incest has fascinated viewers since its first performances in the early 1600s, the play's symbolic layers offer even more intrigue, inviting generation after generation of theatregoers to search for meaningful parallels between their own mortality and this richly allusive text.

Chief among these important themes is *ars moriendi,* or "the art of dying well," which finds its echoes in Hamlet's preoccupation with dying, his famous contemplation of Yorick's skull, his meditations on suicide, and the play's incessant emphasis on death—beginning with old Hamlet's murder and culminating with the spectacular final scene, where the stage is laden with bodies. Composed and first acted during the plague years of 1599–1606, the script was strongly influenced by fear of "the sweating sickness," which raged through London and its environs, killing people abruptly and indiscriminately. In 1603, in fact—the year of Elizabeth's demise and the accession of James to the throne—more than forty thousand people in the city succumbed to the disease.

Not surprisingly, Shakespeare's audience was constantly searching for emotional solace during this time of increased vulnerability to the plague, which *Hamlet* ironically provided through its intense theatrical preoccupation with death and dying. According to popular ars moriendi tradition, people who wished to die well could prepare themselves through a variety of contemplative exercises that forced them to confront death in much the same way that Hamlet broods over the skull of his dead jester. Fortified by coming to terms with their own mortality, they could therefore meet death with dignity and spiritual support. This same theme surfaces in other Shakespearean plays like *The Tempest*, where Prospero retires to Milan where "every third thought shall be my grave" (5.1.311), and *Julius Caesar*, where Brutus stoically receives news of his wife's suicide by explaining, "With meditating that she must die once, / I have the patience to endure it now" (4.3.190–91).

Closely connected to this ars moriendi trope is the presence of the gravediggers, whose occupation of uncovering dead bodies parallels the play's larger symbolic fixation with unearthing the truth, excavating cultural memories, and revealing unresolved Oedipal traumas in the royal family of Denmark. Set within its comic context, the gravediggers' scene mirrors the play's more serious preoccupation with digging up the truth on a variety of crucial topics: Hamlet's relationship with his father and mother, his distaste for Uncle Claudius, his love for Ophelia, his desire to become king, and his morbid fixation with death. Just as the gravediggers go about their grim business of unearthing long-dead bodies so fresh ones can be interred, so, too, does Shakespeare's play systematically uncover the ambition, pride, lust, jealousy, and attendant sins that have been buried for years under layers of courtly intrigue and deceit.

Another seminal death image that signals the first and most important murder in the play is the poisoning of Hamlet's father as he lies sleeping in his orchard. Echoing throughout the play, the poison poured into old Hamlet's ear reappears in the players' reenactment of the crime, the poisoned sword and wine at the conclusion, and all the metaphorical poison poured into ears throughout the play: gossip, suggestions of revenge, slander, and evil thoughts that visit sickness and disease upon the entire court of Denmark. In selecting this particular method of killing the king, Shakespeare was once again exploiting contemporary Renaissance scientific knowledge—in this case, Italian physician Bartolomeo Eustachi's discovery in approximately 1570 that a hollow structure of bone and cartilage extending from the middle ear to the rear of the throat—now called the Eustachian tube—can carry fluids from one location in the body to another. Like the author of an early-day *Friday the 13th*, Shakespeare capi-

23. *Hamlet*, 1997. Victoria Adams as Ophelia and Martin Kildare as Hamlet. Photo by Karl Hugh. Published with permission of the Utah Shakespeare Festival.

talized on this novel method of killing the king, which reminds us of all the other poisonings in the play, both literal and metaphoric.

Hamlet's grief over his father's gruesome death and his eventual meeting with old Hamlet's ghost comprises only one of four important father-son relationships in the play, all of which relate to death and dying. The others include Polonius and Laertes, old and young Fortinbras, and Uncle Claudius as surrogate parent to the young Hamlet while his absentee father was away smiting "the sledded Polacks on the ice" (1.1.63). Perhaps some of this emphasis upon fathers and sons is indebted to the fact that Shakespeare's own son, Hamnet, died in 1596 at the age of eleven—approximately four years before Shakespeare wrote this play.

Though the names of Hamnet and Judith, Shakespeare's twins, seem to have been inspired by his neighbors, Hamnet and Judith Sadler, and the title of the play certainly owes a debt to the principal character, Amlethus, in the source material, Saxo Grammaticus's *Historia Danica,* the parallel between the name of Shakespeare's hero and his recently deceased son is too tempting to ignore. One possible hypothesis is that Shakespeare, while mourning his son's death, wrote a play that helped expiate his grief through an exploration of the relationships among four different sets of fathers and sons. Adding to the intrigue is the persistent rumor that Shakespeare the actor may have played the part of the ghost in early productions of the play, which could explain why this morbid character has such an expansive and dramatic role.

One final theme that helps us understand the many references to death and dying in *Hamlet* is the text's emphasis on the art of acting. Viewed within this metatheatrical context, Shakespeare's play offers an intriguing range of dramatic life-or-death situations. Although the play-within-the-play is the most blatant of these, Shakespeare encourages us to interpret a number of other elements in his text in the same morbid fashion: Hamlet, for example, feigns madness in his attempt to learn the truth about his father's murder; Claudius pretends to be innocent of the crime to save his life; Polonius falsely impersonates a devoted father and public servant and ends up being killed for his duplicity; and Rosencrantz and Guildenstern counterfeit as sincere friends, which leads to their bloody executions.

One result of such an emphasis upon the artifice of the play is that we as spectators are invited to consider the extent to which our lives are self-consciously theatrical. What is the crucial difference—Shakespeare seems to be asking—between the stage world and the real one? Between illusion and reality? If "all the world's a stage," as Jacques's well-known *theatrum mundi* commonplace from *As You Like It* suggests, how much of our own behavior, like Hamlet's, is spent dissembling the truth to discover the truth? And how often do we become actors to save our own identities?

All these central themes relating to death and dying are woven through the fabric of Shakespeare's play like a profusion of multicolored threads in a beautiful Renaissance tapestry. Which of these images will emerge most vividly in director Howard Jensen's 1997 production of the script? Which will allow us to see with clarity "the skull beneath the skin" of our own mortality.[1] As Hamlet might say, "the play's the thing" (2.2.633) that will help us learn how to die well, no matter which century we inhabit.

1. T. S. Eliot, "Whispers of Immortality," *Collected Poems (1909–1935)*, in *The Complete Poems and Plays* (New York: Harcourt, Brace & World, Inc., 1971), 32.

"All My Travels' History"

The Moral Geography of *Othello* at the 2002 Utah Shakespeare Festival

Geography plays a major role in Shakespeare's *Othello*, as it does in many of his plays. Caught between the two markedly different locales of Venice and Cyprus, the events prove the old adage that "people change places, and places change people." Such characters as Othello, Desdemona, and Iago are forever transformed by their journey through these disparate worlds, just as these dramatic places are permanently altered by the characters' presence.

One of these locations, Venice, was the crown jewel of sixteenth-century Italy. A major Mediterranean seaport and center of commerce, it was also home to the incredible richness of literature, painting, architecture, music, and all the other art forms that flourished during the Italian Renaissance. At the same time, it symbolized the depths of political intrigue, decadence, and moral depravity that were unfortunately typical of Italy during the same time period. Characterized, on one hand, by Baldassare Castiglione's *The Courtier* (1528), a testament to the importance of civilized, courtly demeanor, it also produced Niccolo Machiavelli's *The Prince* (1514), a cynical, pragmatic, amoral treatise on the uses and abuses of political power. Polluted by prostitution and other social ills, Venice was an overcivilized, licentious, ingrown society that carried within it the potential for its own destruction.

The other location, Cyprus, a fortified outpost on the edge of Christian territory, is a very different world from Venice. Infinitely more barbarous, it is a bastion of male power, where Desdemona—alone and isolated from her Venetian support system—is vulnerable to the machinations of a highly skilled manipulator like Iago. This is a savage, warlike milieu where such admirable military virtues as quick decision making and an inflated sense of honor work strongly against Othello and his new bride. Ironically, Cyprus was also revered as the birthplace of Venus Aphrodite, the goddess of love, who was reputedly born in ocean foam and washed ashore near Nicosia. In keeping with this amorous deity, Cyprus provides the perfect location for Iago to convince Othello of his wife's sexual infidelity.

Because of this geographical dichotomy between Venice and Cyprus, Othello and Desdemona move from an urbane, civilized, and somewhat-depraved Italian city-state to a barren military encampment whose claustrophobic confines intensify Iago's unrelenting psychological assault. Also conspiring against the lovers is Othello's naïveté concerning the subtle charms of Venetian ladies. Like Venice itself, Desdemona carries with her the seeds of her own demise. Transplanted into the new terrain of Cyprus, her innocent sophistication confirms her as a "cunning whore of Venice" (4.2.87). In the same fashion, after a storm destroys the Turkish fleet, Othello becomes that perfect oxymoron, a *miles amores* or "soldier of love," whose warlike nature is dangerously out of place on an island devoted to Venus.

The physical geography of *Othello* is underscored by a deeper, more symbolic moral geography, where Iago and Desdemona fight over the soul of the hero. Torn between these two extremes—the evil of Iago and the goodness of Desdemona—Othello's mind slowly degenerates into murderous passion. As Bernard Spivack argues in *Shakespeare and the Allegory of Evil,* Iago descends from the medieval vice character, whose role in such well-known morality plays as *Mankind* and *The Castle of Perseverance* was to beguile the hero into acts of depravity that would eventually endanger his immortal soul. In these early plays—as in *Othello* itself—evil starts with a tiny seedling of doubt or jealousy, then proliferates into a forest until the moral atmosphere of the play is overgrown with sin.

The physical and moral geography of *Othello* is supported by a vast number of important themes and images that bring currency and realism to the play's symbolic landscape. Chief among these are the relatively small cast of characters, the compressed storyline, the lack of a subplot, and the vivid contemporary setting: the Turks attacked Cyprus in 1570,

24. *Othello*, 2002. David Toney as Othello and Susan Shunk as Desdemona. Photo by Karl Hugh. Published with permission of the Utah Shakespeare Festival.

approximately thirty-three years before Shakespeare's play was written and first produced. An additional topical influence was the fact that the newly crowned King James I of England was fascinated with Turkish history while his wife, Queen Anne, once asked Ben Jonson to write a play about Moors *(The Masque of Blackness)* in which she played a role in "dusky" makeup.

Enlivened by other significant elements like contemporary racism, the uses of verbal and psychological poison, the changing roles of women, the lust for revenge, images of foreignness, the tempest on sea and in Othello's mind, the isolation of an island universe, the reversion to brutish behavior, and the ironic importance of the handkerchief, Shakespeare's play takes us on a geographic and psychological journey into the wilderness of the human heart. If we truly give ourselves over to the mystical experience of theatre, we can become one with *Othello*—navigating through the landscape of the play, alternately seduced by good and evil—and change the world we live in as it inexorably changes us.

The Rhythm of the Kiss

Poetic Seduction in *Romeo and Juliet*

When staging a production of *Romeo and Juliet*, actors and directors often give considerable attention to the precise moment when the title characters kiss during their first meeting in act 1, scene 5. This intersection of lips and hearts, so crucial to the lovers' journey in the play, forecasts their romantic destiny through several intriguing factors, including the number of times they kiss, the duration of the kisses, and exactly when they occur during the metrics and rhyme scheme of the sonnet that encloses them.

The answers to these questions require not only a careful reading of the text but also an acute sensitivity to the theatrical conventions that inform the lovers' meeting. If we read the scene through this new and very powerful lens, we can become much better classroom teachers of the play as we understand how the subtle clues embedded in the text encourage us to reevaluate the relationship between this ironic and often-misunderstood scene and the entire play.

Despite the fact that such amorous poetic devotion feels comfortable and familiar to modern viewers, the insertion of a sonnet into the body of a play would undoubtedly have been seen as an alien intrusion by the more literate members of Shakespeare's audience, who would have been vastly more sensitive than twenty-first-century aficionados to such an awkward fusion of genres. While the intelligentsia could have enjoyed the plays both in print and onstage, most of Shakespeare's audience would have encountered his work only in the theatre, where a lack of reading skills was little impediment to appreciating his dramatic genius. A modern literary student may argue about the sprinkling of sonnets throughout the play, "It's all poetry, right? Shakespeare's just shifting from one verse form to another. Why all the fuss?" The effect, however, would have been much more startling to Renaissance viewers used to *reading* sonnets but *seeing* plays. It might be somewhat akin to a speaker suddenly yodeling in the middle of his talk. "Where did *that* come from," a listener may rightly ask, "and what is this guy trying to accomplish through such an odd mixture of oratorical skills?"

Today's audience members are so accustomed to watching the lovers' courtship begin via this well-known sonnet, in fact, that some further attention to the shift in genres may be useful. More specifically, how would Shakespeare's audience have interpreted the appearance of such a foreign poetic form in a play written mainly in unrhymed iambic pentameter? It must have struck them as strange, perhaps even off-key and somewhat disingenuous. The fact that the insincerity of poetry is a common theme in Shakespeare's canon would have further complicated this unexpected appearance of the sonnet. This is nowhere more clearly articulated than in act 1, scene 5 of *Twelfth Night,* when the Countess Olivia declines to hear Viola's courtly praise of her beauty because she doubts its honesty. "Alas" says the heroine in disguise, "I took great pains to study it, and 'tis poetical," to which Olivia tartly replies, "'Tis the more like to be feigned" (1.5.206–7).

Such exchanges make Shakespeare's occasional infusion of conventional poetic patterns into his plays more intriguing because the artificiality of intricately rhymed verse is a shocking and suspicious intrusion into the more "realistic" blank verse and prose of the dramatic event. This fact is heightened when one realizes that most of the rhyming lines in *Romeo and Juliet* come from characters other than the two lovers, which makes their shared sonnet an anomaly within the context of the play.

MAKING THE WORD FLESH

To enfold this rhyming, eighteen-line section (94–111) into *Romeo and Juliet,* written and first produced around 1595, Shakespeare had to reach back to his earlier apprenticeship as a writer of sonnets and long narrative poems, generally believed to have taken place in the late 1580s and very early 1590s. Much like a novice post player in basketball who develops a drop-step move in the key—never knowing exactly when and where he will use it—Shakespeare the poet was able to import sonnets into his plays because he had perfected the genre during his youthful training. He already had the "move"; he just needed an opportunity to display it. This poetic invasion also betrays the author's proclivity for including everything but the proverbial kitchen sink in his early plays, which were largely experiments in seeing how his growing audience would respond to a variety of verse forms. If it worked, he kept it; if not, he discarded it, much as he did with the brief resurgence of the sonnet within his plays. His use of the sonnet in *Romeo and Juliet* also allows Shakespeare a moment of self-congratulatory reflection where he references his early poetic training and accomplishment through his newly adopted dramatic career.

This convenient marriage of genres, containing something old and something new, allowed Shakespeare to recreate the sonnet form brilliantly by taking an apparently outdated poetic device and bringing it to vibrant and reanimated life through accomplished performers in front of live, appreciative audiences. In short, the only improvement Shakespeare could make on the sonnet was to dramatize it, to make it flesh through the immense performative potential of actors, costumes, music, staging, and all the other elements of live theatre that make dramatic poetry so memorable to such a wide range of viewers.

A similar synthesis of genres occurred around the same time in the history of theatre when the bishops of London banned verse satire in 1599. Due to an eerie etymological confusion, the word *satire* (which was spelled "satyr" during the Renaissance) came to personify the verbal assaults of half-men, half-goats who launched violent and abusive attacks on members of the social establishment (see, for example, Alvin Kernan's *The Cankered Muse)*. This ban effectively silenced the genre, but the dramatists—keenly aware that the proclamation didn't extend to the stage and always on the lookout for innovations to their theatrical repertoire—immediately absorbed the satirist into their plays, begetting such famous literary figures as Jacques in *As You Like It,* who carried on the tradition of verse satire for Shakespeare's delighted viewers.

A FUSION OF GENRES

In the same fashion, the author's incorporation of sonnets into his plays redefines this poetic structure and employs it for a completely new purpose, which is often antithetical to its original use. In *Romeo and Juliet*, for example, Romeo's artificial, pseudoliterary, and extremely conventional introduction of the sonnet as a wooing technique—with its rather precious pun on the Latin *manus* or "hand" as he encloses his lady's fingers within his own—eventually gives way to a much deeper and more meaningful reality as the adolescent beginning to the lovers' relationship spirals toward their tragic deaths. Later in the play, when Romeo attempts to swear by "yonder blessed moon" (2.2.107), Juliet jolts him back to reality with "do not swear at all" (112), proving—as women have explained to men for centuries—that females are always more mature than males in affairs of the heart. Set within the play's tragic context, Romeo's attempt to woo Juliet with an old-fashioned poetic device resurrected from the author's earlier literary career is much like a young man trying to seduce his lover by bludgeoning her into submission with a one-thousand-page romance novel. Thus, Shakespeare's use of the sonnet betrays a devotional idealism that is simultaneously the glory and the downfall of his ill-fated lovers.

This awkward fusion of literary genres, especially apparent in such early plays as *Love's Labor's Lost* and *The Two Gentlemen of Verona*, both rife with poetic flourish, reaches its zenith in *Romeo and Juliet,* where the sonnet is used no fewer than four times in the play: once by the chorus in the prologue, a second time during the initial meeting between Romeo and Juliet in act 1, scene 5, a third time in the prologue to the second act, and a final, truncated, six-line sonnet delivered by the prince at the conclusion of the play. In the central sonnet in act 1, scene 5, Romeo reaches out to Juliet—both literally and figuratively—using religious iconography to deify his love for her and frame his adoration as a holy pilgrimage. This traditional and antiquated courtly wooing scene, which begins with a fairly typical fourteen-line English sonnet rhyming ABAB CBCB DEDE FF, ends in a four-line coda or rhetorical caboose rhyming GHGH that follows the previous train of thought. In short, the alternating rhymes of the first three quatrains end with a couplet, then devolve into another quatrain that concludes this initial meeting between the tragic lovers, intertwining their lives in the same breathless, intimate moment that the meter and rhyme scheme of Shakespeare's poetry coalesce. Set within this poetic context, Romeo and Juliet appropriately fall in love by completing each other's rhymes. They join together in the creation of a sonnet through witty wordplay, mimicking a modern animated conversation where two excited participants eagerly finish each other's sentences. The entire event is not unlike a contemporary musical, where a boy and girl are compelled to break into song to express the great devotion they have for each other. In Shakespeare's play, the lovers break into a sonnet instead.

Despite the apparent harmony of their initial meeting, Juliet rightly rejects Romeo's insincere poetic assault later in the balcony scene, insisting instead that he adopt a more realistic, honest mode of courtship that actually fits within the dimensions of the play in which they both live. An ironic device from another literary world, the wooing sonnet is useful only insofar as it betrays the artificiality of Romeo's initial proposal and signals its contrast with his eventual evolution into a lover worthy of Juliet's romantic attention. In modern terminology, the sonnet is his pickup line, one that undoubtedly worked well on earlier lovers like Rosaline but is now clearly inadequate with a woman of Juliet's obvious intelligence, maturity, and amorous sensitivity.

Structurally the final four-line coda following the regular fourteen-line sonnet provides a tantalizing hint that something is off-key in this poetic seduction: the rhyme scheme has taken a disastrous wrong turn after its more traditional beginning. The first fourteen-line sonnet comes to an abrupt halt, and then another sonnet begins immediately with the line, "Thus from my lips, by thine, my sin is purged" (109). Instead of ending the lovers' meeting on a perfect rhyming couplet at the conclusion of the first sonnet, which suggests future harmony and concord, Shakespeare concludes this literary rendezvous with an additional four lines in alternating rhyme that predict an unhappy ending to Romeo and Juliet's fledgling love affair. The nurse interrupts this beginning to the second sonnet in much the same way that the feud assaults their marriage and death separates the lovers forever at the conclusion of the play.

As further proof that the wooing sonnet comes from another time and place, most modern directors of the play highlight—sometimes literally—the eighteen-line meeting between the lovers by having the rest of the actors go into an upstage freeze or a slow-motion dance while the love scene takes place down center. Similarly the rest of the stage is often darkened while the lovers bask radiantly in a small pool of light. The forward motion of the play stops—in both literary genre and staging—while these two young people fall in love. Such common directorial decisions reflect not only the poignancy of the lovers' initial wooing scene but also the instinctive realization that Shakespeare is somehow shifting gears in the poetic machinery of the play.

An even more intriguing disconnect between Shakespeare's regular blank verse and the abrupt and artificial insincerity of the sonnet would have been available to a Renaissance audience through the realization that the adult male actor playing Romeo was kissing a boy actor impersonating Juliet, creating a theatrical *trompe l'oeil*—a passionate delusion—where the promise of future intimacy between the two characters was undermined by the unisexual and emotionless embrace of the actors playing the roles.

THE RHYTHM OF DESIRE

So what about those kisses? How do they fit into the artificiality of the sonnet? And to what extent do they help predict the play's tragic conclusion? Not surprisingly, Shakespeare is often quite specific about times when his characters kiss onstage—in *Romeo and Juliet* and many other plays. Some of the best examples of these implicit stage directions occur in *Othello*, particularly in act 2, scene 1, when the Moor lovingly greets Desdemona after their perilous voyage to Cyprus:

> I cannot speak enough of this content.
> It stops me here; it is too much of joy.
> And this, and this, the greatest discords be
> That e'er our hearts shall make! (198–201)

Most directors infer two kisses between the lovers, one after each time "this" occurs in line 200. Othello hopes the sweet sound of their lips parting—"And this [kiss], and this [kiss]"—will be the "greatest discords" their love ever suffers. Later, in an ironic, macabre echo of this earlier embrace, Othello kisses his sleeping wife four times before he kills her:

> I'll smell it on the tree [kiss].
> O balmy breath, that dost almost persuade
> Justice to break her sword! One more [kiss], one more [kiss],
> Be thus when thou art dead, and I will kill thee,
> And love thee after. One more [kiss], and that's the last. (5.2. 15–19)

And finally, of course, Othello embraces his wife one last time as he is dying: "I kissed thee ere I killed thee. No way but this, / Killing myself, to die upon a kiss [kiss]" (5.2.369–70).

Since most of these kisses take place at the ends of lines, they break the tempo of Shakespeare's iambic pentameter, which briefly goes on hold during each embrace. If modern actors require approximately three and a half seconds to deliver a line of verse (which equals about a thousand lines per hour of stage time), the inclusion of even a two-second kiss after a rhythmic ten syllables is enough to extend a line to nearly twice its normal length, focusing the audience's attention on its dramatic importance. In plays like *Othello* and *Romeo and Juliet*, therefore, time stops with every kiss, effectively freeze-framing the moment and alerting the audience to the play's halting, yet inevitable, progress toward its tragic conclusion.

Sometimes, however, similarly crucial stage actions occur within the very rhythm of the lines, such as in act 3, scene 1 of *Julius Caesar*, where Caesar is killed on a troche (78). After being stabbed by the other conspirators, he staggers into the arms of Brutus, who gives him the coup de grace on the line, "Et tu, Brute?" In most productions of the play, the initial thrust of Brutus's knife occurs on the first stressed syllable of the word "Brute," giving new and horrific meaning to the phrase "a stressful situation." In this one instant onstage, the regular iambic rhythm of the text (the words "et tu") reverts to a murderous troche ("Brute"): the meter we anticipate changes to its polar opposite, and the world of ancient Rome alters inexorably as the iambic rhythm of Caesar's heartbeat is stopped forever.

These examples remind us that the creation of dramatic meaning has much to do with the alternation between expectation and reward, between the regularity of the verse and the sudden, intricate surprises in the text that mark Shakespeare as a consummate theatrical genius. In *Othello*, for example, we assume the Moor's speeches will continue their usual metrical pattern, yet the normal progress of the play is interrupted by the placement of kisses between and within lines that must pause reverently to accommodate them. In *Julius Caesar*, our tacit anticipation of a regular metrical foot is brilliantly reversed in a way that mimics the upheaval in the city-state: art imitates life as iamb turns to troche. In contrast, however, our expectations in the first meeting between Romeo and Juliet are modified by the added complexity of the kisses happening within a fourteen-line English sonnet. In short, we have not only the rhythm to consider but the elaborate rhyme scheme as well.

Most directors plan three kisses in the scene: (1) one after the fourth line—"To smooth that rough touch with a tender kiss"—when Romeo attempts to kiss Juliet's hand, which she withdraws to stop him; (2) another after the couplet in the fourteenth line: "Then move not while my prayer's effect I take," where Juliet first allows Romeo to kiss her lips; and (3) a third in the middle of the eighteenth line, after "give me my sin again" as Romeo kisses Juliet on the mouth a second time—perhaps longer and more passionately—after which she exclaims, "You kiss by the book," meaning either that he is an expert, well-practiced lover who's been reading all the right manuals or that he has used the iconographic religious imagery of the Bible ("the book") to court her.

FORECASTING DISASTER

Since the first of these kisses occurs at the end of a line, the second punctuates the conclusion of the fourteen-line sonnet, and the third occurs in the middle of a shared half-line at the end of the last aborted quatrain, a subtle shift becomes apparent, leading from regular meter and rhyme to a sudden disruption of the final line of this poetic section. A further interruption comes from the nurse, who breaks off the lovers' dialogue with "madam, your mother craves a word with you" (112); Juliet leaves, and Romeo learns unexpectedly that his new-found love is a Capulet. In other words, the broken line within a broken sonnet forecasts the eventual demise of the lovers soon after the artificiality of Romeo's proposal has betrayed the insincerity of his immature love. All signs—including the antiquated poetic device intruding on the play's blank verse, the second sonnet truncated by the nurse, and the placement of the kiss in an awkward position in the last line of the new quatrain—predict disaster.

These poetic prophecies lead relentlessly to the lovers' suicides at the conclusion of the play. As in *Othello,* a final embrace seals their dramatic fate when Juliet attempts to "die with a restorative" by kissing Romeo's poisoned lips, yet finds them "warm," which is surely the most heart-wrenching line in the entire play (5.3.166–67). In tragedy—as in life itself—timing is everything: if only the feud had never happened; if only Tybalt had not killed Mercutio, or Romeo had not killed Tybalt; if only the letter from Friar Laurence had been delivered on time; and if only Juliet had awakened a few seconds earlier. But we can't say that Shakespeare doesn't prepare us. As the interruptions in the wooing scene forecast, the timing between the lovers is all wrong. From the broken quatrain to the awkward midline kiss, the prophetic warning in the prologue is supported by all the rhetorical power at Shakespeare's command and echoed by the prince's aborted six-line sonnet at the conclusion of the play.

In the end, truth speaks to us ironically through the sonnets—the most artificial and literary devices in the text—as if channeling some arcane secrets from the author's distant past. There's life in Romeo and Juliet's final kiss, however, as there is in Othello's dying tribute to his Desdemona since each time these wonderful plays are produced and the Neoplatonic kisses are performed, the lovers are reborn into a theatrical world of promise and excitement. Shakespeare seduces his audience in much the same way that Romeo seduces Juliet—through passion, wit, and humor—as the insincerity and awkwardness of the wooing scene gives way to a deeper and infinitely more moving parable about the value of love in our lives and the ways that we move from infatuation to maturity in our most cherished relationships. Sometimes, as the old song reminds us, "a kiss is just a kiss." But when Shakespeare is involved, nothing is quite that simple.

ಐ V ಜ

The Romances

All Corners of the World

Cymbeline at the 1988 Utah Shakespeare Festival

When director Kent Thompson and I had our first meeting to prepare for his summer 1988 production of *Cymbeline* in Cedar City, Utah, we both confessed we were overwhelmed by the immense scope of this obscure and difficult play. Fifty-four characters (thirty who have speaking roles and one who literally loses his head for love) range over England, Wales, and Italy in a narrative that weaves together twenty-four separate plot developments—all summarized at the end of the play in a single, breathless scene covering more than five hundred lines. Conflating events from such eclectic sources as Holinshed's *Chronicles*, Sidney's *Arcadia*, Boccaccio's *Decameron*, *The Mirror for Magistrates*, Spenser's *The Faerie Queene*, an anonymous play entitled *The Rare Triumphs of Love and Fortune*, and native folktale motifs about wicked stepmothers and long-lost sons, Shakespeare's text seemed nearly impossible to stage. How, we wondered, could we ever make coherent theatrical sense of such a rambling, disjointed, crowded, and episodic play?

One early discovery that helped us immensely in categorizing and understanding the play's diverse elements was that the mythic universe of *Cymbeline* is clearly divided into four unique worlds, each of which adds something important and necessary to Shakespeare's complex plot. England, the first locale, is a barren, artificial environment dominated by the evil queen and her choleric son, Cloten. In Italy we find the sensual, wealthy, Machiavellian domain of Philario, where Iachimo wagers with Posthumus over Imogen's chastity. Rome, represented by Caius Lucius, is a coldly logical, orderly, classical society devoted to the twin gods of

25. *Cymbeline*, 1988. *Left to right*: Liisa Ivary as the queen, Martin Robinson as Posthumus, and Monica Bell as Imogen. Photo by Michael Schoenfeld. Published with permission of the Utah Shakespeare Festival.

money and power. Finally, Wales is a natural, fertile land characterized by courage, wisdom, and nobility—the moral and ethical center of the play.

Once we had identified and defined these four distinct worlds, the play's designers were able to differentiate each geographic area through set, costumes, music, lighting, and other production elements. Set designer Ron Ranson envisioned Britain as a pair of gnarled, silver trees that turned into columns as they ascended into the Utah sky. Immediately dubbed "trolumns" by the production staff, these characterized the queen's garden as a sterile, sinister environment within a highly stylized, iconographic society. Philario's lascivious Italian mansion featured a long wooden table that slid out from the inner below on a slip stage and a sunken Roman bath complete with prostitutes clad in skimpy bathing attire. Rome was depicted by columns, banners, eagle emblems, and staffs topped with *caducei* while the cave of Belarius in Wales was a leafy scrim traveler masking the inner below. Each place was further distinguished by the rotation of huge, seven-foot golden disks on the upper stage and the inner below that revealed in bas relief a tree intertwined with snakes representing Britain, two nude lovers for Italy, symbolic vegetation for Wales, and a Druid sun god for Rome. In the fifth act, a strong, vibrant Roman eagle displaced the limp, sickly bird earlier associated with Britain.

Costuming by Linda Roethke was rigid and metallic in the British court with pale blue and silver hues predominant; Italy was marked by brighter colors, filmier silks and chiffons, and an abundance of naked flesh; Rome featured the conventional military white togas with red, gold, and burgundy trim; while Wales was all natural earth tones, primitive woven fabrics, and animal skins. Christine Frezza's music not only identified each of these geographical locations but added seasonal definition to them. Britain was the wintry sound of trombones and chimes, a dying culture; Italy was the summer of low, sensual brass and double reeds; Rome was autumn with its trumpets and drums; and Wales radiated the warmth and richness of spring through recorders, lutes, and strings. All the instruments reconciled harmoniously at the end of the play as the various musical motifs combined to bestow life and happiness on Cymbeline's kingdom. In a similar fashion, Liz Stillwell's lighting design brought the cold, stark domain of Britain, the reds of Italy, the warm yellow and straw colors of Rome, and the green fertility of Wales into lovely fusion at the end of the play as the silver columns reflected hues from each of the four worlds and military banners fluttered in the air like new-grown leaves.

Once we discovered these four separate worlds, the moral geography of *Cymbeline* started to take shape as well. We began to understand that Imogen and Posthumus go on a symbolic journey toward awareness and maturity in the play. If they appear in the first act as fairy-tale heroine and hero—the archetypal Snow White and Prince Charming—they must be demythologized as the story unfolds. Through Shakespeare's theatrical shock therapy, each dies and is reborn into a better, happier world at the play's conclusion. To illustrate this on the physical level, the normal geometric design of the Utah stage was softened and rounded by adding a series of platforms on the downstage side, which created a forced curve for the actors to travel and helped symbolize the journey from one world to the next.

On the moral level, we determined that both Imogen and Posthumus were incomplete characters at the start of the play. As portrayed by actress Monica Bell, Imogen was only an *image* of virtue: smugly chaste, yet obsessed with unresolved sexuality. Like Juliet, she was burdened by beauty "too rich for use, for earth too dear."[1] Posthumus, played by Martin Robinson, was insecure and threatened by his wife's latent sexuality; consequently, his foolish boasting about her virtue brought trouble to both of them. Each of these flawed, two-dimensional characters needed desperately to be humanized by the action of the play.

In their movement through the four separate worlds of *Cymbeline*, Imogen and Posthumus take on the best characteristics of each locale as they strive to become morally and spiritually worthy of each other: true sexual awareness and vitality in Italy, patriotism and rationality in Rome, and nobility, strength, and courage in Wales. They confer all of these upon Britain—now cleansed of the evil queen and her son—which becomes a strong and vital composite world at the play's conclusion. When Jupiter appears in act 5, scene 4, we learn one of Shakespeare's principal lessons: only through suffering can the characters in this play, and the society where they live, find real happiness. Jupiter's motto—"Whom best I love I cross" (101)—suggests that life is a trial that strengthens and ennobles the participants. As a result, the journey that Imogen and Posthumus be-

1. *Romeo and Juliet*, 1.5.49.

gin and end in Britain is circular since its ultimate goal is the discovery of their true selves, unsullied by false praise and artificial piety.

The production resulting from these theoretical assumptions about *Cymbeline* was extremely successful, playing to packed and appreciative houses during its entire two-month run. While I do not think many spectators were consciously aware of our dramatic intent in depicting the four worlds of Britain, Italy, Rome, and Wales, I am convinced the concept helped audiences intuitively understand a play that appeals more to the emotions than the intellect. In a grotesque and ghoulish fashion, Cloten's decapitated corpse teaches all of us to respond to this mythic, sprawling play, not with our heads but our hearts—a domain where symmetry and structure are often most profoundly satisfying.

"This Rough Magic"

The Tempest at the 1995 Utah Shakespeare Festival

Shakespeare's *The Tempest* (1611)—like so many of his later plays—features an intense storm that profoundly restructures the plot and characters within its dramatic universe. Through his "so potent art" (5.1.50), Prospero causes a shipwreck as the action begins, marooning on his island not only his two most bitter enemies but also the future husband of his beloved daughter, Miranda. Suspended between his lust for revenge and need for regeneration and renewal, Shakespeare's magician hero forgives his adversaries, gives his daughter to the future king of Naples, and then abjures his art by breaking his magic staff and drowning his book of charms "deeper than did ever plummet sound" (5.1.56).

Not surprisingly for a play so devoted to tempests both physical and emotional, Shakespeare's comedy has elicited a storm of controversy from a number of different sources during the past four centuries. Even the long-accepted conventional interpretation of the play as Shakespeare's farewell to the stage—complete with Prospero as playwright renouncing his theatrical magic—has recently come under close scrutiny by bibliographers, who believe the play was written before *Henry VIII* and *The Two Noble Kinsmen* and may even have preceded *The Winter's Tale*. So much for dramatic tradition!

Five areas of disagreement that are particularly fascinating to modern readers and theatregoers are characterization, colonization, images of the New World, magic, and the masque. Through his soaring poetry, Shakespeare dramatizes the inherent conflicts within each of these elements, organizing his play around a series of debates that are as intriguing today

26. *The Tempest*, 1995. *Left to right*: Harold Gould as Prospero and Brian G. Kurlander as Ariel. Photo by Wesley Bernard and Marielle Hui Wilkes. Published with permission of the Utah Shakespeare Festival.

as they were nearly four hundred years ago. Since *The Tempest* is a theatrical script, however, it is only completely realized through performance. Solely in that artistic venue can the infinity of choices available to readers be narrowed and refined to a single vision, unique to the particular place, time, and audience of the Utah Shakespeare Festival during the summer of 1995 in Cedar City.

This wide range of interpretations is nowhere more startling than in the contrast between such characters as Prospero and his "abhorred slave," Caliban. Prospero, for example, has been described variously in recent theatrical productions and scholarly books and articles as a noble ruler, tyrant, necromancer, Neoplatonic scientist, imperialist, and magician while portrayals of Caliban have ranged from ugly, deformed savage to sensitive, victimized New World native. The precise degree of interpretation of these and other seminal characters like Ariel, Miranda, Ferdinand, Antonio, Alonzo, and Gonzalo depends, of course, upon the director, design team, and individual actors at the festival this summer since they make the decisions that transform the play from page to stage.

Likewise, any good theatrical performance of the script must on some level respond to the charge that Prospero has stolen the island from its original inhabitants in the same manner that Renaissance England was slowly beginning to colonize much of the civilized world. Caliban, whose name is an anagram of "cannibal," had previously owned the island with his dam, Sycorax, and his power and authority over the territory were usurped in much the same way Antonio stole Prospero's dukedom in Milan. As the great popularity of Montaigne's essay "Of the Cannibals" (translated into English by John Florio in 1603) indicates, the colonization of relatively unspoiled lands where prelapsarian natives led an Edenic existence had become a wildly controversial topic by the later stages of Shakespeare's career. What were the moral responsibilities of colonial exploration? And what obligation, if any, did the invaders have to educate and Christianize the primitive inhabitants they found during their travels? Perhaps—the play seems to suggest ironically—the Europeans are the savage, predatory, and inhuman ones in their enslavement of indigenous citizens like Caliban.

Such Shakespearean debates about colonization are always played out within the larger and more provocative context of images of the New World. As Gonzalo's utopian monologue in act 2, scene 1 implies, Renaissance Europeans were fascinated by the concept of discovering a pristine paradise that would provide a fresh opportunity to experiment with laws and social customs not already encrusted by centuries of English tradition. In 1607, just four years prior to the first performance of *The Tempest*, in fact, British explorers had founded Jamestown, and in 1609 they sent a fleet of four hundred new colonists across the Atlantic, who—after being lashed by a ferocious storm—were forced to land in Bermuda, where they spent the winter. Prospero's island, hard by these "still vexed Bermudas" (1.2.229), provides a wonderful island laboratory where the various theories of colonization and civilization popular during the Renaissance could be dramatized before an attentive audience.

Much of Prospero's political and moral power is accomplished through magic, of course, which introduces yet another important area where modern productions of the play must make specific choices between interpretations that are often quite contradictory in their aim and scope. In one sense, the magic of *The Tempest* is Baconian in origin: a systematic study of nature, which leads to the understanding and control of all its forces. On another level, magic can be portrayed in the play as pure theatre and illusion: a true source of power for Prospero the artist. And finally, magic can be associated with the black arts—as it is in *Macbeth* and other plays—where it is often depicted as profane, irrational, unholy, and malicious. Prospero's theatrical magic may, in fact, contain elements of all three of these aspects of enchantment, though each actor playing the role must at some point decide which of the three he should weight most heavily in his performance.

One final dramatic element in *The Tempest* that requires careful and deliberate choices by the production team is the illusion of the masque in act 4, scene 1—the magnificent culmination of Prospero's magic that can either be a genuine celebration of Miranda's betrothal or a boastful display of power from a retiring sorcerer who desperately wants to preserve his authority and position in Milan by providing a priceless bride for the royal husband of his choice. As Sir Walter Raleigh's selection of the name Virginia for his new American colony implies, virginity is considered an attribute of power, a possession worthy of royal monarchs like Queen Elizabeth. In this sense, Prospero's masque may also be viewed as a victory celebration for safeguarding Miranda's chastity from Caliban's lustful desire to populate the island with their children. Through such extratextual elements as music, costuming, lighting, set design, props, blocking, and dance, each different production of the play creates its own masque with the unique and special blend of illusion, celebration, braggadocio, and ceremony appropriate to the director's concept and the actors' skills.

The brilliance of Shakespeare is that all these interpretations—and others too numerous to mention in such a brief article—coexist harmoniously within the text of such a play. Conversely much of the agony and exhilaration of directing *The Tempest* accrue from the fact that the production is sequentially defined by the choices made among these different interpretations at each phase of the rehearsal process. This is, of course, the collaborative "rough magic" of theatre. Are these choices the same ones you would have made? Do they fulfill your expectations of the play, or do they challenge, amaze, and delight you with their distinctive creative energy? There's only one way to find out, of course: come see the show!

"It Is Required You Do Awake Your Faith"

The Winter's Tale at the 1990
Oregon Shakespeare Festival

The Winter's Tale is classified in most anthologies as a problem play, which generally means that modern audiences have a problem knowing how to respond to this sprawling, episodic, and perplexing product of Shakespeare's later years. To be sure, the text stretches credibility through a number of fantastic and startling events: Leontes's sudden jealousy; Hermione's death and the famous statue scene; the mauling of Antigonous by a bear; the fictitious creation of a seacoast in land-locked Bohemia; and—perhaps most unsettling—the intrusion of a sixteen-year interval that separates disjointed halves of the play into two entirely different locations, character groups, and time sequences.

All these elements, however, are typical of a theatrical genre known as *romance* that was much better understood in Shakespeare's time than our own. Its stock conventions included children abandoned to the elements, princesses raised by shepherds, handsome princes in disguise, sea voyages, and other implausible, but entertaining, events accompanying a typical journey from separation to death to joyful reunion. Like such other late plays as *Pericles* and *Cymbeline, The Winter's Tale* invites an entirely different audience response than do the author's comedies, histories, and tragedies. Though it offers illusion rather than reality, allegory and myth instead of literal fact, its artifice leads inexorably to some of Shakespeare's most profound and enduring insights about the human condition. As Picasso argued in another context, such art provides us with "a lie which leads to the truth."[2]

Our production seeks to capitalize on the conventions of romance by focusing on Paulina as the wise and articulate storyteller who guides us through a sad tale most appropriate to the winter of our lives. Like the shaman of tribal ritual, she is a magician, a medium, an educator, a healer, and a mystic whose communication with the spirit world brings seasonal renewal and affords the play's principal characters a miraculous and unexpected second chance at happiness. Her dramatic universe exists outside of time, deliberately composed of mythic images collected from William Blake, English pre-Raphaelite artists, nineteenth-century Viennese paintings, Gustav Klimt, Greek and Roman emblems, and an eclectic fusion of other Judeo-Christian symbols.

The resulting narrative moves less from place to place than season to season, from death to life, and from tragic error to divine reconciliation. Like the mythic Proserpina, Hermione returns from death in a way that confounds rational analysis; by doing so, she teaches us that we must endure winter before spring can come, that sorrow ultimately begets happiness, and that the natural cycles of life bring spiritual awareness and comfort to us all.

Viewed from this perspective, Shakespeare's play is strangely satisfying. It speaks eloquently through the language of disguises, transformations, miracles, rituals, and other metamorphoses that allow the characters—as well as the audience—to feel firsthand the healing power of reconciliation and self-knowledge. The experience of the play is, in fact, much larger than our linear, logical conception of reality. When Florizel and Perdita (whose name literally means "the lost child") marry at the conclusion of the play, their union symbolizes the potency and fertility necessary to turn the winter of Leontes's old age into a new spring with the reborn Hermione. If a problem exists in *The Winter's Tale*, then, it is not located in the text but in our peculiar twentieth-century reaction to this mythic journey into the uncompromising seasons of the human soul. As Paulina counsels, we must awake our faith to respond rightly to Shakespeare's unique pattern of theatrical convention. If we listen carefully, the play whispers softly to our hearts, rather than our heads.

2. Pablo Picasso, quoted in "Picasso Speaks," *The Arts,* May 1923.

VI

Shakespeare's Contemporaries & Other Playwrights

Food for Thought

Volpone at the 1991 Utah Shakespeare Festival

Ben Jonson's primary source for the plot of *Volpone* was undoubtedly the well-known Aesop fable "The Fox Who Feigned Death," where a crafty fox covers himself with red mud, lies motionless on the ground, and pretends to be dying. When the birds of prey begin to circle around him, he waits until they are within reach, then seizes and eats them. In like manner, Volpone tricks each of his feathered suitors into thinking he is near death, then feasts upon their avarice and stupidity.

This central image of feeding upon foolishness embodies Jonson's satiric philosophy, according to which the abundant fools and sinners of the world exist principally as nourishment for several types of hungry diners: (1) the witty characters of the play, like Volpone and Mosca, who delight in exploiting the greed of their feathered prey; (2) Jonson himself, whose artistic talent depends on the crafty way he exposes such social aberrations as covetous lawyers and husbands begging to be cuckolds; and, finally, (3) the audience, which happily devours the comic meal presented onstage before it.

If this theatrical feast of sin and folly simultaneously sustains the plot, exhibits Jonson's skill as a dramatic satirist, and charms the audience, it also nourishes its viewers in a deeper, more meaningful way. Like the classical Greek and Roman dramatic models the author so proudly emulated, Jonson's satiric comedy claims to cure its audience members of their own reprehensible behavior by holding up a dramatic mirror where their worst flaws are reflected in exaggerated caricature. The rapacious greed and lust of the play have reduced most of the major characters to

27. *Volpone*, 1991. Jeanne Homer as Gobbo and Richard Kinter as Volpone. Photo by Jess Allen, Rich Engleman, and Richard Maack. Published with permission of the Utah Shakespeare Festival.

bestial parodies of their better selves; they have descended one level on the great chain of being, which theorizes that humanity is precariously suspended between the angels and the animals. The more foolish people's actions, the more beastly they become.

Like Scoto of Mantua's mystical elixir, Jonson's comedy offers its audience a cure for a wide range of moral and spiritual imperfections that metaphorically turn lawyers into vultures, greedy men into sly foxes, servants into parasites, and English travelers into silly, chattering parrots. The secret to comic reformation—the author seems to say—is seeing our flawed behavior for exactly what it is: the degenerate action of beasts. All the playwright must do to cure his audience, therefore, is expose sin and folly whenever they appear. Thus, Sir Politic Would-Be's discovery within his tortoise disguise is a symbol for the entire play, which promises that each character's flaws will eventually be revealed and punished in a highly didactic fashion.

As a result of this careful theatrical mixture of pleasant comedy and serious satiric instruction, *Volpone* affects many theatregoers like a modern-day, timed-release medication: it slides easily down our throats, yet withholds its medicinal effect until a later, more opportune moment. Typical of such other Jonsonian efforts as *Epicoene*, *The Alchemist*, *Bar-*

tholomew Fair, and *Every Man in His Humour,* the comic catharsis of *Volpone* strikes when we least expect it, when the laughter has vanished, when we begin to slip downward on that great chain of being and the beast within us rears its ugly head. At that moment, we are still nourished by Jonson's comic banquet, which delights and sustains us long after the curtain has fallen.

Awl's Well That Ends Well

The Shoemaker's Holiday at the 1994
Utah Shakespeare Festival

Thomas Dekker's comic masterpiece *The Shoemaker's Holiday* seems at first glance to be a late-sixteenth-century version of "The Beverly Hillbillies Make Reeboks in the Renaissance." Loosely based on part one of Thomas Deloney's *The Gentle Craft,* a collection of stories celebrating the exploits of famous shoemakers in England, the drama's main plot chronicles the meteoric rise to fame and fortune of Simon Eyre, an ambitious, madcap entrepreneur who—through hard work, clever deception, and magnificent luck—becomes lord mayor of London. Attended by Margery (his somewhat ditzy wife), Hodge (his industrious and kindhearted foreman), Firk (a journeyman addicted to bawdy puns and cheap ale), and a gaggle of good-natured, but unsophisticated, cobblers, Eyre ascends to prominence in a delightful dramatic parable that rewards virtue over social status, industry over aristocracy, and love over law.

Garnishing this central story are two romantic subplots—each dealing with love lost, then found. The first involves one of Eyre's journeymen, Ralph Damport, who is conscripted into the army and sent off to fight in France. Returning wounded from the wars, he finds that his young wife, Jane, thinking him dead, has left Eyre's shop and moved to a different section of London, where an unscrupulous gentleman named Hammon is courting her. In the other subplot, a young aristocrat, Roland Lacy, disguises himself as a Dutch shoemaker so he can avoid going to war and instead court the beautiful Rose Oatley, whom he loves against her father's wishes.

Dekker describes Simon Eyre's Horatio Alger, shoe-leather-to-riches story of working-class triumph—with its two attendant love stories—in a dedicatory epistle as "a merry conceited comedy" where "nothing is proposed but mirth." Yet beneath the play's comic surface lie a number of important themes that provide insight into the economic, social, and political milieu of London during the years 1598 to 1600, when the play was written and first produced. Chief among these is the ascent of capitalism, by which Eyre's dramatic elevation to lord mayor and his accumulation of an immense personal fortune emblemize the upwardly mobile middle class in England during a time of great financial opportunity and expansion.

All the major characters in the play, in fact, are engaged in buying and selling goods. Eyre, for instance, makes his fortune principally through purchasing a shipload of foreign merchandise and reselling it for enormous profit; Lacy bribes his way out of the service so he can be with Rose; and Hammon tries to buy Jane from Ralph by offering twenty pounds in gold. Even during the play's denouement—when the king honors the shoemakers by visiting their banquet on Shrove Tuesday—Eyre manages to raise the specter of commercialism when he talks his sovereign into giving him a special patent to buy and sell leather products two days each week in the newly named Leaden Hall. Eyre's economic triumphs—set against this swirling background of money won and lost—signal a victory for the bourgeoisie at the expense of indolent and snobbish aristocrats like Hammon and Lacy's pompous and insufferable father, the Earl of Lincoln. True human value, Dekker seems to argue, comes not from riches and social prominence but from the honest labor, vitality, patriotism, and camaraderie personified so vividly by Eyre's gallant shoemakers.

Closely allied to this theme of nascent capitalism is the play's emphasis on the development of guilds—early trade unions, each with its own particular language, group identity, mythology, and patron saint. Based on Dekker's intimate knowledge of contemporary working-class conditions in London, the play offers a delicious feast of cordwainer jargon. "Hark you, shoemaker," Firk asks Lacy, who is disguised as a Dutch cobbler, "have you all your tools? A good rubbing-pin, a good stopper, a good dresser, your four sorts of awls, and your two balls of wax, your paring knife, your hand and thumb-leathers, and good Saint Hugh's bones

28. *The Shoe-maker's Holi-day*, 1994. Brian G. Kurlander as Roland Lacey and Laurie Birmingham as Margery. Photo by Wesley Bernard and Marielle Hui Wilkes. Published with permission of the Utah Shakespeare Festival.

to smooth your work?" (4.78–82). This is a world where people take immense pride in their craft, and they are often rewarded for their diligence in mysterious and unexpected ways. Ralph, for example, is reunited with his wife when he recognizes a pair of sandals he once gave her:

> This shoe, I durst be sworn,
> Once covered the instep of my Jane.
> This is her size, her breadth. Thus trod my love.

These true-love knots I pricked. I hold my life,
By this old shoe I shall find out my wife. (14.45–49)

In knowing the size and breadth of Jane's feet, Ralph has captured the
dimensions of her soul. As the Cinderella motif implies, marriages—like
comfortable footwear—need a perfect fit to be successful. Jane eventually
rejects Hammon because he doesn't measure up to the same moral standards displayed by Ralph and the rest of the good lads in the Shoemakers' Guild, who are loyal to their union brothers and mutually supportive
in a manner that the play's aristocrats can never understand or duplicate.

Focused so tightly on commercialism and the emergence of industrial
guilds, *The Shoemaker's Holiday* also centers, not surprisingly, on the city of
London: the familiar, bustling, real-life locus of action that serves as a scenic backdrop for the fictional characters and events of the play. Eyre and
his imaginary cohorts move through a dramatic landscape that includes
such well-known places as St. Paul's Church, Leaden Hall, Watling Street,
the Guildhall, Tower Street, and many other locations—particularly in the
East End of London, the heart of trade—that would have been immediately familiar to Dekker's audiences. The milieu of the play seemed like
home to viewers in 1600 because it *was* home to them. In the same manner,
the drama's concentration on urban events also helps define it as one of
the earliest examples of a popular and influential literary genre we now
call *Jacobean city comedy*, which traditionally included sexual intrigue, class
mobility, and the obsessive pursuit of wealth—in short, all the seamy ingredients of today's most popular movies and television shows.

Other important themes in *The Shoemaker's Holiday* include the rich
and exotic uses of language, particularly in Eyre's highly imaginative,
rhetorical, and alliterative verbal flourishes; Lacy's pseudo-Dutch dialogue; Hammon's courtly, fashionable discourse; and Firk's rambling ob-
scenities concerning the erotic possibilities of the "tongues," "laces," and
"tightness" of women's shoes. Also of interest are the holiday aspect of
the play, in which the three central plots move from union to wandering
to joyful reunion at the conclusion; the employment of scapegoat figures
like Hammon, Oatley, and the Earl of Lincoln, whose mean-spirited antagonism is defeated by the comic progress of the drama; and the gradually richer clothing that Eyre and his wife wear as they rise in social and
financial prominence. Most intriguing, perhaps, is the odd amorality of

the world of the play: Eyre illegally impersonates a city official to purchase the shipload of valuable merchandise and then ascends to the position of lord mayor following an unlikely scenario where "seven of the alderman be dead, or very sick" (13.35–36); Lacy deserts from the army only to be pardoned later by his strangely unperturbed king; and Jane and Ralph appropriate all Hammon's wedding gifts because, as Hodge argues, "The law's on our side. He that sows in another man's ground forfeits his harvest" (18.63–64).

In the final analysis, however, *The Shoemaker's Holiday* may tell us even more about its author than the world where he lived. Thomas Dekker was a popular playwright, though hardly a wealthy one. Unlike Shakespeare, who, as a shareholder in his own theatrical company, earned a great deal of money on the plays he composed, Dekker was a "jobbing" dramatist who moved from one employment to another as his services were needed. Though he wrote several well-known pamphlets—including *The Wonderful Year* (1603), *The Seven Deadly Sins of London* (1606), and *The Gull's Hornbook* (1609)—and had a hand in at least five other plays, he lived in continual poverty and was frequently cast into debtors' prison. Incredibly, he earned only three pounds for writing *The Shoemaker's Holiday*, his best and most influential play.

Viewed in this light, Dekker's "merry" comedy presents life in early-seventeenth-century England as more of a dream than reality. Simon Eyre's London is an idealized dramatic universe where hard work and perseverance are always fairly rewarded with royal favor, financial security, true love, and good fellowship: here even unsophisticated cobblers and minor dramatists can enjoy sweet success. Dekker has, therefore, stitched together with his playwright's awl a compelling, seductive, and very stylish piece of social propaganda. If only his impoverished life could have imitated his art!

The Heart of the Matter

'Tis Pity, She's a Whore at California State
University, Bakersfield, in 2006

Pssst! Wanna see a show about moral degradation, murder, and brother-sister incest? No, it isn't the Disney Channel gone berserk or Jerry Spring-er on location in the Ozarks. It's John Ford's *'Tis Pity, She's a Whore*, one of the best late English Renaissance plays you've never heard of. Although the play was first performed and published in the early 1630s, it has a dis-tinctly modern feel, inspired, no doubt, by its abundant violence, corrup-tion, treachery, and adultery—all staple ingredients that contemporary audiences hold in high regard. In fact, in his review of JoAnne Akalaitis's 1992 production of the play at the Public Theater (one among many recent trendy revivals), *New York Times* critic Frank Rich asked how "a work with language so frank and nasty and sexual politics so sophisticated [could] have been written almost four centuries ago?"[1]

Set in Parma, Italy, the play's multiple plots ricochet wildly between the impassioned love of Giovanni, a brilliant young scholar, for his chaste sister, Annabella, and a series of intrigues involving the following charac-ters: Florio, Annabella and Giovanni's father; Putana, Annabella's guard-ian (whose name translates as "whore"); Friar Bonaventure, Giovanni's wise, if ineffective, religious tutor; Soranzo, a nobleman who marries An-nabella before realizing she's pregnant with her brother's child; Bergetto, a half-witted suitor for Annabella's hand; his servant, Poggio; Grimaldi,

---

1. Frank Rich, *"'Tis Pity She's a Whore:* Jacobean Tale of Lust and Revenge Updated to the Fascist 1930s," *New York Times,* April 6, 1992.

another of Annabella's suitors; Vasques, Soranzo's clever servant; Madame Hippolita, Soranzo's former lover; and a gaggle of bandits or *banditti*. Like most Renaissance revenge tragedies, the play spirals down into a spectacular, bloody, Grand Guignol conclusion that rivals the best of today's *Friday the 13th* films.

Though Ford was obviously pandering to his jaded Caroline audience, whose members thought they had already seen every possible depravity onstage, his shocking subject matter and outlandish finale cloak a deeper and more profound reality. In a world this sordid, the pure and selfless relationship between Giovanni and Annabella seems almost innocent by comparison. Despite the well-known taboo against incest in most societies, it was occasionally celebrated in the Greco-Roman world, in mythology and folklore, in Icelandic and Norse legends, and even in the biblical story of Lot and his daughters, which lends virtue and credibility to the love between brother and sister, though the play's brutal and bloody climax is a forgone conclusion because of Giovanni's selfish arrogance and murderous instincts. As in Shakespeare's *Romeo and Juliet* (which also features young lovers, forbidden romance, a meddling nurse and friar, and a horribly tragic ending), the sweet, passionate love between Annabella and Giovanni dignifies their relationship and stands in stark contrast to the decadent world in which they live. Theirs is a relationship that exists against all odds and despite social conventions, a love that endures even in the face of its tragic conclusion. Like John Webster, whose metaphysical drama looked for "the skull beneath the skin,"[2] Ford reaches deeply into the heart of his play, which still pulses to a familiar modern rhythm after all these years.

---

2. T. S. Eliot, "Whispers of Immortality," *Collected Poems (1909–1935)*, in *The Complete Plays and Poems* (New York: Harcourt, Brace & World, Inc., 1971), 32.

Invalids, Real and Imaginary

The Imaginary Invalid at the 1989
Utah Shakespeare Festival

The comedies of French playwright Jean Baptiste Molière offer convincing proof of the maxim that great art often imitates life. His last play in particular, *The Imaginary Invalid* (1673), is interpreted most clearly in the context of the author's biography. Its bitter satire of doctors, for example, results not only from the deplorable state of medicine in seventeenth-century France but also the fact that inept physicians had cost Molière a mother, two sons, and several close friends. Likewise, the avaricious and scheming stepmother Béline may owe something of her character to Molière's own stepmother, Catherine Fleurette—who, like her stage counterpart, had two daughters. In fact, the author's preoccupation with fathers and daughters—in this play and others he wrote—may give credence to rumors that he married his own daughter, Armande, the beautiful and mysteriously illegitimate child of his principal actress and former lover, Madeleine Béjart.

The most telling parallel, however, between the stage and real world is that both Argan and Molière were dreadful hypochondriacs. The author was a sickly man whose hard work and obsessive concern with his health invited constant ridicule, most notably in rival playwright Le Boulanger de Chalussay's *Élomire the Hypochondriac*, or *The Doctors Avenged* (1670). Like Argan, Molière was addicted to physicians and took many bizarre and noxious remedies to rid himself of a wide assortment of real and illusory ailments.

29. *The Imaginary Invalid*, 1989. Cal Winn as Argan and Monica Bell as Toinette. Photo by Michael Schoenfeld. Published with permission of the Utah Shakespeare Festival.

Viewed from this angle, *The Imaginary Invalid* is less a satire of medical charlatans than a fascinating self-portrait of the author as patient. Within the comic caricature of Argan, we see Molière's attempt to explore and treat his own psychological malaise. The result was both ironic and fatal. During the fourth performance of the play on February 17, 1673—after a scene when Molière, playing the part of Argan, had feigned death—art immediately translated into life when the playwright had a seizure onstage. Though he managed to finish the performance, he was rushed home, where he lay gravely ill. Because of his past attacks on religious hypocrisy and medical incompetence, no priest or doctor would come to his aid, and he died that same evening.

The ensuing funeral ceremony and burial were dogged with controversy. Since he had not formally renounced the acting profession prior to his death—a ritual required by the Catholic Church—he could not be buried in consecrated ground and was instead interred in a remote section of the cemetery reserved for suicides and stillbirths. According to popular gossip, Molière deserved his tragic ending: he had counterfeited illness and death onstage, and Death had avenged himself by snatching the author from the happy world of theatre and hurling him into the deadly seriousness of the Last Judgment.

Molière's sudden demise also helps explain the awkward mixture of genres in a play that yokes together commedia dell' arte characters, ballet, farce, interact skits, Egyptian dancers, and figures from classical mythology in a "comedy mixed with music and dances" written to please King Louis XIV. The author's usual habit was to compose his plays rapidly, get them onstage as soon as possible, and then revise them according to audience response. In this case, however, Death preempted the revision. What we are left with is undoubtedly a play in progress, a rough draft of a delightful experiment that begins as a comedy of character, establishes a clever plot, evolves into a debate, careens wildly into melodrama, and finally degenerates altogether into an operatic finale featuring pig Latin and a chorus of singing, dancing doctor buffoons: a literary demolition derby where the last genre still rolling at the conclusion is the winner.

This odd, deconstructive journey is surely a chronicle of Argan's disintegrating mind, but it also reflects, on a deeper and more profound level, the psyche of Molière—hopelessly ill, distrustful of physicians, fearful of death. In his own inspired way, however, the author has turned his macabre and brooding life into joyous, brilliant comedy. By recognizing the ultimate absurdity of his situation, he converts fear into farce, pain into pleasure, and satire into the healing release of laughter. As a result, the happiness forbidden to Molière in his life exists forever in his art.

A Modern Jacobean Comedy

A Mad World, My Masters at the La Jolla Playhouse in 1983

Like any good wedding, Barrie Keefe's *A Mad World, My Masters* contains a mixture of something old and something new. The older, borrowed element of the play is Keefe's use of a dramatic style that we now call *Jacobean city comedy*. Popular in England from approximately 1598 to 1612, this theatrical genre was a descendant of fifteenth- and sixteenth-century morality plays, Latin comedies by Plautus and Terence, the Italian commedia dell'arte, and native English verse satire. Selected plays by Ben Jonson, Thomas Dekker, John Marston, and Thomas Middleton—the best-known city comedy playwrights—display a number of characteristics typical of this kind of drama.

As the name implies, city comedies were an exposé of urban life; since the city was assumed to be the absolute center of lust, greed, and corruption, it offered a perfect setting for dramatic satire. Consequently this brand of comedy habitually presented a wide spectrum of characters, each flawed to some extent and dominated by a specific *humour* or behavioral idiosyncrasy. Another distinguishing feature of city comedy was that the plays were marked by fast-moving, multiple plots that intersected on several levels. The principal themes were usually money, lust, and power—often in combination—and the play often explored the various connections among these three seductive sins. Finally, city comedies were heavily ironic: characters usually got the opposite of what they were striving for, and a clear sense of poetic justice insured that everyone received his proper reward or punishment in the end.

192

A Mad World is typical of city comedy in many respects. In fact, Keefe's manipulation of this inherited Renaissance genre reveals his penchant for using traditional forms to deal with contemporary issues. Two of his other plays, *Frozen Assets* and *Bastard Angel,* are indebted to Dickens and Chekhov respectively (though his best-known work, *Gimme Shelter,* is entirely unique in plot and structure). In *A Mad World,* the scene is London—more specifically, the East End, where Cockney dialect and working-class families are the norm. Furthermore, Keefe's characters are all dominated by distinct humours: one, for example, is crafty and sly; another is unrelievedly cheerful; a third is lethargic; while a fourth is cocky and pugnacious. The different plots move at a furious pace, splicing together at several unexpected points while money, lust, and power are the principal themes. Even the play's title (though nothing of the plot) is borrowed from a Middleton comedy written around 1610.

The new additions to Keefe's marriage of city comedy and twentieth-century London result from the play's unique attention to social class and the complexities of game playing. Out of the clash between the industrialist Claughton and Grandma Sprightly tumbles one of the play's great moral and social lessons: the British notion of class structure hasn't changed much over the last four hundred years. Game playing is also a recurrent motif in the play, especially the "cons" (as Superintendent Sayers would call them), which are at the heart of Keefe's comic milieu. Blood sports such as cockfighting, boxing, and hunting serve as minor background scenery to a dramatic universe where social status and sexual conquest have become the greatest games of all.

In the final analysis, Keefe's play is itself a con. His modern, satiric version of life, wrapped in city-comedy form, portrays the mad world that entraps each one of us. As Graham Parker's theme song for the play echoes, "You're in the race; you've got a place. But that's what they all say."

ॐ VII ॐ

Acting Shakespeare

Roundtable Discussions with Actors and Directors

Measure for Measure AT THE 2003
UTAH SHAKESPEARE FESTIVAL

Featuring Elisabeth Adwin (Isabella), Scott Coopwood (Angelo),
Michael David Edwards (Lucio), Henry Woronicz (Duke), and
Michael Flachmann (festival dramaturg)

FLACHMANN: Good morning. My name is Michael Flachmann. I've been company dramaturg here at the festival for eighteen years and was fortunate enough to be dramaturg on this summer's production of *Measure for Measure*, directed by Liz Huddle.

As I'm sure everyone knows, the members of the production team—including the actors, director, and designers—ask ourselves many of the same questions that intrigue scholars about difficult scripts like *Measure for Measure*. Because of the demands of our profession, we don't have the luxury of juggling a lot of different interpretations and theories about the plays. We have to make choices, which then focus the script and crystallize audience reactions.

Actors, I think, do just as much research as scholars. Some of it is literary, and some of it happens in rehearsals. Much of this research is emotional and instinctive. As a result, what we are doing today is taking a different doorway into the play than we have for the past two days with all these wonderful scholarly papers. I think this is an avenue of inquiry that Shakespeare himself would have welcomed.

To begin with a question for the actors, most scholars view *Measure for Measure* as a problem play. Yet when you see a first-rate production of the script, like yours, many of the so-called problems seem to disappear.

So I'd like to start off with Henry and ask what you see as the problems in this script. And how has this production solved them?

WORONICZ: There are a number of what we would think of as classical structural problems in *Measure for Measure* from an actor's point of view. They have to do with threading through the story and starting with the motivational events that help define the characters. The big question for any actor playing the duke is why he does what he does. Why doesn't he just stop everything and change the laws? He says, "I've given the city permission to behave badly for fourteen years, and I don't want to look like a tyrant." So this conflict begins his whole journey.

As an actor, you process this to find all the little touchstones that Shakespeare uses in the script. There are two especially important ones for me in terms of his arc in the journey. In one of the earliest scenes when he is explaining what he is trying to do, he begins by saying, "Oh no, no, no, believe not that the dribbling dart of love can pierce a complete bosom." Then, at the end of the play, he is asking for Isabella's hand in marriage, so something has changed in the course of his journey. He doesn't feel complete anymore. He needs a partner: this young woman that he has fallen in love with in the course of the story.

FLACHMANN: So you learn in the play that you need Isabella?

WORONICZ: The big scene with Isabella, when he explains about his plan to trick Angelo, is always difficult for me because there is an important chunk of that scene where he interrupts right after Claudio and Isabella talk, and she is going to let her brother die to protect her chastity. As an actor, I am always trying to make sure I can differentiate in the audience's mind when this guy is telling the truth and when he is not because the spectators know he's in disguise. How do you find the honesty of what is true and what is false to the people around you? If he knows that Angelo had been betrothed to this lady and, as they say in the souvenir program, "jilted" her, [laughter] if he's aware of this, why didn't he do something at that time to solve the problem? He seems to be afraid of getting involved with the law. He loves "the life removed" like Prospero, like many other rulers in Shakespeare, who step back from the general business of running the state, and they get lost in their books. Why doesn't he do something about that?

FLACHMANN: So you've got all these layers. You're an actor playing a role, and that character acts in the play.

WORONICZ: Yes, that character acts, too. That's always true. He also seems to be very well acquainted with Mariana at the moated grange. Shakespeare likes the plasticity of time and stretching things out. At one point, he said the duke is going to be here in two days, and then in the very next scene, he says he is going to be here tomorrow. Then Lucio comes in seeming to know that the duke is going to be here tomorrow. As an actor, that is always one of your problems when you have to make sense of the passage of time. Sometimes you just ignore the problems. Against all instinct, you go that direction strongly and fully anyway to help make the play happen. So when he comes to Mariana and she says, "Oh, here's a man who's long been my comfort...," Liz Huddle, the director, and I decided that she is used to being visited by friars. [laughter]

FLACHMANN: All those friars look alike anyway. [laughter]

WORONICZ: Yes, in their robes, and they are always blessing people. And then there's the moment I wasn't convinced was going to work—but I think it has worked for me—where he asks for Isabella's hand at the end of the play. And it's very deliberate. Shakespeare to me is the most deliberate of writers. If he has an opportunity to say something, he will. And when he has a character keep quiet, that's an important choice. When Isabella doesn't speak at the end of the play, that seems to me an awkward choice. The duke deals with Angelo and wraps things up, but then comes back to her again. I think we have found a way to play this with him as a supplicant to her. He is asking for completeness from her.

Now what's she going to do? That's the test. He is going to see what she is made of, to see what kind of person she is. When she turns around and begs forgiveness for Angelo, that's an important moment in the play. The greatest of human qualities is to ask for mercy. She says, "I will forgive this man. I will be bigger than my circumstances and 'look on this man as if my brother lived.'" And at that moment, I think the duke is falling in love with her. When he first sees her, he says, "The hand that hath made you fair hath made you good." His first response is how pretty she is. So Isabella completes the duke.

That difficult ending has always been a problem in the play, and I think we have managed to make it work. I had played the duke once before, and the ending was much more ambiguous, which I think is another of Shakespeare's great strengths—his ambiguity. If you are directing, it's another point of view. But as a character, you look at the problem that way—what the spine of the play is and how you make sense of it.

I love what we call Shakespeare's problem plays because they don't tie up neatly. They present challenges for the actors and directors to figure out. You know you are dealing with this writer who portrays a certain Renaissance form and style, but at the same time, he is very modern in terms of how people interact with each other. I always think of people watching this play for the first time, and they must be saying, "What the hell is going on?" [laughter] And then there's this whole relationship [gestures toward Coopwood and Adwin]—which you both could speak about—the whole sexual power play that goes on.

FLACHMANN: I think that if the play were crystal clear, we wouldn't even be talking about it. That's one of the joys of the script: it's got some depth and intrigue.

COOPWOOD: Do you think that's why people say, "Oh, it's a problem"—because it doesn't tie up perfectly? It doesn't have a fairy-tale ending unless you create one? And so people say, "Well, there's a problem because it is not complete." But it is complete because that's the way life is. Life is never cut and dried; life is never complete.

WORONICZ: Life is a large problem play [chuckling]!

EDWARDS: But we always ask for much more consistency of our art than we do of our life.

ADWIN: That's right.

FLACHMANN: Scott, any further comments about whether this is a problem play, not only in response to the script but also in relation to your own character?

COOPWOOD: I have gone to productions where I thought, "Yes, there is a problem with this play." And the problem was the direction. [laughter] That was the problem. Or the problem was in a specific performance or in certain choices that were made. And having gone through this experience and watching the world created around me, and then dealing with the audience reaction following that, I don't see it as much of a problem anymore because I think we have struck a balance between the light and the dark and the questions and the ambiguity. I think everything has at least been addressed to some degree.

And I think the performances of the people you see sitting here, not to mention all the other supporting characters who are involved, are all very clear. And I think there is a lightness to the production that counteracts the heaviness and the darkness, that gives it a balance, that lifts it up, and that presents it as what it is. And I was concerned because the script has this reputation. As Joe Cronin [who plays Pompey] will tell you, he was involved in a production that was so dark and so depressing, the comedy was almost an afterthought.

ADWIN: I saw that.

COOPWOOD: You know what I mean? That is a director problem. It is not a problem with the script. I think for Angelo, specifically, the biggest problem that I have is not why he does what he does, but why he did what he did. You hear in the script about the relationship with Mariana. Obviously, there has to be some event, something had to have taken place. I don't see Angelo as a bad guy. He's not the villain. It would be too easy to play him as a villain. It wouldn't be interesting to watch, and it wouldn't be interesting to play. I could just phone it in, but it wouldn't be fun. And I'm having a blast with this production, so obviously there's a struggle there.

Something is taking place that's making me work every night to get where I need to go. And that's the joy of doing what we do. There has to be something about the relationship with Mariana that you only hear about through Henry as the duke. And I don't even know if the duke is telling the truth [chuckling]. You know the brother was killed in a shipwreck, and he had all this money, and Angelo allegedly said to Mariana, "Well, you don't have any money now, so I don't want you anymore." That's way too simple for me. So I had to create something, and we talked about this, Michael [Flachmann] and I, when we started rehearsal. What is it, what happened? So I had to create this whole backstory about the relationship between Mariana and myself, and that is what I created to get me where I need to go every night so that when this starts [gestures to Adwin], it's a trigger for a lot of other events.

FLACHMANN: Do you feel comfortable talking about that a little bit more?

COOPWOOD: Sure. Angelo is obviously very, very repressed. And he sees the world in blacks and whites. There's no gray. And he has come to this decision throughout the course of his life as a response to whatever happened to him in his childhood, in his upbringing. But about his relationship with Mariana…I believe they were in the backseat of a car one night, and things went a little too far [chuckling]. So the relationship was consummated, and I believe that event disturbed and disgusted Angelo. That's when he decided that all women were poison, and he created this tunnel-vision worldview for himself. He wanted nothing to do with her any longer because of what he felt she had done to him, what she had let him become.

The laws were on the books at that time. He broke the law; he did the same thing that Claudio did. As he says to Escalus, "I have had such faults." He glazes right over that. So I think that was for me the only way I could get where I needed to go and keep him not completely the villain. He is a real human being, struggling with real problems and real issues, such as this incident in his life prior to the beginning of the play. And for me that incident defines the relationship between him and Mariana, and that's why he leaves her, that's why he abandons her—because he can't face what he did. He feels obviously that he was to some degree trapped into that relationship.

We all have backstories behind what we are doing because they help to motivate us. The nice thing about Shakespeare, though, is that you don't need all this subtext. It's all there in the lines. Shakespeare tells you exactly how to act, when to breathe. Everything is there.

WORONICZ: But he won't go any further; he can't say anything about it. And she won't say anything about it.

FLACHMANN: Speaking of repressed sexuality [gestures to Adwin].

ADWIN: Who says that? [laughter]

FLACHMANN: Any particular problems for you with the character, with the role?

ADWIN: Yes, sure. When you first read a play, it's a totally different experience than when you are performing it. These are scripts, not pieces of literature. So the problems that may pop out at you off the page—when you are first reading it before you have gotten all your muscles and mind in there—are completely different from when you are actually giving it life. And some of those problems just automatically rectify themselves when you begin making choices. The process of going from novitiate to nun is quite extensive, and of course Claudio says, "Well, today my sister is going to the cloister" as if she is signing up with the army or something.

I think the most obvious problem—and certainly one that I have seen in other productions, from Isabella's point of view—is that just because she is passionate doesn't mean she has to be an absolute. Her passion for God doesn't mean that she must be shallow of heart or invulnerable. In other productions I have seen, Isabella can often be very cold and unapproachable. That doesn't really work because the audience doesn't feel anything for her dilemma, and her dilemma is at the very center of the play.

FLACHMANN: And it doesn't give you anywhere to go in your relationship with Henry.

ADWIN: Precisely, yes. And she's got to have vulnerability because this man steps into her life and helps solve her problem. Their falling in love is a wonderful surprise, I think, for both of them. This intimacy that she is experiencing sneaks up on her in the guise of something else. But I think making her too absolute, too unemotional, turns her into a flat and uninteresting character. That was my main challenge, my main goal. When I first read the play, I said, "Oh God, I don't know how I'm going to do this…but I want to play this woman." She's a tough one. She's got so many different levels, and we're getting there. But again I wouldn't categorize it as a problem play. I think it has that reputation because you can't put a label on it. We talked about this before. Consistency is the hobgoblin of little minds.

FLACHMANN: Right. So if you just do the play and don't worry about categorizing it, you'll be in a lot better shape.

ADWIN: Absolutely. I think the problems rectify themselves when you're naturally making choices as an actor. I remember reading about one production that Francesca Annis did for the RSC [Royal Shakespeare Company] in the seventies. When the duke asked for her hand at the end, she gazed out into the audience with this look of revulsion, and then he took his cloak, and he literally enveloped her in it. He metaphorically ate her alive. And I felt that was hard core; that was a really dark interpretation.

FLACHMANN: And you had some religious tutorials. Sister Yvonne, a local Catholic nun, was kind enough to talk with you about how nuns glide.

ADWIN: I did.

COOPWOOD: They glide?

ADWIN: Nuns don't walk. Of course, the first time I put on my costume, I wasn't floating. I aspire to float. Yes, you were kind enough to bring Sister Yvonne for me to meet with. It was fascinating to talk about what nuns' vows mean—especially poverty, chastity, enclosure, and obedience. I wanted to talk to the sister about how she viewed God in Christ and whether there was a certain erotic quality in that.

FLACHMANN: I've got to tell you. The elevator went down about twelve stories in a second and a half. It was a wonderful breakthrough, I thought.

ADWIN: She said she did not view Christ as a lover or husband. What she said was that she viewed Christ as an older brother. I thought that was very interesting. I saw Isabella as a young, hot-blooded, passionate woman. And I don't think she is frightened of sex. I don't think she's in denial about sex. I think she's just making a choice. And that channeling is for God and not other human beings until the end. Although I think this relationship [gestures toward Coopwood]—probably in some subliminal way—awakens all kinds of feelings. There's electricity in it. I was curious about that because I think passion has all different kinds of levels.

FLACHMANN: Thank you, Elisabeth. Michael, I am going to hypothe-size that one of the problems scholars have with this play is the perceived awkward mixture between comedy and the more serious sections of the plot. So what are you doing in this play? What is Lucio's job in *Measure for Measure?*

EDWARDS: I think of the three characters we have spoken about so far, Lucio in contrast to them is much less problematic because his role is principally comic. Within the world of a comic character, inconsistency is a plus because inconsistency generates humor. And I think the comic characters in this play truly embody the humanist spirit in contrast to the world of rules and the kind of puritanical morality that Angelo repre-sents. I see Angelo and Lucio as polar opposites in the world of the play, with the duke and Isabella at the center, orbiting around each other. Lucio is completely amoral, and everything about him is the opposite of what we have seen with Angelo, and I think the contradiction there and the dissonance you've got between the comic and the dramatic is what makes the play great.

Dissonance is what makes art interesting. If everything is consistent and logical, what you get is television. This table is very nice because it is all rectilinear, and it wobbles a little bit, but that's okay. And you know that the wobbling is what's making it interesting [chuckling]. If it didn't wobble, it would be completely invisible. And I think the same thing is true in art. Often our tendency is to categorize, to classify because that is how we make sense of the world. But when art is truly great, it defies classification. And that's what we like about it.

I think what we are talking about here is the clash of different points of view. The duke has a point of view; Angelo has a point of view; Isabella has a point of view; and Lucio has a point of view. And they're all in conflict with each other. The play happens when you throw those people into a particular situation and see how they respond. That's what Shakespeare was really brilliant at: taking these different points of view and not only making wonderful rhetorical arguments but giving them a very interesting and dynamic dramatic voice.

The scenes between Lucio and the duke are brilliant dramatically because not only do you get to see Lucio weaving the web of his own destruction, but it's a great way to reveal what the duke thinks about himself because he's watching this guy who is completely repugnant talk about him. And what he is saying is totally opposite to what he has thought of himself. It's a great opportunity because in the very next scene, the duke is asking Escalus what the duke was like: "What did people say about the duke? My God, does everybody think I'm like that?" This is a great opportunity for self-discovery. And that comes about in a comic scene.

We don't normally think of comedy as being an avenue for self-revelation, but in this play it is. And I think that's another element that makes the play so great. It's messy, and it's about life. The problem of the play is that this guy is going to get killed because he got his girlfriend pregnant. And how do we react to that? The play deals with that problem in a messy way, and the conclusion is messy as a result. You know, this play is about what it means to be alive and how we react to moral quandaries. Should we condemn this man for impregnating his fiancée? They were going to get married anyway. Most modern audience members would say, "What's the big deal?"

WORONICZ: But this is going on in Jacobean times. You know once the vows had been made, that's the end of the trail.

COOPWOOD: That's not the law, though [chuckling].

EDWARDS: Change the law.

WORONICZ: The other big messy thing is that we've got this ruler who can't pull it together himself, so he gives his power to someone who he knows is a puritan, and then he decides to hang around and watch [laughing]. There's this whole thing about the duke being a voyeur. I think he is fascinated by the intricacies of life that Michael [Edwards] talked about. He's almost like a scientist, like Prospero: he's involved in his books. He wants to put people in certain situations and then see what they do. He wants to listen to Claudio and Isabella talk.

FLACHMANN: Yes, we have all that eavesdropping.

WORONICZ: Yeah, your sister is a nun, and she's come to give you comfort. "Oh God, let me hear what they are saying." He wants to watch.

FLACHMANN: Do the Lucio-Duke scenes work for you in much the same way that Michael [Edwards] has explained them? I mean, do they help you find your character or discover the perception the other characters have of you?

WORONICZ: Yes, I think he's taken aback—first by the audacity of this guy—as when he says, "Oh, I'm intimate with the duke." And he asks him what pleasure the duke was given to. There's a sadness in him, I think, when he asks if the duke was addicted to any kind of pleasure? "What was he like?" I don't think he knows himself very well. I think he's like anyone searching for the truth—he's always looking for the next answer. But there are no definitive answers. There are only greater observations as you go out into your circle of life. And so I think that's what he's involved with in terms of his relationship with Lucio. And Lucio puts him on that path a little bit. And Isabella also puts him on that path from a physical as well as a spiritual point of view. So the psychological elements get very Byzantine in the course of the play.

You know, actors are interpretative artists. We take what a playwright has given us and we say, "What does this say to us at this time and to this particular audience?" And we take it from there. I remember as a kid, I was given a leather jacket or a bag or something with a tag on it that said it was made from "fine leather." It said you may find imperfections in this garment, and that's part of it being fine leather. It's a genuine, authentic thing. And I always think of the odd bumps and twists and turns in a play as Shakespeare's little tag saying, "This is authentic." That's one of the joys when you are able to do some of the plays uncut. We get all those little bumps and imperfections that usually get cut out. You can see the whole piece in front of you, the whole textured canvas. That rarely happens these days because some of Shakespeare's plays are so long. If we hadn't cut eight hundred or so lines out of *Richard III*, we'd still be in our seats [laughing].

FLACHMANN: One of the topics we've been flirting with is the legislation of morality. And we have had several good papers on that topic in this symposium. What do you think this play teaches us in modern terms about attempts to legislate morality?

EDWARDS: You can't. We try. We have been trying for thousands of years. We don't seem to be able to. Just because you pass a law doesn't mean we are going to stop behaving the way we behave. I don't think anybody in this room hasn't broken the speed limit.

COOPWOOD: Just because you pass a statute, that doesn't mean there aren't breasts in the world. [laughter]

EDWARDS: I think Pompey speaks the most truth in the play. He asks Escalus, "Are you going to geld and splay all the youth of the city?" It doesn't matter what the law is. You know people are going to behave like people behave, and they will change their behavior when as a group they decide that their behavior needs to change and not when somebody gives them a law. Usually rules follow behavior; they don't lead to it. People are doing something, and then we say, "Oh, we wish they wouldn't do that, so we are going to make a rule that says you can't do that." So the only thing that happens is that more people get punished. But nobody really changes his or her behavior. We get speeding tickets, but we still speed. It is a mistaken assumption to think that you can create a set of rules a priori of behavior. I think rules are generated out of consensus.

COOPWOOD: And for a lot of people, we have to come to them individually. I think we understand and change our behavior as we grow up. But who am I to tell you what you can do in your house? It's none of my business.

EDWARDS: Rules are appropriate for a three-year-old because they don't know. It's our job as parents to teach them.

FLACHMANN: I think this question impacts all the characters—this distinction between our natural inclinations, our yearnings and urges, and the rules we're surrounded by. But I'm particularly interested in the way they affect Isabella, especially in terms of your desire for a "more strict restraint." How do you deal with what many people see as an unconscious sexuality in your language? How did that fit into your portrayal of this complex character?

ADWIN: Sexual language is certainly inherent in some of her speeches. As far as playing them as an actress goes, I don't think about that at all.

30. *Measure for Measure*, 2003. Elisabeth Adwin as Isabella and Scott Coopwood as Angelo. Photo by Karl Hugh. Published with permission of the Utah Shakespeare Festival.

I think of it in terms of passionate metaphor. But I'm certainly not aware that she is intentionally trying to arouse anyone.

FLACHMANN: Maybe you could talk a little about your backstory, if you have one, on why you are entering the nunnery—especially one that has such rigorous standards.

ADWIN: I feel that you have to make a strong choice for her history; otherwise the play probably doesn't work. In the Renaissance, most nunneries were not particularly desirable places to go. In terms of thinking about it for the sake of this production, in my own mind, I had to envision positive reasons for entering a nunnery. Otherwise it wouldn't really be true. So I believe that she and Claudio probably lost their mother in childbirth and that they were both very attached to their father, who has recently died. So they have lost both parents, but there was a very close relationship with the father. I think they grew up very Catholic, very devout. Perhaps in her father's illness a lot of the money that would have been part of the dowry was lost. And perhaps—because of her beauty and intelligence—she had some suitors, but they didn't appeal to her. She's a very fussy girl.

WORONICZ: High standards.

ADWIN: Yes, and I think she's very spiritual. I think between getting married to somebody you don't really love and going to a place where you could be contemplative and spiritual, that a nunnery ideally would appeal to her. I don't think that's a stretch at all based on those choices that I made.

WORONICZ: Nunneries provided a refuge for a lot of people.

ADWIN: They did.

WORONICZ: Choices were limited, in particular for young women.

ADWIN: Absolutely.

FLACHMANN: What about the arc between the passionate devotion to the nunnery that we see at the beginning and—in our production anyway—the passionate devotion to the duke at the end?

ADWIN: Actually the first thing I said to Liz Huddle [the director] when I had a meeting with her was, "Okay, what about the end?" Because it could go so many different directions. And she said, "Well, they're getting together." [laughter] For a second, I was a little disappointed because the play is Jacobean. But she said, "No, I want this." And I said, "Well, okay, then the challenge for Henry and me will be to find those moments of bonding and love and friendship." We are finding new opportunities every time we do it. And it's wonderful. That was a real challenge. And I would like to think that we succeed in that. So I don't believe—based on my preparation and the way we've addressed that issue in this particular production—that this arc is especially odd.

FLACHMANN: You really have to build that bridge, though.

ADWIN: Yes, and I think we talked about this before: she is filled with all this passion and these wonderful ideas about her own morality and what is appropriate within justice and mercy, and yet she's got this huge journey to go through, and the duke helps her get there.

WORONICZ: And he also has a journey to go through that she helps him with.

ADWIN: That's so sweet. Something is happening to me. And you're [to Woronicz] responsible.

FLACHMANN: I think what we're seeing so far is that great productions and great actors solve difficult problems, and that these problems are at the heart of what makes this a terrific play. It's the inconsistencies: the leather jacket with the flaws in it.

WORONICZ: Yes. I'd like to return to something Michael [Edwards] touched on earlier. One of the most important issues I think Shakespeare is dealing with in the play is how society functions. In the scene between Lucio and the duke we were discussing earlier, Lucio says, "Can you tell me if Claudio is going to die or not?" And the duke has an interesting line here. He says, "Why must he die, sir?" Lucio's answer is, "For filling a bottle with a funnel." We changed the line a little bit.

FLACHMANN: We changed "tundish" to "funnel."

WORONICZ: Yes. This is a moment where the duke suddenly starts to look at these laws in a different way.

EDWARDS: "The Duke yet would have dark deeds darkly answered; he would never bring them to light."

WORONICZ: And the duke suddenly hears something about himself that he hadn't heard in all this previous talk. Claudio is condemned for "untrussing." Sparrows do this in the eaves. I think this realization pulls the rug out from under the duke concerning what the law is about. And then when he gets to the last sweep of the play—when he is doing this test—he is talking about an "eye for an eye, a tooth for a tooth," which is the old code. "Measure still for measure": this is how it works, right? And he realizes that you must do what is best for people in specific situations. You can't just lay down these laws as you were taught. As humans, as creatures, we are messy, and we need to talk and converse and sort things out. And I think there's a moment there that is important for the arc of the play about law and morality and rules.

FLACHMANN: I love your line, too, about caring for "a thousand bastards."

EDWARDS: "Ere he would hang a man for the getting a hundred bastards, he would pay for the nursing of a thousand."

WORONICZ: He's a passionate conservative. [laughter]

EDWARDS: Obviously Lucio is a liar and doesn't know the duke. He describes a man who was of the same appetites as Lucio, who "had some feeling of the sport; he knew the service, and that instructed him to mercy." This is the most important part of that line. You've got to have some compassion. For all of Lucio's immorality—and he is a liar—the one thing he cares about in the play is Claudio. He loves Claudio.

ADWIN: Kind of a crush there [chuckling]?

EDWARDS: Yes, and that makes him angry. Because Lucio sees the world as it is, not as it should be. And he is angry because his leader is not seeing the world as it is. I mean that's what all "this ungenitured agent will unpeople the province with continency" is about. It's absurd; this man is being condemned for taking his clothes off. It makes me angry when those kinds of things happen. So I think for all his amorality, he's really angry that we are punished for simply being what we are.

WORONICZ: There's one other character in the play who sees the world exactly as it is and lives his life according to it, which is Barnardine. That odd little grace note is one of the imperfections in the play. Suddenly, Barnardine comes out, and the duke says to him, "You just look at the world as it is, and you live your life accordingly." I think there is something about that in terms of what the duke has gone through that he admires and respects. People should live their lives according to what they see around them. And he pardons him for that.

ADWIN: That's right.

WORONICZ: And he's got no reason to pardon him, other than the fact that he's just being generous. Well, why does Shakespeare put Barnardine in there? Again it's growth on the duke's part. Same with the pardoning of Lucio at the end. There is a lot of testing that happens in that last sequence of the play.

FLACHMANN: I want to ask Scott, what in particular do you find intriguing about Isabella in the play? Are you attracted to women in uniform? [laughter]

COOPWOOD: Well, first of all, she is very beautiful, and she is very passionate, articulate, and committed. And those qualities are attractive: intelligence, intensity, and passion. He has managed to sequester himself away for the last five years since the "incident," we'll call it.

FLACHMANN: The backseat?

COOPWOOD: Yes. He has managed to sit in his chair, read his papers, and look at the laws and wish they would be followed [chuckling]. Why does he say, "Let her in"? That's the question. The sister of the man condemned wants to see you. There's a long pause there. He never thought of Claudio as having a family or being a human being. He has a sister; he has parents. This might be problematic. He is a person. Why does he say, "Let her in"? I think probably because Shelby [Davenport, the provost] says, "She's on the verge of becoming a nun. She is very devout, and you should probably see her." All right. Now all he would have to do is to say, "No. I am not talking about it to anybody. This is black and white. He dies." But we don't have a play if he does that.

ADWIN: There you go.

COOPWOOD: But she comes in, and she is everything he is afraid of. But also everything that is exciting. And we all want what we can't have. There are so many different layers to that attraction. And I think he is so repressed, and that incident before scarred him so much. Somebody gave me this quote from Gielgud explaining that—when he acted the part in 1969—"he felt Angelo was so repressed that the first time Isabella got close enough to touch him, he had an orgasm right there." That was it; it was over. And from that point forward, he had to have her again. He would do anything to have her. I thought that insight was really interesting because that's kind of the way I had felt about the whole relationship. To look back thirty years ago, on one of the greatest actors in the history of the stage, and to find the character the same way was a really wonderful experience for me.

WORONICZ: A great line you have that always jumps out at me is "she speaks, and it is with such sense that my sense breathes with it," which is in an image of copulation. And in the Catholic mind, as soon as you thought about it. . . .

COOPWOOD: It was done.

WORONICZ: Yes.

COOPWOOD: So the sin has been committed. Once he starts down that road, there's no turning back. Macbeth says the same thing: "so far stepped in blood," you know, and Richard III says it, too. Very often Shakespeare's characters feel that they have to live out their fate, whatever that may be. When he says, "Blood, thou are blood," he looks at the audience, and he seems to say, "I'm just like you. Get over it." To me he struggles with it, he still tries to say no. That whole scene is about the struggle. Shakespeare writes it in there as a struggle, an intense battle.

FLACHMANN: Well, I love the way Shakespeare separates those two scenes. He's got you coming down the stairs in our production, still brooding about this decision, about this choice. "What am I going to do?" And you are obviously obsessed.

COOPWOOD: Well, I don't know, depending on the elasticity of time, how long it's been. I don't think he's slept at all. He is really tormented.

FLACHMANN: I want to make sure we get to one of the scenes I think is the most fascinating—the Isabella-Claudio "you're going to have to die" scene. Do you want to talk about that a little bit, Elisabeth? What is your motivation there in terms of why you tell him about Angelo's proposition and why you value your chastity, your immortal soul, more than his life?

ADWIN: Well, that's a huge question in the play, especially for a modern production and a modern audience. How do you get your head around her decision? And you know again, people find it a problem play because that scene appears somewhat archaic and ridiculous. Back then, of course, audiences would have found it extreme but not unbelievable.

COOPWOOD: The immortal soul is more important. It's easy. That's what they believed.

ADWIN: It's a very tricky scene because of the ironies. Audience members get very uncomfortable in that scene, and occasionally it prompts snickers or laughter. And that's just something that as a performer you have to ride through. The way I justify it is that her chastity represents control over her own body, which is a basic right that should never be violated. She thinks, "This is my right as a human being." And women back then expected the men in their lives—their fathers, their brothers—to protect them in every capacity: emotionally, physically, and spiritually. And she's lost her father. She's lost her family. Her brother is the only man she has. Based on their upbringing, she expects Claudio will understand and will be brave and will do this for her.

And it doesn't seem to her to be an absolute question. I think it's incredibly difficult for her, so she walks into the scene with two primary emotions. "Oh no, God, I have to tell him. This is killing me. I would die for him if it were my life, but I can't do this. I just cannot bring myself to do this." Her life she's ready to give. But this is different. This is a right. "I hope he understands. Oh, it's killing me." And he's hoping, of course, that with her persuasiveness and articulateness, her female charms, Angelo will have mercy on him.

Of course, she has to break the bad news to him. I know when we looked at the scene, you [Michael Flachmann] and I, we broke it down and noticed great structure; it's a brilliantly structured scene. When she comes in, she's skirting around the issue. Some very elaborate, flowery metaphors are used. And it's quite verbose in a beautiful way, some extraordinary work. But he says, "Let me know the point." He's using very terse, monosyllabic statements to counteract that, and he's asking a lot of questions. I find that very interesting. Then as soon as the secret comes out—"Can you believe this? He wants me to sleep with him"—the whole scene shifts.

As Claudio realizes that she cannot go forward with this, he starts getting frightened, and he gives one of the most beautiful speeches on death ever written. He breaks into verse, which is quite exquisite. Who has the power in this scene? Who has the information? I just think it's such a beautiful scene—terribly, terribly difficult. And every night I do it, I don't know what to expect from the audience because you make yourself so vulnerable, and you hope that people will go on the journey with you. And most people do. I don't think those laughs—if and when we get them—are cruel laughs. I think they are laughs of recognition and ironic laughs. But it is hard. As far as owning her body, it's a basic right.

WORONICZ: How much does her entering the sisterhood influence her decision in this scene?

ADWIN: I think it's a huge influence because chastity is one of the vows she is about to take. Absolutely, so that's another issue, but even beyond that is the fact that rape is totally unacceptable.

FLACHMANN: I've often heard actors say that they take a little something with them from each role they've played. If this is true for you, what insights into your own life has this play given you?

COOPWOOD: I've never had a problem with forgiveness and mercy in my own life. But I think every time you stand in front of the dramatic mirror, it strengthens you, or it gives you a resolve to go back and look deeper and make certain you really have those qualities. And this play for me is about forgiveness and mercy and what it is to be human. I am a little less judgmental these days just for having played this part because I see—on a fictional level, in my artistic world—how poisonous that can be. Hopefully I am a better person for having a little more restraint before I pass judgment on anybody about anything. And it's easier to forgive and easier to be more merciful in that forgiveness. I think this play again is perfect for the times we are living in, too.

ADWIN: It's really made me look at my faith or lack thereof, at how I view the universe and God. So for me this has just been a revisiting of those issues. And it has been positive, very positive in that way.

EDWARDS: Watch out what you say to people; you never know who they really are [chuckling].

FLACHMANN: That's right.

EDWARDS: There is a lot to learn through playing a character like Lucio because the role offers a wonderful freedom and license. And there is something very pleasurable about being able to explore the boundaries of freedom and license in a fictional setting. Because I think as much as you can condemn Lucio for his behavior and his attitudes, he has something wonderfully exuberant about him. He is a consumer of life in all its aspects. I find that very vital, and so I receive a lot of energy in playing this character.

For me individually, I think it gives me a shot of exuberance to play Lucio because I feel so joyful doing it. Playing Clarence [in *Richard III*] is a much more introspective journey for me, which allows me to get in touch with experiences like guilt and contrition and repentance. And those are great emotions to explore in a fictional context because you know you have to put the role away after three hours. You can go visit it, and you can have a dialogue with it. That's part of your work, and it's quite cleansing.

And then you can put it away and go home, which is actually very healthy.

FLACHMANN: Henry, do you have any response to that question?

WORONICZ: I have a long and complicated response to that. I think Peter Brook, the British director, said that working on Shakespeare is the greatest school of life that you could know. I've spent most of my professional life working on these plays. One of the greatest gifts about being an actor is that you get to pull the curtain back and experience important events and emotions. It may not be your time to die with your daughter in your arms, but you go through these things in theatre. Working on these plays allows us to get intimate with one of the great minds in the history of the world...someone who is able to articulate the human experience in such a beautiful, complex, and profound way.

So the notion is that you come to these roles at certain times of your life because they are right for you. You have to be able to open yourself up to the play. You cannot play a character you do not have inside you somewhere. That's why you are better at some roles than at others because some just match perfectly with your own life. Taking away that experience of being intimate with this mind and his observations of the human condition is a great gift. And you feel blessed to do that. Lear's "when we are born, we cry that we are come to this great stage of fools" is a perfect line. If I had written that line, I would retire. [laughter] But we not only get to speak that, we get to find our way into it emotionally, intellectually, and in the circumstances of the story that is being told. And that is, I think, probably one of the most human endeavors that you can ever do: to tell someone how you feel and to be so open.

In *Measure for Measure*, the moment that hits me the most is when Isabella kneels and says, "Think about this man as if my brother lived." In that moment, I am aware of the great quality of human mercy. If we could all just forgive people and not be afraid of them and open up to them, we would be capable of much greatness. At that moment, the duke sees that. Actors are emphatic: you've got to feel where you are going within the context of the poetic structure in all its form and beauty. We just get to look behind the curtain a little bit, and then it goes away.

FLACHMANN: What a great incredible thrill and honor to have you all here today. Thank you so much for sharing your lives and your art with us.

COOPWOOD: You're welcome, Michael. [laughter and applause]

Henry IV, Part I AT THE 2004 UTAH SHAKESPEARE FESTIVAL

Featuring Jim Sullivan (director), Michael Connolly (Falstaff), Peter Sham (King Henry IV), Jonathan Brathwaite (Prince Hal), Brian Vaughn (Hotspur), Melinda Pfundstein (Lady Percy), and Michael Flachmann (festival dramaturg)

FLACHMANN: Good morning. I don't believe I've ever seen this many actors up so early in the morning. [laughter] Welcome, everyone, to the actors' roundtable discussion for the 2004 Wooden O Symposium. I'd like to start with Jim Sullivan, the director, if I may, and then move to the actors. I wonder, Jim, if you could talk a bit about the problems, challenges, and rewards of staging a production of this play, especially for a modern audience.

SULLIVAN: The principal challenge is the space, which is very wide without a lot of depth to it. I find that the two plays I've done out there recently for the festival—*Richard III* and *Henry IV, Part I*—were able to adapt themselves to that space from the audience's perspective because of the sweep of things from left to right and right to left, the flow of events, the movement of history. The big issue is clarity: who are these people? Only half of them are called by their given names anyway, and keeping that clear for an audience, particularly a modern audience, is difficult since our ears aren't tuned to that use of language. The first ten minutes is tough with any play, in any production, because the task is to engage eager, excited attention. A good quarter of the crowd had a bad dinner, couldn't find a place to park, had a fight with their husband or wife, their kid doesn't want to be there. Those complexities will lull people into saying, "What's going on in this play? All the characters are calling everyone Henry or Edward. Who are these people?" I think that's initially the problem, but I would say, too, that you can achieve clarity in lots of ways. Getting the feelings of the characters right out there very clearly at the beginning is most important of all.

For the audience as a whole, I know from talking to several scholars here, the language poses the main problem. To know what these characters are feeling—and these actors are so good at that—is of primary importance. I think, too, that our prologue from *Richard II* provides some context to the events and also allows access to King Henry's state of mind, which permits us to see him as a political animal in the three different levels of his world. This is a great challenge in staging any of the history plays because, as you know, except in the broadest of terms, this isn't history at all. If you look at the tetralogy of plays in a general sense, that is what happened. But everything is adjusted to the dynamics of telling a good story.

How the play is made accessible in our times is what especially interests me. The whole story is told in intensely personal terms—fathers and sons, brothers, husbands and wives—so it becomes the history of us all. That's ultimately my paramount concern, which dictates whether we succeed or fail onstage: have we told a story that expresses important truths about the human condition?

FLACHMANN: Jim's question about who these people are is a good one. I'd like to start with you, Michael, and move sequentially to the other actors. Please tell us a little about your character in the play: where he is headed, what his objectives are, and, if you don't mind, talk about your character's arc.

SHAM: We'll all go get some coffee! [laughter]

CONNOLLY: I think anytime you take on a character like Hotspur or Hal or Henry or Falstaff, it's not like stepping into an empty lot. There are architectural encrustations that have taken place in the original domicile that have wrenched it out of whatever proportion it once enjoyed. What I really loved about this process was Jim's insistence that we go back to the script, that we go back to the text and try to explode centuries of tradition that enwrap the play. That meant, at least for me, looking at Falstaff and trying to avoid the trap of playing the clown. I think the most important advice Jim gave me—at least in the early going, even before we went onstage—was "don't worry about being funny," which then allowed me to investigate the dark side, the part of him that is melancholic and troubled, concerned about his own mortality, worried about where he will spend his dying years. I must say I also found him a very admirable person, even though I understand that's not going to be the predominant opinion in our literary seminars.

FLACHMANN: The word "despicable" has cropped up occasionally. [laughter]

CONNOLLY: I think Falstaff embodies a distinctly twentieth-century idea of what a hero is. It seems to me that Hotspur's notion of heroism is very nineteenth century: "I'm standing at the brink of the trench. Follow me, and over the top we go!" If anyone has seen *Gallipoli,* we know where that kind of leadership takes us. In our century, to use a hackneyed example, my dad and all my uncles, except for two, came home from the war. They weren't called heroes; they were called veterans. And when the war ended, they went on with their lives, but by 1988, they were no longer veterans; they were heroes. We called them heroes because we understood that they survived a situation that was horrific, so the very act of survival becomes an act of heroism in the twentieth century. It seems to me that Falstaff embodies that ethos, which is a very modern message, especially the speech about honor, the new "catechism." What do we do for honor?

I'm sorry to wax political, but we are mired in a situation now in the Middle East where we have to save lives for honor. And that includes not just Iraq but Afghanistan, too, where we have twenty thousand active troops.

So it seems to me that Falstaff's journey, in some ways, is a journey from hope at the beginning of the play—hoping that he will be able to coin his relationship with the Prince of Wales into what I'd call the summer home in Florida. I think Falstaff wants to buy a nice house by the ocean and hopefully be waited on by very beautiful young women. He feels that if he could work the relationship with the prince to a certain extent, he will have that little part of Westminster to call his own.

One of the interesting changes that happen in the course of the play is that after act 3, scene 2, Falstaff has less and less contact with the prince and speaks more directly to the audience. In a sense, his isolation from the prince is embodied in the expanded acting role Shakespeare gives him. So

I do think there's a movement from a certain kind of hope that the future will turn out well to a concern whether his future is going to be what he thought it was.

FLACHMANN: Thank you, Michael. We're going to get back to Shakespeare's opinion of war a little later. Peter, do you remember the question?

SHAM: I think so. [laughter] Henry's in an interesting pickle since he put himself into power by usurping the throne. I think his greatest problem in the play is that his son is hanging out with this disreputable old guy and wasting the gift of the kingdom for which his father has given his soul. I found it very difficult to play a king because I don't really know what that means, but what I could latch onto was playing a father. For me the play is very much about fathers and sons; it's about family relationships. How does a father ever know that his son loves him, or how does he say, "I love you," when the parent and the child are in two different worlds? So it was hard bridging that generation gap for me.

A lot of it comes to fruition in act 3, scene 2, because the gap between Hal and his father is so great, and we have that wonderful confrontation scene. It starts out like any father-son argument: "What did I do, God, to deserve this kid?" I was joking around the other day with my four-year-old daughter: "What have I done? Why is she doing this to me? Why am I being punished?" That's what we do as parents. It's really a scene about getting his son to know that he loves him and seeing that his son loves him back, which is even more important. Henry wants to be loved. He wants to be loved by the people; he wants to be loved by his immediate subjects in the palace; and he especially wants to be loved by his son. So it's that relationship that I can really try and flesh out. It's as old as time itself. It's Howard and Ritchie Cunningham. It's Homer and Bart. It's all the same. That was the way I sunk myself into the part. That's amazing: I got Homer and Bart Simpson into the Wooden O Symposium! [laughter and applause]

FLACHMANN: Would it be correct to say, Peter, that at a certain point, especially with a history play like this, you shouldn't worry so much about the reality of history and should focus instead on the humanity of the characters?

SHAM: In true historical terms, Hotspur was much older than Prince Hal. Shakespeare actually takes this from a chronicle history. According to Michael [Flachmann]'s dramaturgical research, it was written by Samuel Daniel in the late 1500s. He made Hotspur and Hal adversaries, which is crucially important in the play. They were real people: they lived; they had families; the families fought. And this is what the story is about: all these families that tried to be the most powerful.

Now you go to a family picnic, and that's exactly what's happening. My Aunt Clarice is on top of the picnic table because her macaroni salad is the best. [laughter] My Uncle Al has shady dealings in New Jersey, so we can't mess with that side of the family. [laughter] The humanity of the characters is ultimately much more important than their historical reality.

FLACHMANN: And that, of course, is my favorite definition of a dramaturg: a scholar who provides research materials for directors and actors to ignore. [laughter] At a certain point, you have to say, "I'm sorry, but I'm going for the humanity of the character. I don't care if Henry had specific medical problems or friction with certain other members of the clan. It's about the humanity of the role."

SHAM: I have a three-ounce rule for dramaturgical research material. [laughter]

FLACHMANN: Thank you very much, Peter. Jonathan, what can you tell us about your character?

BRATHWAITE: I want to follow up on what Peter was talking about: the father-son relationship. That's the first thing that really drew me to the character when I initially read the script. It's the whole idea of a boy choosing his own path in life, and that's the quintessential father-son ideal. A father has a vision of how he wants his son to lead his life, and the son, who is becoming a man, has his own ideas: "No, this is the path I'm going to choose." This happens in households all the time: the boy becoming a man.

And then there's also the prince becoming the king. Breaking from the court to go to Eastcheap, he learns who these people are, which makes him a great king later, when he becomes Henry V, who can talk to the people in the trenches and rally them to fight against unspeakable odds. This power comes from his time with Falstaff, from his experience in that world. He was accepted there, and he always felt rejected in the court. It was there that he finally felt love and respect. He's a "good lad," "a Corinthian."

FLACHMANN: So part of your development as a character has to do with the nurturing you get from Falstaff. Would you say he's a father figure? Does he provide any sort of paternal influence for you?

BRATHWAITE: Of course. Hal is a boy who wants to be accepted by his father, and he's not. He finds this acceptance in Falstaff. They have a good time together. He feels he can truly be himself with Falstaff. There is also the melancholy realization that sooner or later he has to trade in his best friend for his father, his real father. This gives him a deep sadness—knowing that to accept this massive responsibility thrust upon him by birth, he has to say, "'I do, I will.' I will let go of you." And that is exactly what happens in *Henry IV, Part II*, when he assumes the position of king. Anarchy and chaos would result if he stayed with Falstaff, who would take complete advantage of the situation.

FLACHMANN: Peter, is that the way you see your character? Is there a moment at which you accept him in the play?

SHAM: The moment I accept him is when I realize he wants to be accepted. My greatest fear is that he doesn't want to be accepted, and if that is the case, then everything I have given up in taking over the throne is wasted.

FLACHMANN: Well, you have lost your immortal soul.

SHAM: Yes, that's what we're always talking about: if I can get God on our side, then I'm going to be, in the eyes of the public, the rightful heir to the throne. So we have to work a little harder, like Avis [chuckling].

FLACHMANN: You've just ricocheted from the Simpsons to a rental-car commercial! [laughter]

SHAM: I'm just so happy to be in this production. I usually play the king who dies in scene 3 [chuckling].

FLACHMANN: Thank you very much, Peter. Okay, Brian, Hotspur's a lovely role to play. Talk about your approach to the part, will you?

VAUGHN: One of the concepts Peter mentioned earlier was the idea of the image he is trying to create in the eyes of others. I think that's the best approach for Hotspur. He's the successful image of the gallant knight, the leader possessed with an amazing amount of chivalry. In the end, he is essentially writing his own fiction—this ideal that he is unable to possess. One of the ideas I really latched onto was that in the eyes of others, Hotspur possesses the possibility of becoming a great leader. In the eyes of others, he could be a great man. That was wonderful for me because it gave me something to shoot for—the idea of achieving greatness—which always kept me in forward motion.

Hotspur is fraught with contradictions as are most characters in the play, which is what makes them human. Hotspur is obsessed with the truth. He says the truth can change a battle. Yet at the same time, he is writing his own lie, which I think is quite dynamic. I didn't want the character to become too hot tempered, too choleric. I wanted to afflict him with a little bit of fear, especially in the letter scenes. Jim and I talked a lot about these letters. I get this message from my father saying he is not going to be able to join us. By the fifth act, Hotspur refuses to look at any more letters. He says, "I cannot read them now." This fear is something he is constantly fighting against.

In addition, the domestic scenes are so important in this play. There are these intense moments of political posturing, but then you go to these very private domestic scenes. You see this personal side of Hotspur, his love for his wife. He is trying to control her. It's very Mafia-esque: "I can't tell you about my business; I can't tell you about anything" [laughter], yet he wants to. Everything he does is for her; it's all for them together.

The father and son relationship, I think, is also huge in the play. Early on, I only have a couple of scenes with my father, and I dismiss him every time I talk with him. Worcester becomes Hotspur's father figure, juxtaposing their relationship with that which exists between Falstaff, Henry, and Prince Hal. Hotspur only hears what he wants to hear, and Worcester is telling him stories he wants to hear: overthrowing the country, starting a war, achieving greatness. Later, we find that Worcester is using him as a pawn in his own journey, which ultimately becomes a tragedy. He's a fabulous character, though.

FLACHMANN: Melinda, this is a pretty male-dominated play, which makes your role as Hotspur's wife especially important. Talk about how it feels to be engulfed in this testosterone-fueled world.

PFUNDSTEIN: Great! [laughter] All these men make distinct journeys throughout the play. I think it's more important to talk about Lady Percy's purpose in the play, instead of her journey, because you're not going to see that much of a journey with her until part two. Shakespeare doesn't give us an explanation for her arc until this second play. The scenes between Hotspur and Lady Percy help us see the humanity in her husband. Looking at the words on paper, you see this almost abusive, loveless relationship. We wanted to show that it was a loving relationship and that in many ways the two characters are equals. Lady Percy is a challenge to Hotspur—mentally and emotionally—and so the relationship is fleshed out, which makes them a real married couple. It's not just this powerful warrior and his submissive wife. The equality between them is what we wanted to focus on.

FLACHMANN: One of my favorite moments in the production is the scene at Glendower's when you and Lady Mortimer are alone onstage and the lights fade out. Perhaps I should address this question to Jim. What were you looking for in that little tableau?

SULLIVAN: The power struggle in the play has quite an effect on the victims. The scene is about this power, played out in these two marriages. I don't think Hotspur responds well to change. "You used to be more loving. Why are you different?" he asks. "Will you come see me ride off on my horse?" I always have this picture in my head of how glorious he looked. He has the power in this marriage, in this relationship, and he wants it to stay this way as opposed to the way ideal relationships between men and women might exist, which is that two people are willing to change together through time. The last words she is able to say are, "No, I won't sing for you." She's different from Lady Mortimer, who sings a lullaby to put this great warrior, Mortimer, to sleep, to take him off his intentions for a moment. I think the two women have an intuition about what is coming, and I hope that is present for an audience.

FLACHMANN: I've seen some commercials on television recently about gun crimes. One of them has a little kid playing basketball alone, saying, "My brother committed a crime with a gun, and he's in prison. I'm being punished, too." Similarly I'm interested in the effect of war on the characters in this story, especially on the innocent bystanders who suffer. Lady Percy is a survivor. What sort of effect do all these male power struggles have on you and on the play proper?

PFUNDSTEIN: She loses her husband, whom she loves dearly. She put a great deal of significance on their relationship and what they have together, what they've done together. She loses all that because her husband goes off to war.

FLACHMANN: This theme reverberates into a lot of the other characters. Let's get back on the topic of war. I wonder, Michael, if you have any opinion on what Shakespeare is trying to say about war. It's difficult

31. *Henry IV, Part I*, 2004. *Left to right*: Jonathan Brathwaite as Henry, Prince of Wales, and Peter Sham as King Henry IV. Photo by Karl Hugh. Published with permission of the Utah Shakespeare Festival.

to read through a script and find the author beneath it, but I'd love to see you take a stab at it.

CONNOLLY: Oh, boy! [laughter] I want to preface my comments by saying that I think the subversion of hegemonic power that Falstaff vehemently represents in the play is extremely important. That said, I believe he is not quelled at the end of this play. In fact, he is incorporated into the status quo, which is something different than that which usually occurs in a Shakespearean play.

I'm also reminded of Mao Tse-tung's letters, in which he claims that "we live in a world of swirling chaos: excellent opportunities for men like us." One of the elements that Falstaff embodies in the play is the opportunity that war presents for profiteering. Harold Bloom writes at one point that Falstaff has caused no one's death. But that isn't true. Falstaff seems to be rather proud of the fact that of his 150 soldiers, he managed to get rid of 147 of them. This means that after the battle is over, he will probably report 150 present and keep collecting their salaries from the crown as long as possible. So it seems to me that Shakespeare outlines war as a chance for men of few scruples to make a good deal more profit than they normally do, which I believe is a lasting perspective on this business, and I would be happy to argue that point with anyone who wants to talk about Halliburton and its present contracts [chuckling], where overwrites are considered totally appropriate because the government is picking up the tab.

The other important revelation about Falstaff is that I suspect more than a minority of people involved in battle don't really want to be there. Falstaff certainly doesn't want to. He knows he is compelled—he has to do it—but he is not going to do anything more than what will get him to survive. For what it's worth, there was this guy named S. A. Marshall who accompanied the invasion of Saipan in 1943. He started doing after-action reports, where he would go to units, claim he was a statistician, and ask these GIs to fill out questionnaires. By the end of 1945, he came up with the astounding statistic that in any given engagement, only 15 percent of the combat infantry actually fired their weapons. The army took this information, scratched their collective heads, and went to work on how to make our soldiers more efficient. What Marshall was pointing out was that human beings aren't wired to kill other human beings. We don't like to do it.

And I think that in some fashion, before S. A. Marshall started to do the statistical analysis, Shakespeare had some understanding that this encounter called battle is not a normative event. It is not an occasion that most men seek, unlike Hotspur. I think Falstaff embodies that sensibility; he captures the actual reality of combat, which is sheer and unadulterated terror. When you talk to combat infantrymen who survived a battle—unless they were psychotic—they will tell you that the predominant emotion during a firefight is terror. You want to make yourself one with the earth. The hardest thing in the world is to move. In that regard, I think Shakespeare taps into some primal human behavior in the face of battle.

FLACHMANN: Would you agree that Hotspur is using battle to write history, to make a myth, to create a legend, whereas Falstaff is using battle for profit and survival, which is, I think, essentially more human?

CONNOLLY: Yes.

FLACHMANN: Peter, I wonder if your character sees this debate from a different perspective?

SHAM: Henry wants nothing more than peace, and he'll kill anybody he has to in order to get it [chuckling]. That's what he's after, and anyone who stands in his way will be destroyed. He's a great strategist. What's interesting to me every night is that he is worried about people following him throughout the whole play, yet everyone comes to his party. He gets RSVPs, whereas nobody is coming to Hotspur's party. He gets these letters back saying that people are sick or too busy. Because Henry is such a good warrior, or warmonger, he's more at home in battle. He proves a lot to himself in part one. Then he gets this hope of his son joining him in the end. If you go back to *Richard II,* everything has been taken away from him, and that's the reason the conflict in this play has started. As far as Henry is concerned, Richard's supporters are responsible for his father's death. They dismantled everything in his house; they banished him and shamed him. So he is there for vengeance.

FLACHMANN: Jonathan, as Prince Hal, do you have trouble participating in the war effort? Is it a seamless transformation from the tavern scenes to the battlefield?

BRATHWAITE: He's been in Eastcheap, so he knows who these people are. They provide real acceptance for him, a family-oriented feeling, and I think he eventually realizes that he would rather not rule from on high over fearful people but would prefer to be down there with them and rule out of love for them. I think that is why in *Henry V*—just before the battle—he steps in and says, "These are my people whom I have spent time with, whom I know, whom I have this personal connection with, a love for, who have respect for me—out of love, not out of fear." Similarly, when the battle is about to begin in *Henry IV, Part I,* he says, "Listen, if I can save the blood on either side—if I can save my people who are going to die in the thousands—then let me take that chance and go up against Hotspur in single fight."

He learns in the tavern scenes the type of king he wants to be. That's why in *Henry V* he disguises himself on the battlefield and asks his soldiers, "What do you think of the king? How is he doing? Do you agree with the choices he has made?" Most dictators and monarchs wouldn't care: "I'm the law of the land; you will follow and obey." His path is more righteous, and his love for his people is more sincere.

CONNOLLY: I don't know if this has any validity to it, but it seems clear that the fight between Hotspur and Hal is, on Shakespeare's part, essentially subversive. There's a lot of language in the play about Hotspur as a great captain, as a martial figure, but there's very little description until

Hal's speech in [act] 5, [scene] 1 about his readiness to meet his responsibilities as a chivalric figure, as a knight capable of creating mayhem on the battlefield. I think it's subversive to some extent that this kid who seems not very well trained and armed kills this seasoned warrior who is supposed to be famous for his ability to display his knightly honor. It reminds me of an old military aphorism: "It's not the bullet with your name on it that you have to worry about; it's the piece of shrapnel marked 'general delivery.'" [laughter] Hotspur's expectations are that he'll destroy Prince Hal. There won't even be a fight. And yet all those predictions are greatly upset in the chaos of war.

VAUGHN: And that's a really huge theme in the play: how others perceive you. In Hal's first soliloquy—when he looks at the audience and says, "I know you all"—this character everyone thinks is a vagabond, a ruffian, promises, "Wait, trust me. In the face of all this adversity, I'm going to step forward." That is a giant revelation. Another example concerns the controversy Hotspur starts about the course of the river. When they are dividing up the land, he says, "See how this river comes me cranking in, and cuts me from the best of my land." Then he announces abruptly, "I'll have the current in this place dammed up, and here it will run a different course, smooth and evenly." I think that's the meat of the play. This river that is running smoothly all of a sudden gets dammed up and creates this whirlwind, this chaos within, looking for a new flow, a new stream.

That, to me, is Hal's journey. Hal is sitting back in a position he has not chosen. He has not wanted to take on this role; therefore, he has a lot of resentment about the idea that he will one day rule the kingdom. The question, however, is how he is going to rule: "Is it about me? Is it about the state?" And I think that's the concept that separates Hal from everyone else. There's so much personal investment for everyone else in the play: honor and chivalry for Hotspur; war, gain, and money—

SHAM: And for the king, God.

VAUGHN: Yes. And for Hal, it's about the people who are living in the moment, right now. "What can I do for England?" That's the image I think he carries through all three plays. You have to let go of the old life. And it's the same with Falstaff. When Hal is on the battlefield, standing there between Falstaff and the king, that's a central image of the play.

"Which road do I take?" When Falstaff and his father die, Hal has to take the road he was born to travel.

FLACHMANN: While we are on the subject of the battle between you and Hal, I think the stage direction in brackets reads, "They fight." [chuckling] Hundreds of hours go into the planning and rehearsing and choreography of this fight. Robin McFarquhar, our fight director, does this under Jim's wonderful guidance and direction. I wonder if you could talk a little about the physicality of that fight and how Hal seems to be less well trained than you are.

VAUGHN: Yes, I think that survival of the fittest becomes the ideal. Here's this guy who thinks he's a terrible warrior going up against Achilles. And he defeats him because, when it gets right down to it, it's all about survival. Jim and I talked about the possibility that Hotspur might have a death wish: in death he will become greater than in life. I think Hal wins this fight because he's more in tune with himself; he's desperate to win, whereas Hotspur is a little bit outside himself, watching his own ego.

FLACHMANN: The way it's staged, you seem to strut around a bit at the beginning of the fight. And at the end, you appear to be thrusting the sword into your own bowels.

VAUGHN: Jim and Robin and I talked about that moment, which is very samurai—a Japanese moment of honor, self-mutilation to achieve a higher state of being. I'm glad that I look right at him when I do it, too. It's not just his hand; it's my own hand, too. Through a moment like that, you can achieve automatic clarity in your life through death. Many characters in Shakespeare do this.

FLACHMANN: There's also an interesting moment with a favor that we assume Hotspur's wife has given him. A bit of controversy has been swirling around that, especially the brutality connected with it.

CONNOLLY: My father's eldest brother was a member of the second battalion, U. S. Rangers, in World War II. After he died, both sons were helping his widow go through his belongings. Among his mementos were a whole bunch of photographs of German families. I assume he didn't come by these innocently. He was undoubtedly going through the pockets of someone who had been killed—an action that resonated with me in the final moment in the play. What happens to you after you die, especially after you die in combat, may not be very honorable. In fact, it's probably fairly brutal.

As Falstaff I wanted to create some ironic resonance about honor and about the glory of the cause because what always drives me crazy when I hear people talk about the play is what a wonderful man Hotspur is. I'm sorry, but I just don't buy all that. Hotspur is like a second lieutenant in Vietnam going out on his very first patrol and not having coordinated his artillery backup. He just goes out there and does his thing and thinks it's all going to work out. Hotspur is a very dangerous human being. Anything I can do at the end of the play to rub it in, to show that all this garbage about honor and glory is just that—it's garbage—I'll do. He has cost the lives of thousands, and now he's just a piece of meat. That's why I wipe my face with the handkerchief from his wife. After death it's just a piece of cloth, and I'm all hot and sweaty, so I wipe my face with it.

FLACHMANN: As actors you are charged with the responsibility of bringing these characters to life, of making the play flesh and blood. What are some of the principal challenges you've had in this particular script? Brian, any moments for you that were especially tough to stage?

VAUGHN: Well, the entire play is challenging, tough to perform. The biggest struggle I had was trying not to make Hotspur too one dimensional, trying to make him a little more human. The qualities he displays with his wife are quite different from the qualities he displays with the king or with his father or uncle. So that was the biggest struggle. I've seen several productions where things were not equally balanced. He was choleric the entire time. There's a little of that, of course, but added to it should be the honor, respect, and love he has for his wife and his family. All these different qualities add excitement, complexity, and humanity to the struggle.

FLACHMANN: Jonathan?

BRATHWAITE: In examining the relationship between Falstaff and Hal, Jim and I talked a lot about seeing Falstaff as the good and bad in all of us. He should not be played as a fool. We tried hard not to be too judgmental about him.

FLACHMANN: Thanks, Jonathan. Peter, any particular moments?

SHAM: For me it's finding the proper level of desperation and sadness that characterizes the king and what he's going through. He's got this guy who's chewing up his land, who's threatening to take over everything he has built, and he's got this rebellious son. So it's everything at once. And how do you play all of it? We've just got to find the right moments to illuminate each of these elements in the script. I always feel like I'm on loan from a musical-comedy act. I'm a happy guy, so for me that kind of depth is the greatest challenge. I always play it, but to get to the underbelly of the play and to find out what makes this character tick without the musical reprise is very difficult for me.

FLACHMANN: Would you like to hum a few bars from "A Little Bit of Luck"?

SHAM: No! [laughter]

FLACHMANN: Thanks, Peter. Michael, any especially tough moments for you?

CONNOLLY: The toughest thing for me was to consistently forget about what Falstaff was supposed to represent or what he was supposed to symbolize or signify. Instead, I tried to create a three-dimensional character who has realistic relationships with other people, life goals, and other human qualities.

FLACHMANN: So you really focused on specific moments, rather than on an overall concept for the character?

CONNOLLY: That's Jim's job: to worry about the whole package. It's my job to find out how I can get from moment A to moment B in a truthful fashion.

FLACHMANN: Thank you. I have one final question. We have a lot of teachers here, particularly college professors and high school teachers. Do you have any advice for us in teaching these wonderful plays?

CONNOLLY: You need to have your students read them out loud as much as possible. Until we get into our rehearsal room—into a read-through, and we're on our feet with it—it doesn't make total sense. I really don't think it's a piece of literature. It's a play. It's alive! Since it's a living thing, we need to hear living voices embody it to understand what Shakespeare wanted.

FLACHMANN: So get the students up and reading, perhaps even moving around the classroom?

CONNOLLY: I would encourage that, yes.

FLACHMANN: Brian?

VAUGHN: I agree. These plays were meant to be seen—that's crucial. They become clearer and much more specific in performance. I remember when I was in high school and studying Shakespeare, it wasn't until they showed the video of *Julius Caesar* that I really started to understand the play. I think you get lost in the language when you just read it silently. Only when it is recited out loud can you see where the emotions are and what the action is. When you read the script by yourself, you get lost in all those ideas and metaphors. It becomes active only when you read it out loud in response to other people. The actual emotions come right into the room—that's the whole idea.

SULLIVAN: We have to do everything we can to foster more opportunities for that light to suddenly crack through so the dramatic truth is discovered by the students themselves, rather than because somebody told them this is how they were supposed to feel about it. Until you discover Shakespeare for yourself, you can't own it. A principal problem in our culture is that we don't have enough opportunity for these personal discoveries. We can't sell that. We've got to sell you [*The*] *Princess Diaries* 2 instead.

SHAM: That's not so bad. I've got a four-year-old daughter. [laughter]

FLACHMANN: I think that's very true. Theatre is the only art form that people without training can bring to life with their breath. You can't pick up a violin and play anything intelligible if you have no musical skills. You can't take a chisel and a hammer and a block of marble and sculpt anything recognizable without training. Good actors would immediately put us to shame, of course, but all we really need is our breath to bring these brilliant works to life. And that's a priceless opportunity for those of us who teach Shakespeare.

SULLIVAN: By helping your students experience the plays in your classroom, you create the possibility of similar artistic discovery in the future. Without an audience, we're just rehearsing, over and over and over. Good productions of Shakespeare require authentic, real audiences.

And that's the other challenge. You have to create such a mass of energy and money and attention to do these large-cast shows. You need many, many people onstage to lend some level of authenticity to the theatrical experience. When it's authentic, when it's real, people know that, and when it's not, they know that, too. You can't hide it when it's bad. And that's the beauty of great theatre: when it's authentic, it really shines.

VAUGHN: I think a lot of people shy away from the poetic side of Shakespeare, but you can't think of it that way. It's just extended thought.

I think that's something to really try to instill in young people. Sometimes we get trapped in the idea that we're speaking beautiful language as opposed to focusing on the goals we're pursuing in the scene.

FLACHMANN: We've talked about several acting traps, but this is a teacher trap: to look at this language as something lofty and beautiful and unattainable. Characters who are human beings are communicating with other human beings, and that's the heart of any play. The closer we get to that in the classroom and in the theatre, the better off we are. Thanks very much to Jim Sullivan and these talented actors for making this round-table discussion so vibrant and exciting. We appreciate the time you've spent with us, and we wish you a wonderful remainder of the season. [applause]

Romeo and Juliet AT THE 2005
UTAH SHAKESPEARE FESTIVAL

Featuring Paul Hurley (Romeo), Tiffany Scott (Juliet), Ben Reigel (Tybalt), Leslie Brott (Nurse), John Tillotson (Friar Lawrence), Ashley Smith (Mercutio), and Michael Flachmann (festival dramaturg)

FLACHMANN: Good morning, and welcome to the third annual actors' roundtable discussion at the Wooden O Symposium. My name is Michael Flachmann, and I'm company dramaturg here at the Tony Award–winning Utah Shakespeare Festival. Today we have with us six actors from our extremely popular summer production of *Romeo and Juliet*, which was directed by Kate Buckley. Isn't it a wonderful show? [applause] I'd like to start off with Paul Hurley, who plays Romeo, and get each of you to talk about your roles just a little bit. In particular I'm intrigued with the extent to which you as characters feel responsible for the play's fatal conclusion. Paul?

HURLEY: I don't know how responsible Romeo is for the tragedy in the play. I think there's a lot of bad luck that falls upon these two lovers. If all the events went smoothly, this play would end happily. There's a lot of miscommunication, however, and a great deal of misfortune that prevents the two from being alive at the conclusion. The tension in the production, I think, comes from the fact that every time we go see the play, we think that maybe this time things will work out. If the production is done well, we hope the letter will get to Romeo, or perhaps Juliet will wake up just before he takes the poison. The tragedy really comes from the two factions warring against each other and from the fact that the deaths of Romeo and Juliet could be the catalyst that eventually stops the quarrel between the two families. It could have been an entirely different play if everything had fallen into place properly.

FLACHMANN: Thanks, Paul. Ben, does Tybalt's alleged hotheadedness play a role in any of this?

REIGEL: Yes, I think, maybe a little. In a lot of productions I've seen, Tybalt has had more responsibility for the tragedy than he does in this production. When you play a part, you start to identify with the character, and you begin to make excuses for him. I, of course, don't feel responsible for the end of play. That's pretty much out of my hands.

FLACHMANN: That's because you're dead, right? [laughter]

REIGEL: Right, I'm on the slab. [laughter] I think in this production, Mercutio bears a bigger responsibility than in most. He really pushes for all these guys to go to the dance. Granted, I overreact at the party, but when I look at the situation from Tybalt's point of view, Romeo's presence there is a major insult to the entire family. I don't know what he's doing there. Then I write him a letter, which doesn't get answered, and he doesn't respond to it because—in our production at least—Mercutio intercepts the letter. And so I think I have been insulted again by Romeo. Not only did he show up at the party, but he also didn't acknowledge my letter. That's why I go out looking for him. He does his best to apologize, which might have defused the situation, but then Mercutio forces me to fight. He doesn't really leave me much choice.

Tybalt is not a nice guy by any means. He's like so many characters in this play: young people reacting too quickly, whether it concerns love, family honor, or whatever the flash point is at any particular moment. Tybalt has one reaction to everything, which is "give me my sword!" I actually think Romeo is the bad guy. [laughter] He shares a decent amount of responsibility, especially in his impetuousness. Romeo is as much a hothead as anyone in this play. He just expresses it in different ways.

FLACHMANN: I love it! So far nobody is accepting much responsibility here. [laughter] Tiffany, Juliet is a very mature fourteen-year-old. Do you bear any guilt for what goes on in the play?

SCOTT: I don't believe so. [laughter] I think that much of the tragedy comes from this long-standing hatred between the families, this feud that's been going on for longer than any of us have been around. That's mostly what the tragedy stems from, and also, as Paul mentioned, from the bad timing with the letter not reaching Romeo in time. I would say that Romeo and Juliet see past all the hatred. That's the wonderful thing about these two characters: they can see beyond the tragic feud that is happening between the two families and are able to connect on a very personal, human level despite their fundamental differences. So I am not going to accept any of the blame either. [laughter]

FLACHMANN: Thank you, Tiffany. Leslie, any guilt on the part of the nurse?

BROTT: Definitely. I lay so much of it at the feet of the culture, especially the code of honor, where insults must be answered violently. But it's also a culture that encloses women and treats them as objects. Dad is doing a really good job taking care of Juliet within this culture, marrying her to a lovely gentleman.

As the nurse, I'm very shortsighted because I only need to deal with the moment. The nurse is totally pragmatic. Later in the play, when Romeo is banished, I'm thrilled that the friar gets the problem all sorted out. I say, "Oh, what learning is. I could have stayed here all night to hear good counsel" because he thinks further down the road than I do. Later, I say, "Since the case so stands as now it doth, I think it best you marry with the County" because in this world, banishment was a real problem. Romeo wasn't coming back. Juliet needs to accept this because I can't even conceive of her going outside the family compound for any reason other than Mass. And she would have gone to a private Mass in her home, most likely, rather than going out into public.

Juliet is lacking the mechanics, as I do, of how to function in the outside world. I think the nurse's pragmatism that makes her myopic is to blame for much of the tragedy. She makes the best choices she can in the moment, but she sees at the end of the play how her cultural shortsightedness helped create the tragic conclusion. So I take partial responsibility, but I don't take all of it.

FLACHMANN: Thank you, Leslie. John, how does the friar fit into all this?

TILLOTSON: It would be hard for me not to say that I bear some responsibility [laughter], but you need to remember that we have two warring factions. If it weren't for their hatred, my intervention wouldn't have to take place. I get implicated in the ultimate tragedy when I try to become peacemaker. I point the finger at everybody—including the prince—at the end. He's the one who banishes Romeo. Everybody is guilty to some degree. If I have guilt, it is only because I was trying to solve the problem.

FLACHMANN: Ashley, to what extent is Mercutio culpable?

SMITH: Mercutio is certainly the catalyst for the tragic action of the play midway through the story. Imagine if there were no Mercutio in the script and therefore no one for Tybalt to kill accidentally. Then there would be no reason for Romeo to kill Tybalt, for which he is ultimately banished by the prince. The banishment, in fact, is the crucial action that propels the title characters to their ultimate doom. In order for us to empathize with Romeo's vengeful murder of Tybalt, Tybalt must first kill someone who is loved not only by Romeo but also by the audience. It's this empathy that allows us to accept Romeo's actions and follow the play as it turns 180 degrees from comedy to tragedy.

FLACHMANN: Great point. I know Kate Buckley felt strongly that you guys don't know at the beginning of the play that you're trapped in a tragedy. There have been a lot of very interesting comments by audience members about how the first half of the play seems much more like a comedy or a romance while the second half takes on much darker overtones. Does that present some challenges and complexities in playing it?

TILLOTSON: Yes, absolutely. A lot of references to death have been removed from the first half of the play through the director's cuts. It's not until somebody gets hurt that we really have a problem. Even the first big fight—although it's fairly vicious—is far from deadly, and then the play segues into a party scene and becomes much more festive.

BROTT: The play has to function as a comedy in the first half so the audience will be invested in everything working out for the best. Otherwise you see it all coming, and it's downhill from there to the boneyard. [laughter] That's why the prologue, which is not in the first folio, has been removed from the play. Kate didn't use the prologue because it makes all the action passive voice, and the audience isn't really involved in the outcome.

Even after the death of Mercutio, we are still in romance land at the top of part two with all this positive, loving energy from Juliet, and then my character comes in with the bad news. Sometimes it's very difficult for the audience to turn the corner there. They have been trained to see my character in the first half of the play as overly dramatic, and the nurse is definitely the diva of her own opera. But when Tiffany sits next to me onstage, we start to go the other way in the play. Sometimes it's like steering a truck with a really crummy turning radius as we're trying to get that scene to change direction.

FLACHMANN: That must be a major acting challenge, Tiffany, to come onstage at the top of part two extremely happy and then have the scene turn tragic so rapidly.

SCOTT: That's right. I don't know the information that the audience knows when I come on for the second half, so one of the play's ironies is that I'm allowed to dwell in the romance world for a little longer while everyone else is in tragic mode. It does provide an acting challenge to shift gears so quickly when the nurse brings the news of Tybalt's death and Romeo's banishment. But the scene is written so beautifully: Juliet goes from excitement and anticipation of her wedding night, to fear that her husband has killed himself, to shock and anger that he has murdered her cousin, and to grief over Romeo's banishment. There's a lot in that brief scene for me to sink my teeth into.

FLACHMANN: The fight really turns things around, don't you think? It's staged in a comic way at the beginning, and then it turns deadly serious. Can you talk about that a little bit, Ben? How does the fight choreography fit into that moment?

REIGEL: I think that's a challenge, not only in this production but in most productions I've seen. These two guys want to show off—they want to one-up each other—but they certainly aren't out to kill each other.

FLACHMANN: Do you agree, Ashley?

SMITH: Yes, the fight starts out playfully with each person wanting to embarrass his opponent. Mercutio quickly shows himself to be the better fighter because he's less concerned with form and more interested in the practicality of scoring points. But Tybalt doesn't like being humiliated, and he becomes more aggressive as the fight goes on. When Romeo steps in to part the fighters, Tybalt accidentally kills Mercutio. The fight has to start out lightly because the action of the play up to this point has been romantic comedy. The loss of control in the fight is where the plot turns serious. Mercutio's last breath is the beginning of the tragedy.

FLACHMANN: Paul, you've really got three constituencies involved in making the fight scenes in a production like this: the characters themselves, the fight choreographer, and the director. How did that partnership work for this particular production? Did Chris Villa [the fight director] come in and choreograph the whole thing, or did the actors and the director have a lot of input into the process?

HURLEY: For the Romeo fight with Tybalt, we choreographed that in about three minutes, and Kate [Buckley] loved it. That fight just happened very naturally. There was less story that had to be told in that fight. It's pretty clear: good, angry guy kills bad, angry guy. The Mercutio fight had more story underneath it. We choreographed it fairly organically, and then we showed it to Kate, who would say what she liked and what she didn't like. It was a very collaborative process.

REIGEL: When we got sidetracked a little in the fight, Kate would always bring the focus back to Romeo. "This is still the story of Romeo and Juliet," she would say, "so what is Romeo doing when you guys are fighting?" We trimmed it down, which was something I resisted at first, of course, because instead of lines in this play, I have fights. [laughter] As far as making the fight playful, the crowd onstage is a big help with that. When we were first working on it, that's what was missing; as we started adding the crowd into it, their reactions helped clue the real audience into how they are supposed to feel about it.

TILLOTSON: Actually I think the entrance of the friar signals that the play is going to shift from comedy to tragedy. He comes in and starts speaking about the contrast between life and death and good and evil, and none of those topics have been introduced prior to that moment in the play. I'm also the last major character, with the exception of the apothecary, who comes into the play fairly late—in our production, about one-third of the way in, forty minutes after the show has begun.

FLACHMANN: So you are the most important character then? [laughter]

BROTT: Well, you see, it's a play all about this nurse. [laughter]

TILLOTSON: I am the most important character. [laughter] My effect on the audience has been different lately because the evening has been getting darker earlier. Oh, here comes this serious guy. He's in dark clothes. There's a story about Alec Guinness being offered a role, and he said that he would do it if he could come in as if he were death with a scythe. I love the image of that, but it does kind of run counter to what our director was trying to accomplish!

FLACHMANN: I wonder if we could talk about parents and surrogate parents in the play.

32. *Romeo and Juliet*, 2005. Tiffany Scott as Juliet and Paul Hurley as Romeo. Photo by Karl Hugh. Published with permission of the Utah Shakespeare Festival.

BROTT: Sure. Historically, in the culture, I would have been the parent. The nurse—or what we would think of as the nanny these days—did the parenting, and Juliet would have bonded to me as an infant because I was the person who breast-fed her. Lady Capulet has a very large household to run, a position that she would need to maintain in the home with Lord Capulet, a merchant. One of the many nice things about our production is that our Lady Capulet really cares about Juliet. So often you see the role disconnected from her daughter. Our twenty-first-century view of children is that they are the icons of our attention, which was not how the culture functioned during the Italian Renaissance. Juliet's parents are doing what they are supposed to do: finding an excellent marriage for her.

TILLOTSON: I think my relationship with Romeo is a little different; it's more of a teacher-student bond.

BROTT: You have a more mature relationship with Romeo than I have with Juliet, don't you?

TILLOTSON: Yes. I may have known him since he was a little kid, but our interaction has been more formal. I solve problems for him.

BROTT: I try to do that for Juliet, too, but in a different way. When I say, "Romeo is a dishclout to Paris," I don't really believe that. I know the words wound her, and they make me seem disloyal, but the real message is at the very end of the speech. The gold is usually at the conclusion of the speech. When I say, "Your first is dead or 'twere as good he were," I don't see any way around this. That is the cultural reality. Romeo is not coming back. She asks me if I speak from my heart, and I say, "From my soul, too," because I have worked it out in my head that God will forgive her.

FLACHMANN: Tiffany, your take on that?

SCOTT: I believe Juliet sees the nurse's suggestion to marry Paris as the ultimate betrayal, which I think wounds her deeply—so much so, in fact, that she vows to no longer keep counsel with the nurse. At that point, Juliet is on her own. When she deliberately contradicts her parents and tells them she is not going to wed Paris, her behavior is terribly disobedient. She is so strong willed with very deep convictions, and she is willing to make this incredible sacrifice for love.

FLACHMANN: That's awfully brave of you at that moment in the play to disobey your parents.

SCOTT: Yes, and Lord Capulet tells her that he's going to kick her out of the house and disown her. She can't be a member of the family anymore if she doesn't marry Paris. She is determined to be true to Romeo in the face of all this. She's very courageous and very strong in her convictions.

FLACHMANN: That's a pretty terrifying moment in the play. Phil Hubbard [Lord Capulet] is a wonderful teddy bear in real life, but he is very frightening in that scene because he's a big guy onstage, and he gets awfully angry.

SCOTT: He does, and it's suitable, believable anger, too, which is very scary.

FLACHMANN: Right. I want to bring it back to Paul, if I may, and anybody else who wants to respond to this. Can you talk a little bit about speaking the verse, about the challenges and rewards of dealing with Shakespeare's poetry onstage?

HURLEY: Since this is one of Shakespeare's earlier plays, the verse is a bit easier to speak. There are very few full stops that happen midline, which basically means the lines run all the way through, and so the verse is more regular and predictable. Because of this rhythmic quality, the play drives the plot forward with more intensity and passion. When you look at the folio text, you realize that Shakespeare hasn't broken the play down into acts or scenes. It's just one long, breathless rush from beginning to end. So when you are speaking the verse, you have to be especially conscious of always driving through each thought until you get to the end of it. You need to do all the acting on the lines and with the text. If you take too much time—especially in the second half of the script—that's when the play can really bog down.

SMITH: The verse always has to keep moving. If you're going to put a little pause at the end of a verse line, it has to be treated not as a stop but as a springboard to the next line. Actors have to understand what they're saying first and how to phrase the language so the meaning is clear; then they can take it up to speed. Pace is extremely important in Shakespeare, but many actors don't appreciate this fact. Shakespeare wrote his plays to be performed at the speed of thought. You must think as you speak. If you can do this, the audience will never get ahead of you, which can be deadly.

FLACHMANN: We had some good sessions earlier in the week in our Wooden O Symposium about using acting "sides" during Shakespeare's time and trusting the flexibility of punctuation in the plays. I'm interested in how free Kate Buckley allowed you to be with interpreting the punctuation, with putting in pauses and making the text flow from one line to another.

HURLEY: Yes, we had a fair amount of latitude in that regard.

BROTT: Shakespeare had been dead for seven years when the 1623 first folio was printed, so his script isn't like Shaw's, where we can say, "This is the definitive text." In addition, compositors had great control over the way the text was printed. There are a lot of times in the first folio where actors could make a huge emotional choice about the direction the character is going based on a semicolon or a question mark or an exclamation mark. As a matter of fact, most compositors' boxes of type carried many more exclamation marks than question marks.

When actors interpret the folio punctuation, we also pay attention to capitalization, though a letter is often capitalized because the compositor ran out of lowercase type. As an actor, I'm never slavishly devoted to the folio, which contains so many idiosyncrasies. For example, the nurse's first big speech about the earthquake and Juliet's age is written in prose in the folio, but in other early editions, it scans as verse with ten syllables per line.

FLACHMANN: Speaking about memorable monologues in the play, Ashley, you do such a wonderful job with the Queen Mab speech. How do you think it helps further the plot?

SMITH: I've often seen actors play the Queen Mab speech as a show-off piece, a way for Mercutio to convince the audience how fantastical he is. When it's delivered that way, it always appears to exist outside the plot, stopping the action and boring the audience. The clue to its purpose lies at the end of the speech. I see it principally as a means of coaxing Romeo to go to Capulet's party. In order to convince Romeo to ignore his foreboding, Mercutio invents the story of Queen Mab, a fairy who makes certain types of people have certain types of dreams. As Mercutio loses control near the end of the speech, Romeo calms him by saying, "Peace, thou talk'st of nothing." Mercutio then drives his original point home, explaining, "True, I talk of dreams!" Only then does Romeo give in and agree to go to the party. The Queen Mab speech has many facets, but it's primarily a device to get Romeo to the home of his enemy so he can ultimately discover his true love.

FLACHMANN: You guys are speaking today, as I'm sure you know, to a group of teachers, educators, and students. Do you have any advice for us about how we ought to approach Shakespeare in the classroom?

TILLOTSON: It's not as difficult as it seems...except when I'm working on it. [laughter]

FLACHMANN: Thank you, John. Tiffany?

SCOTT: I think you should always read it out loud, which makes the language far more powerful and more accessible to those who are hearing it.

FLACHMANN: Ben?

REIGEL: I certainly agree. I had the wonderful advantage of having parents who are in the business, so I grew up watching Shakespeare from a very early age. It was never meant to be read like literature. It was meant to be seen, to be experienced. I'm a big advocate of watching even a bad production. We were supposed to do *Pericles* at a theatre I was working at a few years ago, and that was one of the few shows in the canon that I didn't know. My father was going to be playing the lead, and he didn't know it, either, so we both tried to read it. He's a twenty-five-year veteran of doing every lead part in Shakespeare, and he couldn't make sense out of it, so we rented a very bad BBC version of it, which helped us understand what the play was about. I think more kids would get into Shakespeare if they got to see it before they had to read it, as opposed to the other way around.

FLACHMANN: Leslie?

BROTT: Absolutely right! Try to maintain as much joy in the classroom as possible. There might be someone like me out there. I'm from a little, tiny town in northern California, where I'm sure people would rather have their eyes gouged out with sticks than read *The Taming of the Shrew* or *A Midsummer Night's Dream* in class, but my freshman English teacher was so enthusiastic that you couldn't help but sense his enjoyment of it, which planted a seed in me. I would try and get students to read it aloud.

I've been acting Shakespeare for years, and the first time I face it, I usually have to read it about fifteen or twenty times. I always read it out loud, but at home in preparation for the first rehearsal, I try to read it at least a dozen times because I get so panicky at the first read-through.

These plays are meant to be spoken. When you just read it on the page, it's like looking at a symphonic score and not listening to the actual music.

FLACHMANN: Thanks, Leslie. Paul, any advice for us?

HURLEY: I was one of those kids who hated Shakespeare in high school. We read *Romeo and Juliet*, *Macbeth*, *Othello*, and *Hamlet*. I never really understood any of them until I was about twenty-one years old and I spent some time in London and got to see lots of Shakespeare productions. This was the first time when the world of that language opened up to me. There are lots of films to see and recordings to listen to. During the Renaissance, people never went to see a play; they went to hear a play. You've got to really listen to these great scripts to understand them fully.

FLACHMANN: How about the BBC Shakespeare video productions? Do you like them?

BROTT: The BBC is state supported. British actors pay British taxes. They can do a wonderful job of it because of all the support they get.

TILLOTSON: I have a problem with our public television not supporting American actors. In the last couple of seasons, we have seen *Kiss Me Kate* filmed in London; we have seen *Oklahoma* filmed in London. We are not seeing enough American productions filmed in America. Our public television and our government are not supporting American actors to produce American productions of these classic plays. That's all I have to say.

FLACHMANN: Amen! Although I feel strongly that the work being done here at the Utah Shakespeare Festival and in other great American theatres is some of the best Shakespeare in the world right now, and I'm really proud of what you guys do. On another topic entirely, what would Romeo and Juliet be doing ten years down the road if they had survived the tragedy?

HURLEY: Two boys, a girl, and a dog. [laughter]

SCOTT: I think it all goes back to a question we often hear in discussions about this production. Is it love or lust between Romeo and Juliet? I think it has to be love. When they first meet, they complete a sonnet together, which betrays a kind of synergy between the two. The wonderful thing about Juliet is that she is able to match wits with Romeo from the beginning. In that first meeting, you can see that the two have true love for each other, a union of souls. So I do believe that they would have had a long and happy life together, were it not for the tragic events that occur.

FLACHMANN: Tiffany, just to refine the question a bit, don't you really teach Romeo how to be a lover? He's certainly romantic at the beginning of the balcony scene, but does he really know how to love someone like you?

SCOTT: Yes, in the balcony scene, she's not willing to hear all those empty vows, those superficial words. She wants Romeo to court her honestly.

FLACHMANN: Paul, did you want to respond? She leaves you so "unsatisfied" in that scene. [laughter]

HURLEY: One of the last things they say to each other really helps us understand the direction of the play. She asks, "Thinkest thou we shall ever meet again?" and his response is, "I doubt it not, and all these woes shall serve for sweet discourses in our time to come." That is, we'll talk about this when we are old and recounting crazy things we did in our youth. I love that prescient moment when the two of them envision the possibility of being together in their ripe old age.

FLACHMANN: Were you all exposed to this play when you were young? And if so, how did that early experience with the script help prepare you for the roles you are playing in this particular production?

REIGEL: My exposure to the play was actually very early. This was the first part I ever wanted to act. I saw my father play Tybalt when I was six. I really wanted to do the sword fights.

TILLOTSON: I am fortunate this summer to be doing two plays that I was exposed to as a child. The first Shakespeare play that I remember seeing was *Hamlet* at the Old Globe when I was maybe thirteen years old. I think these early experiences with Shakespeare give all of us a common bond.

BROTT: I definitely was into the romance of this play. I mean Zeffirelli's production hit me like a ton of bricks. My bedroom had posters of Leonard Whiting and Olivia Hussey. I wanted their relationship to work out because I saw the movie at a time when I had just started to notice boys. Wow, they were great. I felt that big rush of emotion. The performances Zeffirelli got out of these young actors, and the way he cut the movie was so beautiful to look at, and the sound track was overwhelming. I was totally struck by the romance of the play. I still am because who doesn't want to fall in love again that way? And yeah, I still want it to work out. And why shouldn't it? Why does life have to be mired down in tragedy and ambiguity?

I've made a lot of sacrifices in my life just to support my relationship with Shakespeare, Shaw, Williams, and O'Neill, and I've always felt it was worth it. There's nothing more wonderful for me than to hear Tiffany say, "My bounty is as boundless as the sea, my love as deep. The more I give to thee, the more I have, for both are infinite." All my sacrifices are worth it to hear those beautiful lines every night.

FLACHMANN: And on that inspiring note, I just want to say what a great privilege it's been to be able to talk to you actors about your lives and your craft. A session like this really rounds out the Wooden O Symposium because we see the whole other side of Shakespeare's plays—the performance aspect—which brings to vibrant, exciting life much of the scholarship we are doing. I hope the audience understands that everyone who works on these plays does their own important research, and these wonderful actors are just as dedicated to their craft as we are to ours as scholars and teachers. Thank you very much for being here this morning. [applause]

Hamlet AT THE 2006
UTAH SHAKESPEARE FESTIVAL

Featuring Jim Sullivan (director), Brian Vaughn (Hamlet), Ashley Smith (Laertes), Emily Trask (Ophelia), Michael Connolly (Polonius), Leslie Brott (Gertrude), Bill Christ (Claudius), and Michael Flachmann (festival dramaturg)

FLACHMANN: I'd like to welcome everyone to the culminating event in our Wooden O Symposium. We're delighted to have all of you here. I'm Michael Flachmann, the festival dramaturg, and I'm honored to introduce today's panelists from our brilliant production of *Hamlet*. [applause]

As everyone knows, *Hamlet* is performed frequently all over the world, has a great deal of scholarship written on it, and has generated a massive performance history. We've also just spent three wonderful days at the Wooden O Symposium listening to a wide variety of papers, many of which investigated different aspects of the play. Within such an extensive scholarly and theatrical context, how do you make a production like this your own in this special space for this unique audience? In other words, what clues did you find in the script, in the rehearsal process, or in your own life experience that helped you make these characters yours? And in the case of Mr. Sullivan, how do you own this play as a director. Could we start with you, Jim?

SULLIVAN: Sure, thank you. And thanks to everyone for coming this morning and joining us at our festival. It's easy to think of *Hamlet* as Mt. Everest. That's the problem if you're going to work on it. I used that phrase in the initial notes when we began talking about it last fall, and when I shared that sentiment with Brian [Vaughn], he said to me, "That's exactly how I see it." So we agreed that it could be a difficult mountain to climb, given all its brilliance, its extraordinary depth, and its ability to engender conversations on such a wide range of philosophic, political, and social topics, both Elizabethan and contemporary.

Finally, it's all about working in the moment of its performance, and for me that meant making sure we demystified the script right away. We tried to keep all conversation in rehearsal away from everything that *Hamlet* is or has been to people throughout the ages, focusing instead on what the story says to us right now. We were content to leave the ultimate meaning of the play to our audiences.

One comment I did make at the first rehearsal was that I was really sick of all the deception in the world. I'm convinced that the rampant deceit that's running through Hamlet's world—his political and social construct—is a very contemporary issue. If we wanted the play to speak meaningfully to modern audiences, we needed to make certain that it resonated in every way possible within its Tudor staging. So in the opening scene, we purposely mixed in contemporary costuming with Shakespeare's Renaissance context. The guys at the top of the show are in black jeans, for instance. I'm not sure that's entirely evident, and perhaps it shouldn't be. But we wanted to do something that literally put one leg in our time and one leg in Shakespeare's. And I don't know why we would perform these plays if they didn't have one leg firmly in the time of the audience that is watching it. So that was my approach. Our extraordinary company was very amenable and even enthusiastic about that as we set to work on the play.

Staging *Hamlet* is a huge undertaking! The difficulty at this festival, at any repertory theatre, is getting enough rehearsal time, getting the people you need at the hours you need them. This play allowed for that, so we were able to spend significant time on the many scenes involving two or three people—such as the nunnery scene, for instance. And Brian and I spent many rich hours on the soliloquies. I felt that we really had the time—and I know he does, too—to work moment to moment on them. And that made a lot of difference in the process. That was my basic approach to directing the play.

FLACHMANN: Thanks, Jim. We're off to a great start. So, Ashley, how do you own the role of Laertes? How did you make it yours when it's been done so many times before at so many different theatres?

SMITH: I really connected with the idea of family and the sense of loss, with those two concepts combined. From one perspective, this is a story about two families, each with its own tragedy. Although the play is seen from the point of view of Hamlet, the parallels between what Hamlet is going through and what Laertes is experiencing are very interesting. Both these young men are trying to avenge the deaths of their fathers. And the play ends up being a meeting of sorts between the two of them.

We also talked a lot in rehearsal about the fact that since there's something rotten in the state of Denmark, it seems as if the young people are all trying to get out of the country. Although Laertes gets to leave, Hamlet doesn't. This idea of young adults needing to get away from home and strike out on their own and become their own persons is crucial in the play. That's something I could certainly identify with, and I think most people these days tend to have lives like that. It's more common to leave home and end up living somewhere quite far away from your family, although a lot of guilt can go along with that. There's this bond between Laertes and Ophelia. And when the oldest child strikes out on his own, there's always some guilt about leaving the other one behind, that person for whom they feel such deep love. So those are some of the ideas I connected with in the role.

FLACHMANN: Thanks, Ashley. Emily, how about Ophelia?

TRASK: It was really important to me that Ophelia be a real person. Unfortunately, because her role is not actually that large, her character is often just sketched in on the surface. For me it was crucial that she be an intelligent woman. Otherwise why would Hamlet love her? Other than she's the only girl in Denmark. [laughter] So we needed to delve into the heart of her and found immediately that she really did have some soul and some intelligence and some bite, so we worked through and found moments where she was strongly standing her ground. In that time period, she needed to do what her father said, but all the same she also needed to be enough of her own person for that to come through and for the audience to like her. If she's just whining and crying all the time, then when she dies, it's like "oh well, thank goodness she's dead...." So I really approached the meat of the character. I think its all about love for Ophelia: she loves her father so deeply, and loves her brother so deeply, and Hamlet so deeply. So you can define her through her relationships to other people, which tell you a great deal about her character.

FLACHMANN: Lovely job, Emily. Brian, how about the "melancholy Dane"?

VAUGHN: Well, the first place I started was with a great amount of fear about playing the role [laughter] because I think the role is much larger than I am. In fact, the role is bigger than all of us. And I think that's one of the most amazing elements about the play. So I did a great deal of research, certainly, and luckily I found out I was going to be playing the part fairly early—in October of last year, I believe. So the first thing I did was read the play again and then went and read a gazillion commentaries, everything from T. S. Eliot to Harold Bloom. I talked to other actors who had played the part, which was very helpful to me concerning what they had noticed in playing it over long periods of time.

But then it basically became about myself, and I think ultimately that's what the play is about: the recognition of purpose within your own life and Hamlet's journey from the beginning of the play to the end of it. In the midst of this mourning for his father, there is a reexamination of self and those around him, and in that comes this seeking for truth, for immediacy, for the now of all things. That was really what I latched onto, and I think Jim was absolutely fantastic in his design and his ideas about the play's focus on "being" versus "seeming" and "truth" versus "fiction." And in the midst of all of this is, how do we step out of that fictional world, how do we take action against it, how do we ruminate about it, where do we find our true purpose within this plague of pretense?

So that was the real key to me. Also, technically, we spent a lot of time on the soliloquies: when they happen, why they happen, and where they are in the play. I believe that the soliloquies are reaching out to the audience, seeking an answer. It's the moment for the character to ask for help. Then in the second half of the play, there are no more soliloquies. After he comes back from England, he's a changed man; there is a sense of balance and grace and calm about him. And I think he reaches this state of knowing his own self and his purpose. There are so many different facets in playing the role; certain moments resonate at certain times. As one of the other actors said to me, "You'll never get it 100 percent." It's a monster part because it's so rich with ideas about life and humanity and self. It's outside of us, but it also molds to the individual. I think that's one of the most exciting elements about reading the play: everyone becomes Hamlet. Steven Berkoff has written that "we are all Hamlet."

So the thing you have to do in playing the role is to just play it and just be in the immediate moment to moment, the now of it. I think Shakespeare is saying that we have to live in that place of right here—right in this second—and to do that night after night is such a comment on acting and on life. So that's where I started and where I ended, too, I guess.

FLACHMANN: Wonderful! Leslie, tell us about Gertrude.

BROTT: Thank you all for being here today. Thank you for coming and supporting the festival. Gertrude doesn't have a lot of text, but what is there about Gertrude and what Gertrude says about herself and what other people say about her is pretty straightforward. And the big change for me actually came with some help from my director, which was to extract Gertrude from the overall atmosphere that I felt surrounded the play: *Hamlet*, tragedy, heavy. [laughter] Gertrude is living in a really happy place in the first half of the play, and once I realized that, the play started to open up for me.

I am so myopically self-involved with my own life that many times I don't realize what's going on around me, and that's pretty much where Gertrude is living. My friends who know me well can attest to the fact that I'm pretty clueless. Usually people are dating for three or four months before I notice! [laughter] That's actually the case with Gertrude: there are some unpleasantries that she doesn't want to see, and it takes a while for those to filter into her consciousness. But it's also because she would like to fix the problems around her: "Maybe Hamlet's crazy, but perhaps I can adjust that truth." I'm in a happy place, and I don't want to give up that happiness for the corruption and the deceit that's around me. So that's where I started.

FLACHMANN: Thank you, Leslie. Michael, how do you see Polonius?

CONNOLLY: I can attest to the fact that people have to make out passionately in Leslie's living room before she's aware of their involvement. [laughter] That's as far as I will go this morning. [laughter]

I think almost all characters in the canon are like coral reefs. I mean, they are encrusted with tradition and various interpretive choices, and so for me, it's really important to read the text naïvely the first time as if unaware of the various controversies that surround these people. At the beginning, I was aware that there were essentially two schools of thought on Polonius: there's the Pantalone, on the one hand, which really takes care of act 2, scene 2 to Polonius's death; and then there's the Sir Francis Walsingham on the other side, which essentially argues for two scenes in the play.

And so I went to the text and was struck in act 1, scene 3 that even in the folio version, Polonius blesses his son twice. So I began to ask what a blessing constituted in the late-sixteenth and early-seventeenth centuries in both Britain and on the continent. It often constituted a kiss: a kiss on the lips or a kiss on the forehead. For me that was a crucial moment because what opened up for me then was how Polonius as a man loves his children. I wanted that to be the spine of the character. So all the machinations of statecraft—for example, why does he work so hard to position Ophelia as a possible partner for Hamlet?—have to do with his fundamental love for his son and his daughter, along with his desire to further his house, which in that period was a very appropriate way to show love for one's children. In Jim I was lucky to find a director who was interested in approaching the script in that way and who thought that Polonius was a worthy character, and that's where we are.

FLACHMANN: Thank you, Michael. Bill, how did you approach Claudius?

CHRIST: Claudius is a man who is a politician first and foremost, who enjoys power, and who is happy to have gotten power but has done it in a way that is causing him great pain. He loves his wife, the queen, and thinks he can be good for the state of Denmark. What was interesting in working on this with Jim is that we focused on the concept of public and private masks: on the face that Claudius puts on when he is in public to convince people that he is the man who can do the job and do it well, as opposed to those moments where he can reveal the private mask and show the torment going on inside because of what he has done. His guilt begins to creep up on him as things start to unravel through Hamlet's actions or the problems that Hamlet presents in contrast to the neat little scenario that Claudius has set up.

FLACHMANN: Thank you, Bill. I've got some other topics I'd like to guide you through. I know that no one up here is shy, so if you have a comment you want to make, just start waving your hand, and I'll get to you. Brian, we talked about madness this week in the seminar, and there were a lot of references to the "antic disposition" your character puts on. And Emily, there was even a question about the extent to which you actually go mad in the play. Without revealing any "actor-bag" moments here that would make the other participants uncomfortable, I wonder if you could talk a little bit, starting with Brian, about the madness. I haven't asked you this summer, Brian, but are there any moments when you feel Hamlet really succumbs to genuine madness, or is it all a carefully feigned antic disposition?

VAUGHN: Well, I think the antic disposition is a shield for him, a protective armor to seek truth in the midst of all this deception. The words Hamlet uses are his armor; his weapon is his wit. It's as if he's saying, "I will put on this antic disposition to keep everyone off balance about what I'm doing." The first event that happens after he becomes "mad" is the entrance of the players, and he sees clearly the difference between seeming and truth through these performers who are professionally embodying a theatrical reality and doing it so realistically and convincingly. This realization allows Hamlet to go even further with that notion, and I believe that his antic disposition lets him teeter on the brink of control, where he believes he can almost change the "stamp of nature."

Later—when he tells Gertrude to "assume a virtue if you have it not"—his madness has gained some control over him. He goes a little bit into that dark place when he kills Polonius, and then he comes out of it when he goes to England. Like many Shakespearean characters who go into forests or new environments, Hamlet learns a great deal about himself on the voyage to England and comes back to Denmark much saner than when he left. Ultimately, I think that's what happens with Hamlet: he plays with this fake madness, which overtakes him for a time, and then he steps away from it so he can take his revenge.

FLACHMANN: That's excellent. Thank you, Brian. Emily, I wonder about the quality of your madness in the play. Jim has you eavesdropping from the upper stage for some of the scenes involving Polonius's death. How helpful was this in creating your character?

TRASK: The difficulty with Ophelia's madness is that after the play within the play, she disappears for quite a while, and when she comes back, she's singing bawdy tunes and picking flowers. [laughter] So I'm really grateful that Jim added a few key moments for Ophelia to eavesdrop on the other characters. When she overhears that Hamlet "has in madness Polonius slain," the realization hits her that her father is dead. She also listens when Hamlet makes his jokes about Polonius being "at supper," after which she exits immediately. In my mind, I'm the first to find him because I run out there before anyone else.

The eavesdropping gives Ophelia more of a journey to take into her madness. Her love for the other characters is so great that when her brother leaves the country, her father is slain, and she discovers that Hamlet has killed him, she goes mad. I think she has gone through such a slow burn from the closet scene, through the nunnery scene ("Oh, what a noble mind"), and into all these later discoveries and losses that she can't help but go mad.

There's also some debate about whether Ophelia really does take her own life. For me the moment of realization is in the mad scenes when she sings to herself, "Go to thy deathbed." Although Gertrude comes back and says "the limb broke," and it's quite possible that Ophelia just didn't struggle, I think it's a stronger and more active decision if Ophelia takes her own life. When I found out I was doing this role, I was living in Chicago, and I watched people on the elevated train who were having conversations with themselves. Ophelia doesn't know she's mad, so she's trying to sort out her problems. I think that when she really makes the decision to die, that's her sanest moment.

FLACHMANN: The eavesdropping helps me as an audience member because, otherwise, all you have is the out-of-synch "courtier's, scholar's, soldier's, eye, tongue, sword" line to indicate that your mind is starting to degenerate. Jim, Brian talked earlier about the theatricality of his antic disposition. How do you see that fitting in with the lovely device of the actors setting up the stage at the beginning of the show, which introduces the concept of artifice in the production?

SULLIVAN: So much of the play is about theatricality. The text completely provides that motif, most obviously with Hamlet's advice to the players. The business about Ophelia witnessing much of the action of the court wasn't my idea originally; I got that from a production that I read about in Sweden. The idea was to give her more presence so the full weight of Hamlet's killing her father can help break her.

FLACHMANN: Ashley, there's a controversial moment involving you right before the duel when the poisoned and unbated sword is ready for you to grab. Osric sets it up for you, but you deliberately pick one of the

33. *Hamlet*, 2006. Brian Vaughn as Hamlet. *Photo by Karl Hugh.* Published with permission of the Utah Shakespeare Festival.

bated, nonpoisoned swords to begin the fight. Only after you become in-censed do you go back and exchange the first sword for the more lethal one. Can you talk about that decision a little bit? I've never seen it done that way.

SMITH: I'm not sure if it was Jim's idea or Robin McFarquhar's [the fight director]. Robin is an excellent choreographer, and he was not only interested in the moves and the weapons but also in figuring out what story we were telling with the fight. As you may know, the scene is usu-ally done with Laertes taking a bated, unpoisoned sword first from the rack and then making a show of saying, "Oh, this is not the right sword for me; let me see another one." Then he selects the poisoned sword, and that's what he fights with.

But Robin came up with the idea that Laertes is indecisive about whether he can really go through with killing Hamlet. As a result, he initially takes the poisoned sword—as if that was the plan—and then has second thoughts and takes a safe sword, with which he begins the fight. As the duel progresses and gets a little bit out of control and Hamlet begins to humiliate him with his newfound expertise, Laertes starts to lose his cool and grabs the poisoned sword about halfway through.

I thought this was a very interesting choice that showed Laertes as a well-rounded, fallible, insecure person, rather than as a one-dimensional guy hell-bent on revenge. He's conflicted about killing Hamlet, which is realistic because they probably grew up together. Hamlet was the golden boy—the favorite son and heir to the throne—but at the same time, they were no doubt good friends as they were raised, which means there's probably a lot of love there to complicate the issue for Laertes.

FLACHMANN: There's a nice moment in the second scene when you touch Laertes on the shoulder before he and Ophelia exit the stage. I think that was a terrific decision, Brian.

VAUGHN: Yes, Laertes and I are mirror images of each other in our revenge.

FLACHMANN: Michael, I wonder if you could explain a little more about the love Polonius has for his children? I'm also interested in the "neither a borrower nor a lender be" speech, which is often seen by schol-ars as a collection of clichés, but you make it really come alive. Talk about that, would you?

CONNOLLY: Yes, I think you just put your finger on it. It's easy in scholarship to dismiss it as a collection of *sententiae,* easy to poke fun at. And I think this is probably the departure point for many actors and directors about Polonius because they look at the commentary on the speech and infer that he's clearly an egregious, self-important, pompous ass, so let's go ahead right from the very beginning and play him that way.

On the other hand, you could also see Polonius being quite prescient at the moment. I mean, we say good-bye to our children with the assumption that, barring some act of madness, we are going to see them again. In the late-sixteenth and early-seventeenth centuries, however, to say good-bye to someone who was traveling to Paris carried with it no assurance that they would ever return. Polonius is giving advice to Laertes as if it's the last time he will see him, which raises the stakes considerably. He's ensuring a kind of intellectual and moral patrimony, which seems to me the core of it.

I have to look at the speech as an actor. I can't interpret it the way a scholar does; I can't search for all the various sources from which these moralisms are drawn. I have to find my action: What do I want to do with my son, and what am I trying to instill in his character so that when he goes to Paris—the great Catholic cesspool of the world in the early-seventeenth century, right next to Vienna then and only trumped by Rome—he is protected? Why is it necessary for a good Protestant boy to get this kind of advice? I think that's the reason. I don't believe I'm ever going to see him again.

We had to cut the speech significantly in the interest of time. But what I try to do every night is invent it on the spot, as opposed to another production I unfortunately witnessed where Polonius had a crib sheet on which he checked off all the pieces of advice. I really wanted to avoid that. I don't think Polonius is a fool. I wanted to sidestep that naïve interpretation. Does that answer your question?

FLACHMANN: Beautifully! Thank you very much. Bill and Leslie, I wonder if you want to talk about your backstory. Enquiring minds want to know if there was hanky-panky before old Hamlet was killed.

BROTT: If you want to know whether we were fooling around before Hamlet was killed, read John Updike's novel *Gertrude and Claudius,* OK? The ghost says that with his wit and his gifts, Claudius seduced his "most seeming virtuous queen," and I think that's plenty of information for you to devise something in your heads about what went on. It certainly was plenty for me, but you do have to listen to the play. [laughter]

FLACHMANN: That's great. Bill, what percentage of your desire for the throne is lust for power, and what percentage is lust for the beautiful Gertrude next to you?

CHRIST: Well, I would say that the lust for power dominates Claudius.

FLACHMANN: Thank you. Another question that comes up often in seminars of this type is how much of your portrayal of the character is yours, and how much is the director's? Is it possible to parse these things, or is the process so complex and technical that you can't disentangle your role from the director's suggestions?

SMITH: He's in the room, you know. [laughter]

FLACHMANN: Do you want to hold your ears, Jim? [laughter]

SMITH: There's a tricky thing that happens for me: I'll have an idea about what I'm going to do, and then a director will say, "Hummm, maybe we should try it a different way." Sometimes that can rub you the wrong way, but I think a good director is someone who can guide you, rather than imposing his ideas on you. I think Jim is very good at looking at what we are doing and then guiding us to some new ideas and discoveries. Now that we've been running for four or five weeks, I don't actually remember which ideas were originally mine and which were his because I sort of feel like they were all mine. [laughter] I respond best to that kind of direction: being guided, rather than being pushed.

CONNOLLY: I've done three shows with you, Jim. It's always been a cooperative experience. The expectation is that the actor will show up loaded for bear, and that the director is certainly going to be loaded for bear, and then the next several weeks are what the Italians call a *converzatione* kind of exchange. Then when you are running the show, the audience will teach you things as well. At this point in the second week in August, the only time you are aware that "this was Jim's idea," or "this was my idea" is when the idea isn't working, and then you have to negotiate with yourself to find a choice that will work and will satisfy your director's vision and the play's storytelling narrative needs. There's a lot of crap written about actors and their egos, and the bottom line is that there is very little ego involved in this process. We serve the director; we serve the playwright; and we serve the audience. If you let your desires get in the way of any of those three elements, I think that's when you start to become a monster.

BROTT: Jim and I have worked together four or five times, and it's always been a happy association. He really helped me this time because I could not get out from under the weight of *"Hamlet, the Mt. Everest"* thing. I teach acting, but I could not always see how to play the positive choices in each scene. This is what we do in life, of course: we try to fix the situation, to bring it back to equilibrium or a pleasurable balance. I was originally playing the problem because I knew the end of the play. I knew it carried heavy casualties—many bodies on the stage.

I didn't have confidence in my effort, and Jim always steered me back toward believing as a character that the most important thing I could do was to fix the problem in the moment: preventing somebody from being killed, trying to restore somebody to their psychological equilibrium. Whatever I wanted to fix, he kept pointing me back toward the positive. More so than in our other associations, I really had a lot of difficulty getting out from under the weight of four hundred years of scholarship. Usually I'm just brilliant without him, but this time I really needed him. [laughter]

FLACHMANN: Thank you, Leslie. Jim, do you want to chime in on that?

SULLIVAN: When I directed *I Hate Hamlet* at the festival a few years ago—which I really loved doing—David Ivers was in that show, and there's a moment when the television actor is going to be in the Shakespeare in the Park production of *Hamlet,* and he says, *"Hamlet!* Whoa!" That was the Mt. Everest moment again. That show is about the ghost of John Barrymore coming back to coach the guy.

We all need help in life. We need help every day. Mary Tyler Moore used to tell a story about Carl Reiner, who got the Mark Twain Prize for humor for writing *The Dick Van Dyke Show* and other brilliant work in comedy. She said that whoever had the best idea, that's what they went with. And if that meant that the guy who came in to change the water cooler happened to watch the scene and had a great idea, that was what went into the mix.

I think the actors respect me for my eye and my ear because they know I am on the outside of the process watching them, and I respect them because they are the play. If we can be in a situation where we can help each other get to the bigger thing, which is the play, that's all that matters. I have had situations, less than ideal situations, where an actor wasn't ready to give to the others in the cast, and I have had to come in and deal with that firmly. Ultimately, we are playing this play together, and that includes you as audience. When the play starts, the audience has an important voice in the performance. This summer company is a very fine group of actors, and that has made all the difference.

FLACHMANN: Great, thank you. There's so much richness and ambiguity in the script. We've just spent three days with the Wooden O Symposium talking about some of the shades of meaning, and you can't watch a brilliant production like the one we have here without being aware of that. From an actor's point of view, can you play ambiguity? Can you play richness? Or do you have to go for specific moments and let them all meld together into an artistic whole that can be described later as ambiguity?

BROTT: As an actor, no, I don't think you can play ambiguity, but hopefully there will be some ambiguity when you as audience members reflect on the production. If we play specifically from moment to moment, the production supplies its own ambiguity. But you've always got to play the text with absolute concrete specificity so the audience can hear the subtleties.

FLACHMANN: What was the toughest scene or moment for you to do in this particular production?

CHRIST: I don't want to flag anything that the audience can notice tonight. [laughter]

CONNOLLY: There are still a couple of moments in this little role where every now and then I come to the theatre and think, "How's this going to work?"—which I believe is a healthy reaction. There are still two little moments where every night I have a new decision about what is happening, and they both have to do with listening to Brian and responding. That's fun because he comes up with new stuff almost every second, so that's a great ride.

BROTT: The toughest moment for me is trying to figure out what is really bugging Hamlet in the closet scene. I don't want to say the specific lines, but there are a couple of lines where every night I say to myself, "Faker, faker, lousy faker; you should be fired." [laughter] If we could restore about fifteen of Brian's lines, I think I could get it.

VAUGHN: Many scenes are tricky for me to play. John Gielgud said that the most difficult scene for him was the Ophelia-Hamlet nunnery scene. What I find especially interesting in playing the part is the moments where you feel like something is not happening correctly, yet the problem is in the character and not the actor. If you're going through a struggle, more often than not the character is going through the same difficulty you are. That was particularly clear to me in the first part of act 2, where Hamlet comes back after seeing the ghost and begins to put on his antic disposition. In the midst of this, I said to Jim one day during rehearsal that I felt like I wasn't doing anything, that I was just reacting to what was happening to me onstage. While I was playing the truth of these moments, Hamlet begins to talk about the fact that he's not doing anything. And that's exactly what's happening to Hamlet and the actor at the same time! And I think that's frequently true with Shakespeare.

The tricky part about my scene with Ophelia is maintaining the balance of doing one thing to her and feeling another thing inside. That scene is driven by love for her, but in the midst of it, I'm also trying to discover who's plotting against me, so that was a perilous balance to play.

TRASK: What's the most difficult and scary part, other than being lowered into the grave? [laughter] Actually that's not me at all; I get to sit that one out. It comes in the nunnery scene, but it's after Hamlet leaves, which is the only time Ophelia is truly alone with her thoughts. As I explained earlier, in my particular take on the character, it's all about her love for other people—especially Hamlet. To keep that moment honest and active and connected to other people when I am alone onstage is always a challenge for me.

SMITH: For me it's when Gertrude enters in act 4, scene 7 and tells us that Ophelia has drowned. Laertes's response is "where?" It's not the kind of response I would personally make. If I were writing the scene, I probably would have written something like "oh, my God! You're kidding!" I would have written this long speech, but Shakespeare doesn't give me that.

For a while, I just kept trying to figure out what I should be doing there. What's my job in this moment? And finally I talked to Jim about it, and we just tried not doing anything, just being still. When Gertrude is describing Ophelia's death, there's really nothing to do there. But I still get that voice in my head—"Shouldn't you be doing something right now?"—and then I have to reject that and just be still.

FLACHMANN: Great. Jim, did you find any particular moments or scenes that were especially challenging to stage?

SULLIVAN: The hardest moment for the director is when the play opens. You are the most useless person in the room at that point. I love this show. And I love these people doing it. So the hardest thing for me is to let go of it as they would probably confirm. [laughter] I'll be watching a movie or a TV show, and I'll look at my watch and think, "Oh, they're doing the nunnery scene about now."

FLACHMANN: It sounds like Directors Anonymous here. [laughter] What about Hamlet's epiphany in the nunnery scene, when he seems to realize that Ophelia has lied to him?

TRASK: Can I change my mind and say that's the most difficult part in the play for me? [laughter]

VAUGHN: Well, it's a gray moment theatrically. There's a realization that somebody is there—that she's being stage-managed—which is very painful for me because she's the one person in this entire kingdom who, I hope, would be truthful with me. This mixture of deceit and passion is particularly chilling because I know she's a victim in this whole situation. When he sees her being lowered into the grave later, he wants to go back in time and do things differently.

I firmly believe that those two characters have to be deeply in love. So in that earlier nunnery scene, there is such a communion of spirit, of mind, of body, and of soul, and in the midst of that, she can't be truthful. And I have to make a quick right turn in the scene. All this stems from the regret and the loss and the pain.

FLACHMANN: Jim, did you want to add something?

SULLIVAN: I just wanted to say one word about that—he's not Prince Valiant; he's Prince Hamlet. He makes mistakes. He's a human being, not some storybook character, and he's paradoxical. He's noble, but there are times when he has to be vicious. He's all these things, and in the arc of becoming who he is by the end of the play, he goes through that process.

FLACHMANN: You all get so close to these characters during the rehearsal and performance process. Do they ever encroach upon your real lives?

BROTT: I'm really glad Gertrude doesn't blur into my life. There's a fatigue level that affects me, but I'm just a person who wants to go home and go to bed and read a book or have a drink or gab at my friends'. [laughter] I'm glad my parts don't blur over because I've played some scary people. Michael [Connolly] will probably tell you that I actually am Judith Bliss. [laughter] It's my job, and when I take the makeup off and go home and have a shower, I'm done.

FLACHMANN: Brian?

VAUGHN: I agree with Leslie, I don't think you should embody the character. If I were playing the Scottish king, that's the last thing I would want to be doing. Or Iago! Taking him home with you might be dangerous. [laughter] Actors have said to me, "You will be a different actor after you play this part; you will be a changed individual." Laurence Olivier said this play haunted him his entire life. There are insights in the play that I reflect on every single day. One of the brilliant insights about Shakespeare is that his plays are so much about the human condition, and that's why we keep doing them.

BROTT: I tell my students that as an actor you do not have the luxury of living an unexamined life. You have to think about what it means to be alive. I'm not a religious fanatic, but I played one. And I had to do so with compassion. I'm intellectually stimulated 24/7 because I'm an actor.

FLACHMANN: One final question for Mr. Sullivan. When you direct a play, do you ever wonder what Shakespeare would think if he were sitting out in the audience?

SULLIVAN: Well, I wish he were. I have questions. [laughter] First of all, I'd want to know him. I'd want to know everything I could about that heart and mind and the experience of writing these plays. But I also would expect that he would say something along the lines of what Michael Connolly said earlier: all that matters is what works. You know he had a specific company that he wrote for, which accounted for their ability to mount these plays successfully maybe two or three times in a year.

I read a description of Richard Burbage, who played Hamlet. He was violent, truculent, and not very honest, so he probably had a volatility that must have made that first *Hamlet* pretty exciting. Can you imagine creating the role of Hamlet? That's something to really think about. I believe Shakespeare's big idea is that the theatre is the world. As William Saroyan says in *The Time of Your Life*, "It takes a lot of rehearsing for a man to get to be himself." So I think of myself as holding up the torch to that idea as best as I can.

FLACHMANN: I'd like to thank a number of people before we adjourn. Please join me in a round of applause for Mr. Sullivan and his wonderful actors. [applause] It's such a joy to have you share your craft with us. We discover again—as we always do with these roundtable discussions—how bright and engaged the actors are and how incredibly hard they work at bringing these productions to life. And I want to thank Michael Bahr for setting all this up: he and his staff do a wonderful job with the Wooden O Symposium. [applause] And finally, thank you to the audience for supporting this place that we all love so much. [applause]

King Lear AT THE 2007
UTAH SHAKESPEARE FESTIVAL

*Featuring Jim Sullivan (director), Dan Kremer (King Lear), Carole Heal-
ey (Goneril), Anne Newhall (Regan), Shelly Gaza (Cordelia), Michael
Connolly (Gloucester), James Newcomb (Kent), Tim Casto (the Fool), and
Michael Flachmann (festival dramaturg)*

FLACHMANN: Although *King Lear* has always been popular in the twentieth century, we've recently seen an unprecedented surge in productions
of the play with major mountings of the script during the past two years
at the Denver Theatre Center, the Goodman, the Milwaukee Rep, the New
York Shakespeare Festival with Kevin Kline, the Chicago Shakespeare
Festival, BAM with Ian McKellen, and the Stratford Festival with Brian
Bedford. Why such a renewed interest in the play at this particular time
in our history? What special truths does the script have to teach us? What
is it about this play that speaks so eloquently to us today? Jim, if I could
start with you, sir?

SULLIVAN: Of course. Thanks to everyone for coming to our festival
and being here for this symposium. The critic Jan Kott said a generation
ago that of all the plays Shakespeare wrote, this was the most shockingly
contemporary. I don't think he used the work "shocking," but I think we
would have to do so now in retrospect, and he compared it brilliantly to
Beckett's *Endgame* and Ionesco. There is a remarkable irony when you
look at this wonderful creation of Shakespeare's poetic Renaissance imagination four centuries ago in juxtaposition to the disturbing video clips
we see nightly on CNN highlighting the results of personal and political
miscalculation, barbarous torture, and human cruelty. The world we live

in with its imperious leadership and self-annihilating acts of terrorism is reflected in Shakespeare's play when a seemingly banal act at the beginning of the story ruptures this perilously thin membrane between chaos and civilized order and sends the narrative hurtling down the hill. This is precisely what makes the play so perfectly relevant—beyond even the extraordinary genius of the author's poetic imagination and the truth of the human condition. We are constantly bombarded with information and surrounded with images that are present in this four-hundred-year-old play.

I believe that the theatres you mentioned, Michael, have responded in kind to the reality of our existence as theatre always ought to and as theatre is uniquely equipped to do. It ought to jolt us with how meaningful it is and please us with how well done it is. I like for both to happen, and I think by and large we deliver these truths here, but the jolting is what I'm most interested in as a director. I think that's why this play has reemerged the way it has lately.

KREMER: I don't know that I have a great deal to add to that, except for the hope that a play that deals at its core with clarity of vision and an individual's refusal to see the truth in front of him might have significant resonances for us as a population right now.

HEALEY: I've had the privilege of being in this play three times, and each time some new revelation has been presented to me. In this production, those revelations are coming on a nightly basis. When I'm not on-stage, and I'm on the deck listening to this play, waiting for my entrance, it thrills me. It's such a difficult play to do because you almost feel as though you could never come up to the genius of this work, and you feel that you fail nightly because you can never, ever come up to the perfection of this play. But on the other hand, the struggle to speak this play and to embody this woman, Goneril, and to present her force in the world is such an exciting challenge. I keep saying to myself night after night to just be there—be present with these words—and push him out into the storm. That's my job, and I am trying to stop being conscious of myself.

I've been on these panels before, and I spend my entire time defending Goneril's actions. There's a line that Regan says to Gloucester: "Oh, sir, to willful men/The injuries that they themselves procure/Must be their schoolmasters. Shut up your doors." I realize that the people who have hurt me deeply in my own life have been my greatest teachers. And

Lear could never realize, could never come into the clarity of vision he achieves, without these schoolmasters.

FLACHMANN: That's excellent. Anne, any response to that first question?

NEWHALL: Theatres, when they are struggling to reach their audiences, often try to give them an umbilical connection to the text itself. For me this play deals with aged parents, as I am doing in my own life right now. That perspective helped me identify with playing one of the daughters. It seemed to me to be the most vital connection from Regan's point of view. We don't know much about Lear as a father. But we—my fellow sisters and I—have all, of course, found our own arcs concerning what that might be and therefore what our jobs and points of view are in the first part of the play. That is how the play spoke to me. I think that avenue illuminates a reason why theatres might want to do such a classic as this, especially right now when their audiences are dealing with aged and infirm family members and such attendant concerns as living wills, Alzheimer's, and many other similar problems.

GAZA: A main reason this play speaks to me so eloquently today has to do with how Cordelia feels about what her father is doing to her and to her country. Frankly, without getting too political, I feel that very much in my daily life today. I feel love and loyalty toward my country, even though I feel betrayed of late by those in power. And even though Cordelia is betrayed by her father, who is the ruler of the country, her loyalty remains steadfast. The idea of feeling disappointment in the authority in which we trust our lives seems particularly pertinent today.

CONNOLLY: For those of us who were alive from 1987 until 1991, I think what we experienced with the failure of the last Soviet coup attempt in 1991 was an opening up of a possibility of a new kind of world, a new kind of arrangement with the failure of the Soviet Union and the disassembling of the Warsaw pact. I think that is one of the reasons why this play is back in business—because of the aggregation of "n" words in Lear, especially "no" and "never." I think for many people, today's future is not bright, is not wide open with possibilities; it is, in fact, rather grim. And this, to my mind, is the grimmest of all Shakespeare's plays.

This is the third time I've done it. The second director I had said something that has stuck with me for some time now, which is that the next characters to walk onto the stage after the end of *Lear* are Vladimir and Estragon from *Waiting for Godot.* That seems to be an appropriate way of dealing with the ending of this play, and it embodies the attraction of it at this particular historical moment.

NEWCOMB: The great existential questions about artifice and authenticity run throughout Shakespeare, but they are most profoundly expressed in *Lear* and *Hamlet.* All eras suffer fatally from the conceit of permanence—from the sense that our world will always be thus—and history, of course, has proven that's not the case. I guarantee that during the first century in Rome they thought there would never be a time when Rome wouldn't exist. I think this concept is particularly true in the heath scenes in *Lear,* which I have found to be really extraordinary. I think for anybody who's ever played the Fool, Kent, Edgar, or Lear, there should be a "Brotherhood of the Heath." [laughter] There is something extraordinarily profound about that emptiness, that alienation from the world.

Of course, the storm is an expression—a manifestation of what's happening in Lear's mind—but the concept is also true for many people in this country, particularly for those who are one paycheck away from homelessness. And here is a man who was king of the country, and he's alone in the wilderness. He has that profound sense that we all have, the "3:00 a.m. syndrome," when you wake up and ask, "Why am I here? Why have I made the choices I've made?" And Shakespeare doesn't do this to bring us all down. [laughter] But these plays really put you into that framework, that mindset, and make you reevaluate who you are. They ask the greatest existential question about identity: what's real and what isn't?

CASTO: I actually agree with everything you said about the heath. There should be a brotherhood of those who have had to do those scenes because they are quite exhausting. [laughter] The reason I think *Lear* is being done so often is that the violence is a result of the dysfunction in the play. For me that's a mirror of what's happening in our society right now. I agree with Shelly: I've been on the heath for a great number of years now, and I think directors around the country know they can use this play to make a personal statement.

FLACHMANN: Excellent. Thank you, Tim. We see, as we always do, that the greatest productions are founded in current events, even if the scripts were written four hundred years ago. Anne brought up character arcs. I wonder if we could talk about those a little bit. Carole, I know you have some strong feelings about your particular character's journey in the play. I think it's appropriate to talk about this because we all paid forty-eight dollars to see the show, and we want to be witnesses as the characters change and mature; beyond that, I suspect all of us in the audience want to change and mature through a kind of theatrical osmosis.

HEALEY: Almost everyone I meet after the show in the courtyard says to me, "You were so evil," and I just want to hit them [laughter] because I realize I didn't do my job very well if that's what they think. If they can't see what it was like—if they can't use their imagination and listen to what Lear says to his daughters—then they're not paying enough attention. When he first asks us to tell him how much we love him, this is how he addresses the three girls: "Goneril, / Our eldest, speak first." "Our dearest Regan, wife of Cornwall." "Now, our joy."

FLACHMANN: And that bothers you? [laughter]

HEALEY: How do you think that would make you feel? And then shortly thereafter, he's divided the country in three. Now traditionally the eldest would get the biggest share or the whole shootin' match, especially if she has shown clearly that she is extremely intelligent and a powerful leader. I think Goneril inherited those characteristics from her father. And I know she would be an excellent leader of the country. She's politically savvy; she's always thinking two steps ahead of everybody else. Instead, he gives her—in our production—a northern patch, quite small, and there's this laaaaarge swath [laughter] in the middle that has London in it, you know. And then there's this other southerly patch, where it's warmer. I get the cold north near Scotland.

And then, after I see what he does to his favorite daughter—how he treats her, how he banishes her forever, displaying the cruelest, harshest, most insane behavior—I say, I think rather prudently, to my sister, "We've got to stick together. 'If our father carries authority with such disposition as he bears, this last surrender of his will but offend us.'" If your father exhibited that kind of behavior to his favorite child, wouldn't you be a little bit afraid for your own life?

Then he shows up at your house with one hundred knights and squires, and now that he's retired, he's ready to party. [laughter] He shows up with guys who are screaming for dinner: "Let me not stay a jot for dinner, aaaah. Get it ready, aaaah." Can you imagine coping with that kind of company in your house? Your father showing up with a hundred guys—not his own age, who might want to go to bed at a decent hour,[laughter] but with a hundred young guys who are egging him on to more and more frat-boy behavior. And when I ask him to a little disquantity his train, he says, "Degenerate bastard! I'll not trouble thee…Detested kite! thou liest," and he starts defending his men without ever considering that my request made any sense whatsoever. Never for a moment does he say, "Oh, I'm so sorry. You know what, let me send fifty of my guys just to a house down the road. Are we keeping you up? Are we upsetting your other servants?" [laughter] Not for a moment. [more laughter]

KREMER: I need to take a second and straighten her halo. [laughter]

HEALEY: But after I take away fifty of his knights, he says, "Into her womb convey sterility;/Dry up in her the organs of increase." Can you image a father saying that to a daughter? To someone who obviously has no children? I'm sure he went exactly for the most vulnerable, hurtful, painful part of her life. So given all that, [laughter] I think Goneril has a bit of a point, don't you? [laughter and applause]

FLACHMANN: I'm thinking maybe Mr. Kremer would like to respond to that. Am I right on that, Dan? Would you like a little equal time here?

HEALEY: Just don't call me names. [laughter]

KREMER: She didn't mention that little part about poisoning her sister, did she? [laughter] Actually everything Carole said is quite accurate. And I think that productions achieve power when characters are not played in a stereotypical way. I've never seen the play very successfully done when you just have two evil sisters who team up and throw their father out of the house. The depth of characterization comes from understanding the motives of human beings. Goneril believes she's right, which sets in motion a believability of situation that allows all the characters to deepen and strengthen their roles in the play. From his perspective, Lear is right and justified in his actions as well.

The complexities of these relationships are so intricately woven, it's difficult for me to explain an overarching line of action. These are relationships that we discovered in the course of six weeks of rehearsals, working with one another moment by moment through the play. Each character behaves one way in one scene and then is affected by someone else and acts a different way in another scene. So as far as giving a picture of a character's arc through a story, I don't feel able to articulate that, but I do think that this production is greatly enriched by the talents of all of the actors up here and the actors who are not here today with us: the soldiers, the servants, the other characters who give the play such a living fabric, such a humanity. We all bring the play to life onstage.

FLACHMANN: Thank you, Dan. Anybody else want to talk about character arcs? Jamie?

NEWCOMB: I think Carole's adamancy about her perspective on Goneril is one of the reasons why her performance is so strong. You have to believe in the reality of your character in the play. I do find it interesting, though, that the contract is made concerning the division of the country at the beginning of the play. Lear expressly reserves a hundred knights, and he has given his daughters each a third of the kingdom. The kingdom! [laughing] He's probably not the easiest guy to live with, and he's getting worse and more mercurial as time has gone on, and there are indications about the fragility of his mental state at the very beginning of the play. Regan and Goneril say in [act] 3, [scene] 1, "Well, how about twenty-five knights; how about ten; or why do you need even one?" And then suddenly there's a storm brewing, and the daughters don't say, "You know, the weather looks bad, Dad. How about if you just come in until the storm passes?" So there is—for whatever reason—a true vindictiveness in the daughters that gets more pronounced as the play goes on. Whatever the provocation may be, the fact that the daughters send their father out into the wilderness in a horrific storm is cruel.

FLACHMANN: Let the record show that Ms. Healey was shaking her head no during that whole dissertation by Mr. Newcomb. [laughter] Anne?

NEWHALL: I am the understudy for the role of Regan, having joined the cast in performance immediately following opening due to a medical emergency in the family of the wonderful actress, Carey Cannon, originally slated to appear and who is blessedly returning to the show for the last three weeks of the run. I share this because I needed to define Regan very quickly with no rehearsal and on my feet in front of an audience during performance. And so what I did was in confluence with the blocking as I understood it to be. I'm not certain I understood it initially, but I was very kindly shoved by various actors [laughter] out of their light [more laughter] on certain nights. I needed to find my way not only as the middle child, the middle daughter, but I literally needed to find the acting path between what would have been already taken up by these two lovely ladies [referring to Healey and Gaza]. I needed to learn how to survive as a middle child would between these two.

And there were moments of identity with both Cornwall and Edmund that helped me move toward the developments that happen in our part two [Shakespeare's acts 3, 4, and 5]. Regan's acme, her brief moment of triumph, is the counting down of knights with her sister in [act] 2, [scene] 4. Goneril and Edmund become her obstacle and obsessive compulsion, respectively, in part two as she devolves into a disaffected, violent creature of bloodlust. She learns her sadism from Cornwall and the bloodlust from Edmund, whom Cornwall brings into their household, their camp, and with whom she falls into violent infatuation and more.

That's how I found my arc, by nightly learning from both audience and fellow company members on my feet what I needed to contribute to the storytelling. I am not certain there is yet an inevitable logic to her arc. I don't think I'm in a position to know because I'm still learning at such a fast and furious pace. I cannot yet be as fierce an advocate for my character as I would like to be, but I do think that's always our job.

FLACHMANN: Thank you, Anne. That was great. Michael, you have a fascinating arc as Gloucester. I think you move from fairly blunt comments about your bastard son to "I stumbled when I saw." Anything you want to talk about there?

CONNOLLY: In *The Casket* by Plautus, the prologue says, "Get up and stretch your legs. A long play by Plautus is about to begin." But I'm going to talk movingly about the most underappreciated character in the play: Gloucester. No, I'm not. [laughter] After you get the call and you have the contract to play Gloucester in *Lear,* you try to wipe your slate clean and pick up the text as if you'd never read it before and just react intuitively to the situations he's in. One searches in vain for serious critical treatment of Gloucester's life. I mean, there just aren't any, so you go ahead and do a search, and there aren't that many articles about Gloucester.

When you read the play, you pretty much know why because for three acts there's not a lot of memorable poetry. In the two other productions I've been in, the memorable poetry in [act] 3, [scene] 7 [the blinding scene] was cut to the bone. What you get out of your mouth is "because I would not see thy cruel nails/Pluck out his poor old eyes," and we move to the blinding. Thank you, Jim, and thank you, God, for giving those fifteen lines their full weight!

So, for an actor playing Gloucester, the most immediate thought that comes into your mind is how to honor the structural demand of this character, which is that the Gloucester-Edmond-Edgar part of the play, that triangle, must have some presence, and I think that's what I start off with. What is the key to this guy that will give an arc to the play and will also hopefully create a character whose contribution to the narrative enriches and renders more complex that theatrical experience? Luckily, somewhere around early March, I actually opened my ears again and heard the phrase "our good old man." And from that point on, I tried to construct textually the nuances of this first scene in which he's not a very good old man, talking about his bastard son in the way he does. What is good about Gloucester? And when do the wheels fall off the cart, and what happens as a result of that?

So that's the fun part, and then you bring all that homework into rehearsal on the first day, and you see what Jim has in mind. Because you know that's really what it's about. It's about this extended conversation or negotiation, in some cases, with your director and with your colleagues because you're not a solo act. That's what I love about the theatre. You're in there plotting out your particular piece of business before, and it's like Clausewitz's first dictum on war: you know, all plans evaporate at the sound of the first bullet; similarly all planning evaporates at the moment of the first rehearsal [laughter] because then you've got to be open to the experience, you've got to be able to say "yes" to everything that's going on around you. Happily in my case, a lot of the long-term thinking about Gloucester bore fruit because I was in a place where people were willing to deal with the homework I had done. And also the wonderful thing about playing a character like Gloucester is that not too many people pay attention to him, so there aren't very many hard and fast ideas about how the role ought to be played.

FLACHMANN: Excellent. Thank you. A few literary scholars who don't know much—nobody at this conference, of course [laughter]—have argued that *King Lear* is unactable, unplayable. As someone involved with the rehearsal process, I would say the script is admittedly challenging and difficult but certainly actable. I wonder if you could talk about which scenes were the toughest to stage and why.

SULLIVAN: I think most recently it was Harold Bloom who said that, and he was echoing Charles Lamb, who, I think, said it first. I look to

34. *King Lear*, 2007. *Left to right*: Shelly Gaza as Cordelia, Dan Kremer as Lear, and James Newcomb as the Earl of Kent. Photo by Karl Hugh. Published with permission of the Utah Shakespeare Festival.

Granville-Barker on this question, who points out that Shakespeare was a very practical man of the theatre. He wrote the play to be acted. That ought to count for something. [laughter] Every character in the play is conceived as a part of the theatrical puzzle; everybody makes sense in the universe of this play. Peter Brook observed that Shakespeare doesn't take anybody's side; he makes everybody right in his or her own mind. That's because Shakespeare was both a writer and an actor.

It's one thing to read the play and be struck by its force and beauty—its nihilism and its power—but relying on the read only removes one from the mimetic force of the play. Being physically present to that language onstage, among each other and in the audience, takes us beyond the sublime experience of reading the play into an entirely different world of grandeur and excitement. Nobody owns this work. Each one of us comes to it in our own time, and it will surge on beyond us and last because of its strength as a piece to be performed.

FLACHMANN: Wonderful. Dan, the toughest scenes to do? Could you pick one and tell us how you solved it? Or is the whole play just immensely difficult? [laughter]

KREMER: I think the scenes on the heath and that world of increasing madness and isolation where chaos reigns is one of the strangest experiences to go through as an actor onstage and is sometimes physically disorienting. I think early on we found that coming out of those scenes was a little jarring. It just upsets everyone's equilibrium and rightly so. I hope that is the effect those scenes have on the audience, too.

FLACHMANN: Thank you. Carole?

HEALEY: The Fool has this line that he says to Kent when he's in the stocks: "Let go thy hold when a great wheel runs down a hill lest it break thy neck with following [it]." For me that's the sensation of the inevitability of the play. Jamie and I did a very rigorous hike on Sunday, one of those hikes in which you had to look carefully where you were placing your feet or you might break your leg. It was strewn with boulders and branches and other hazards, and every now and then you would stop and look up, and it was so majestic and beautiful that you had to catch your breath. But then you had to go back to that task of placing one foot in front of the other and overcoming each obstacle, each boulder. That's what it's like to be in this play, I realized. It's like going down a precipitous, dangerous path every single night.

In our first scene when Dan says, "How now, daughter? What makes that frontlet on?/You are too much of late i' the frown," I love what Shakespeare does because he has this very strange line ending, and I realize if I'm very strict with the verse, I do myself a great service in terms of the acting: "Not only, sir, this your all-licensed fool,/But other of your insolent retinue/Do hourly carp and quarrel, breaking forth/In rank and not-to-be-endured riots." The line ends with the word "sir," which implies that she stops herself because all this anger and frustration is tumbling out of her; the injustice of what's she's had to endure is tumbling, tumbling, tumbling, and she has to stop herself on that line ending as if she's on the edge of a cliff. There's never any time to think in this play. The action is always on the line and with the line and through the line. And if you stop to have a moment as an actor, you do the play a horrible disservice. The sheer inevitability, the force of this play, will take you on an amazing journey which makes it hard to breathe. It's difficult physically to act these scenes, but the play will take you where it wants to go.

FLACHMANN: Thank you Carole. Anyone else have comments about scenes that are difficult to stage. Jamie?

NEWCOMB: I found it tough to commit fully to the circumstances of the heath scenes until we had an audience. We sort of halted, bungled our way through it, dropped lines; it never had any consistency or flow to it until we were actually able to commit to being in that storm and in those circumstances, which were physically exhausting.

One of my insights about the function of Kent is that he's like Horatio in many regards: he's the audience. He watches a great deal of the play as you do. We see him and see the action of the play though his eyes as well. The first scene with the disowning of Cordelia is a terrible event, and then my own banishment follows because I can only speak truth to power. Kent is a pragmatic man. I've always been able to speak directly to Lear, but suddenly I'm banished and make a statement about how I'm going to shape my "old course in a country new." So Kent is the essence of loyalty.

But one of the truths I find interesting about the arc of Kent is the analogy of the wheel of fortune. You think life can't get worse, and then it does. When you think the wheel has made its turn to the bottom, oftentimes it hasn't. And the glorious moment of reconciliation between Cordelia and Lear when he comes out of madness and sees her—recognizes her for whom she is—and apologizes is a stunning moment, and there's a feeling that the wheel has finally moved back up for Kent, and of course that's not the case. In the end, I think Kent becomes the audience for the play.

FLACHMANN: Thank you. Michael, perhaps a word from you, sir?

CONNOLLY: I just want to make a comment about whether this is an actable play. Margreta de Grazia did a great job on her deconstruction of the Shakespeare industry in the nineteenth century, on the *primus principia* of critics taking over the study of Shakespeare as opposed to letting it live in the theatre, where it was actually having quite an interesting life at the time. And one of my old mentors, Roger Hertzel, made a very good case both in class and in print that if ever a play text were the detritus of a live performance, we have it in Shakespeare. This is totally unlike Ben Jonson, who oversaw the publication of his complete works because he was bucking for poet laureate. We're actually dealing with texts that may be several removes from their original author, so to privilege textual examination over theatrical performance is an incredibly old-fashioned idea that we really don't need to get into anymore. I have colleagues teaching in the English Department who refuse to deal with Shakespeare's texts as playhouse documents, who will not allow questions from our students about the theatrical history or the theatrical moment in which these plays were produced, and I just think that's probably not very constructive. [laughter]

FLACHMANN: Could you have them strung up as soon as possible? [laughter] Tim, do you see the Fool as standing for some particular trait within the character of Lear?

CASTO: No. The reason I say so is because as an actor that isn't something I feel I can play. What I am able to play as the Fool is that my fate is tied to Lear's fate because he has been my benefactor, and I love him. As he rose, I rose with him. I function as a truth teller, not unlike Kent. I think I get away with a lot more than Kent because I am the Fool. I have a license to tell the truth. So I have to think of myself as the truth teller. What happens to Lear is what happens to the Fool. If he loses his power and his place, I lose mine, too.

FLACHMANN: I think that's a brilliant answer that illustrates the fascinating gap between literary questions and theatrical solutions to those questions. Thank you, Tim. Jamie, what's loveable about this old man?

NEWCOMB: When Caius [Kent in disguise] first meets the king, he asks if I know him, and I reply, "No, sir, but you have that in your countenance which I would fain call master." He has an innate nobility, the authority of a king, which everyone recognizes and respects. This is all backstory, which is something interpretive that can be conceptualized in many different ways in that first scene. What I play is that there have been signs of deterioration. I remember him from earlier days. And this decision to split the country up and give away his power is not a wise choice in my opinion. There are three truth tellers really. The Fool, Cordelia, and myself speak the truth and are punished for it ultimately. So it's an intangible quality that Lear has, and I am loyal to that to the end.

FLACHMANN: Great. Michael, do you want to add anything to that?

CONNOLLY: In answer to an earlier question, did you see *Der Untergang (Downfall)?* It's a German film that came to America, I think, two years ago, which features Bruno Ganz playing Adolf Hitler in the last two weeks of the Reich. There's a brilliant scene where Magda Goebbels goes to her sleeping children who have all been drugged and puts cyanide capsules into their mouths and holds their little jaws together so the children will all die. I mean she kills her children, and this is a loving mother! So it seems to me that *King Lear* begins with these kinds of inconsistencies. If you were in Germany in the 1920s when it was riven by internal dissent—if you were there when your country was humiliated at the Versailles Treaty—and this charismatic person came along and said, "Here's the future; I can make it happen," to be at that moment is one thing, but to be at the end of that sequence is another thing. Shakespeare very clearly gives two titles to Lear's two daughters: one in the farthest southwest of the kingdom and one in the farthest north of the kingdom. So there's this implicit sense in the play that Lear has been a unifier. He has created a kingdom out of nothing, and the people who were there at the beginning in the "Beer Hall Putsch" of the reign are Kent and Gloucester, the last two survivors standing.

So we've had lifelong loyalty to this man, and Gloucester has a habit of loyalty, a habit of allegiance. So even when Lear retires, Gloucester still tries to find a way to move his house forward in the power system and in [act] 3, [scene] 3 makes his first real moral decision in the play when he says, "No, I'm not going to go along with the way they're treating Lear; I'm going to try and save my old friend, the king." So I think there's sufficient evidence in the script for Kent and Gloucester and the Fool that they have been part of an enterprise that was flourishing, positive, and beneficial for everyone, and there was also a great deal of personal loyalty forged in that relationship. It's not just about the accumulation of power.

FLACHMANN: Thank you, Michael. Shelly?

GAZA: Cordelia knows her father well enough, I believe, to realize that he's not himself in that first scene. When she returns from France to search for her father, she hopes to find the man she remembers from her childhood, the man who has been absent for so long. In the end—no matter what he has done—Cordelia will always love Lear because, most simply, he is her father.

FLACHMANN: Is there a pecking order among the three daughters?

HEALEY: Where are all the mothers in this play? Because there's no one else around, I think Goneril certainly mothers Regan. We decided during rehearsals that Cordelia was always just a little different than the other girls. She was what we called "a tree hugger." [laughter] There's obviously a deep-seated love between Lear and Cordelia. When he banishes Kent in our production, Lear picks up his sword and says, "O vassal! Miscreant!" It's a very violent moment in the play. Regan rushes to me, and I protect her. And Jim has always had Cordelia be a little bit separate onstage from her sisters.

In that first scene, there's a lot of fear in terms of what's going to happen. He starts laying down the law, and my feeling is "whatever you say, Dad. I will do whatever you say. Just don't kill me. Don't hit me. Don't banish me. Don't take everything away from me. I will agree to anything you say. And I will be obedient." Now all Cordelia had to do was to say, "I love you, Dad," and everything would have been fine. [laughter]

NEWHALL: Since I was not part of the rehearsal process, I made my own psychological peace with how I should act as the middle sister. I was the absolute darling of my father's eye till the death of our mother, whom my father does mention in [act] 2, [scene] 4 to me. I know my sister is coming to join us, but Dad doesn't. This helps me anticipate the strength and support I'm going to get from Goneril, my surrogate mother, when she finally does arrive. I know I'm his darling (relative to her), and I feel those early speeches in [act] 2, [scene] 4 with my father show that he sees a remembrance and devotion to my mother as a weakness in me, which provides a way for him to get to me—to secure me on his side—until, of course, Goneril does arrive and the dialogue between the two sisters reveals their collusion one with the other. That's how I placed her as the middle sister.

FLACHMANN: How about Shelly and then Jim?

GAZA: Carole brings up a great point: Cordelia, like Goneril and Regan, is very like her father. She's strong headed and willful and doesn't always say the right thing, which gets her into trouble. She's not just a nice, sweet, come-and-save-your-father-at-the-end-of-the-play kind of character. She has grit to her that she shows when she says farewell to her sisters. She also displays it when she tells Burgundy off for rejecting her. She certainly is her father's daughter in that sense.

However, being the baby of the sisters means that she was probably loved and coddled by her father in a way that her other sisters weren't. So she inherited the strong willed part of her father, but she also got emotion from him, too, which is probably why she's capable of having more of an emotional arc than the other sisters have. That's how being the baby changed her.

SULLIVAN: I just want to make a couple of short observations about the family relationships of the play. It's a circle that comes back to Lear from oldest daughter through youngest daughter. And they are all alike. The first storm of this play is in the first scene, in which Cordelia says, "I will be patient and say nothing." And in the storm on the heath, Lear says, "I will be patient and say nothing." Whatever love was once there and whatever loyalties existed based on what Lear did for the country, all that is now changed. This is an eighty-year-old man who is no longer able to reign. All of these ideas I agree with.

Whatever that backstory is, the one constant is the need for love, the human requirement for love. When you read the Old Testament in the patriarchal story of the prophets, there's a constant demand of Israel from the "all-loving God," and the primary sin is loving somebody else or having another idol before him. The wheel of the play is that you have an enormous sense of universal forces being played out in individual fears and passions. And this is what makes it emotionally stunning.

FLACHMANN: Carole and Shelly, how has inheriting a new middle sister affected the dynamic of the play?

HEALEY: Yes, it was a huge change. Anne is such a different actor than Carey, even though she is doing the same blocking and making the same choices Carey made because Anne didn't participate in the rehearsal process. But she has to connect her own humanity to the character of Regan, which makes everything different. I feel in so many ways more protective toward Anne as Regan. She's more vulnerable than Carey was. Carey was slightly aloof—as if she wasn't going to show all her cards to me. I feel Anne is much more vulnerable and in need of protection, and I have that instinct to take care of her more.

In the scene with Lear—when he says, "I gave you all," and she responds, "And in good time you gave it"—it's like she's pulling a knife out of her heart. It hurts her terribly to have to say that to her dad. Carey played it more strongly, and she justified her action because she had to wait so long for her inheritance. Intellectually she said that's why I'm justified in doing what I'm doing. With Anne it's more of a painful choice for her. So you have two actresses taking a very different approach to this particular moment in the play. You put a different actress into that middle role, which is so pivotal, and everything changes. It's fascinating!

GAZA: Well, the problem about Cordelia is that she doesn't actually interact very much with anybody in the play except for Lear and Kent. Anne and I just have a very brief conversation in that first scene. So a blunt answer to the question is that it didn't affect me much because we don't get a chance to act very much onstage together.

But the process has been very interesting for me because most of my play is backstage. I come on in the first scene, and then I have an hour and fifty minutes off to make tea and hang out in the Green Room, [laughter] and I listen to the show over the monitor. Much of my show is based on what I hear, which has been a really interesting experience for me. I've never gone through a play in quite that way before. In regard to how having Anne in the cast has affected the chemistry of the play, I notice subtle differences in the character of Regan, but the overall dynamic of the play has remained essentially the same for me.

FLACHMANN: I can't possibly thank you guys enough for taking time out of your busy schedules to come here and talk with us today. How about joining me in a hand for these wonderful actors and this great director? [applause] You're all so incredibly articulate and insightful, and listening to you talk helps us get inside the play and inside your skins for a little while. We appreciate that opportunity very much. I also want to thank Michael Bahr, Matt Nickerson, Jess Tvordi, and everyone else who's helped put together the Wooden O Symposium. And thanks so much to everyone for supporting our festival. [applause]

Othello AT THE 2008
UTAH SHAKESPEARE FESTIVAL

Featuring Jim Sullivan (director), Jonathan Peck (Othello), Lindsey Wochley (Desdemona), James Newcomb (Iago), Corliss Preston (Emilia), Justin Gordon (Cassio), and Michael Flachmann (festival dramaturg)

FLACHMANN: Welcome to the culminating event in our Wooden O Symposium, the actors' roundtable discussion about *Othello*. I'd like to begin with a question for the actors, and then we'll come back to Mr. Sullivan for his opinion. With a play produced as frequently as *Othello*, how do you make these roles your own? How do you balance the demands of the script, the director's vision, and your own innate ability and life experiences to take ownership of these roles? We'll start off with Jonathan, please. You've done the role twice before, right?

PECK: Actually two and a half times. The first one was ninety minutes in Knoxville, Tennessee. Four actors did the show, which was very strange. [laughter]

FLACHMANN: Aside from that production, Jonathan, how do you make this role your own when it has been done so often, with so many films and videotapes available and so much information about past performances?

PECK: Number one, you try to avoid watching other actors do the role. You're going to steal, of course; [laughter] you're going to borrow from other actors, but I've found several cultural idiosyncrasies to personalize my characterization of Othello. For instance, if you spend time in Africa, you see people squat on their haunches while they wait for buses. And African men have no qualms about walking down the street holding hands. You also see this behavior depicted in Egyptian paintings. I didn't want to go as far as using an accent or dialect, which I think sometimes distracts from the words you are saying. And then you end up working with some really amazing directors who…oh, I've already got the job. [laughter] You come in with your own ideas, and then you collaborate with people you trust. I guess that's pretty much it.

FLACHMANN: Great. We're off to a good start. Lindsey?

WOCHLEY: I like to begin with the text—with what I have that's solid in front of me—and then take into consideration the other actors I'm working with and the director's vision of the play. Desdemona is nineteen, and she's very fantastical. In this production, she daydreams most of the time and is very happy with Othello. She loves him with all her heart.

FLACHMANN: Good job. Jamie?

NEWCOMB: Yes, I also begin with the text, but you have to understand that in regional theatres in this country, most of the conceptual decisions about the play are made long before the actors start the rehearsal process. I have occasionally been part of the initial design conferences—that's always a joy to be involved in from the beginning—but it doesn't happen very often. So you have to be very careful about any kind of rigid choices you make as you approach the text. I started working on Iago last December. For such a massive role, you have to be pretty familiar with the language before you come into rehearsals—especially here, where you have about two and a half weeks of actual rehearsal that is spread out over seven weeks.

But I also couldn't be too rigid in decisions I had made about the character since I was going to be collaborating with the director and with other actors. So much of the joy in the process is in what we come up with collectively. Corliss and I met early in the rehearsal process for breakfast and came up with a very interesting idea about the relationship between Emilia and Iago. Then you just have to take your best shot. You make a series of assumptions in the rehearsal room as you conceive the play, and then you hope that the audience will affirm your assumptions by the way they respond to the play. That's pretty much the context in which we work.

FLACHMANN: Thanks, Jamie. Corliss?

PRESTON: Yes, I agree with Jamie. I was cast in February, and I know from working here before that I need to get on the text immediately. I try to learn the role before I get here, just so I have it inside me, and then when I hear the design concepts and what we're going to cut, I let go of pieces of the play I learned, but I still keep them in my head. I already know different pieces of the puzzle that I can incorporate, even though they may be cut. I've seen this show a lot, and I've always found Emilia a bit of a puzzle. There's such ambiguity to her until the end of the play, when she gains clarity and you get to see who she really is. I love that arc to her character and tried to make it as exciting as possible. And I did get together with Jamie so we could discuss a lot of our choices. They weren't set in stone. And I also like to go to museums and just look at paintings and sculpture and see if anything hits me instinctively. I also did a lot of research. I love to see what's out there. I think it's very important to have your own ideas before you enter into rehearsal and then be ready to let them go. But I think about the role beforehand so the ideas can gestate inside me. And also Michael [Flachmann] is a wonderful resource with all the research he has done on the plays.

FLACHMANN: Thank you, Corliss. Justin?

GORDON: I approach plays in a similar fashion. I always begin with the text and see where that takes me, but I try to be as open as possible when I arrive at the rehearsal process. And then I really begin to look for the parallels between myself and the character I'm playing. I found Cassio very eager to begin his new career—much in the way that I, too, am beginning my career as an actor. The eagerness and the desire to do well are parallels that I found between myself and Cassio.

FLACHMANN: Excellent. Let's move the microphone down to Mr. Sullivan. Jim, are the problems of making a production your own vastly different for a director than for an actor? You start with the script, of course, and have a direction in which you want to proceed. Jamie has said—I think quite accurately—that some of the most important conceptual decisions are made before the actors are onboard. So how do you as a director approach a play like this that's done so frequently and has such a rich production history behind it?

SULLIVAN: Well, at this theatre, of course, I think the actors have much more conceptual input, especially those who have been here before. If the play is being done in the outdoor Adams Theatre, the architecture, based on the recollection of a Tudor theatre, encourages a playing style that enhances the relationship of the actor to the audience through the natural light that is available for the first ninety minutes of the performance. In fact, we're now seeing [in August] lighting cues at this point in the summer that we set after midnight in late June! The work on the outdoor stage at the Utah Shakespeare Festival is generally going to be—for want of a better word—"traditional."

First and foremost, most directors want the play to mean something right now. So all our decisions are made with one foot in Shakespeare's time and another firmly planted in our own. Costume designer Bill Black has supported this concept with contemporary trousers on the men in this production that are actually black jeans or black leather pants; all this, I think, helps make the issues of the play sadly tragic and frighteningly contemporary for a modern audience.

FLACHMANN: Thank you. Several of you have said that you start with the script, and then your relationship with the script is changed through the rehearsal process. I wonder if you can share specific examples without revealing any dark secrets about the production. Can you think of any moments that were changed because of your interaction with Jim and the other actors?

WOCHLEY: In [act] 1, [scene] 3, my relationship with my father actually changed a lot. At first I was playing the lines as if I cared about him. [laughter] But I found out through rehearsal that she really doesn't care at all. He wasn't there for her in her life. Othello is all I need now. I don't need my father at all. He's just a weight around my neck. After Jim and I talked about that relationship, my understanding of the scene changed a lot.

FLACHMANN: Lindsey, is the insight that your father hadn't cared for you textually supported, or is it a backstory that you and Jim came up with in rehearsal?

WOCHLEY: I think the text is ambiguous enough that you can interpret it in any way you choose. So I guess I would have to say it's a backstory.

FLACHMANN: Jamie, any special moments for you, sir?

NEWCOMB: Jim and I had talked a lot about the scene on the dock in Cyprus at the beginning of act 2. I had this idea about Iago's relationship with Desdemona and how she's a catalyst for Iago's growing villainy and malice. This prompts the question about his motivation, which is one of the great ambiguities in Shakespeare. I don't actually think his motives are ambiguous at all. There are a lot of reasons why he behaves the way he does. It's an accumulation of circumstances that lead to a specific decision to go deeper into his plot. I think he's certainly immoral and unethical, but opportunities that are available to him allow his further unscrupulous behavior.

One of the most crucial moments for me is on the dock with Desdemona when we're waiting for Othello, and she prompts me to entertain her. I tell a series of bawdy jokes, but I'm also wooing her because I think she's quite attractive. Desdemona has qualities no other woman possesses, and every guy who sees her is smitten with her, and Iago is certainly one of them. And then he has this very unfortunate epiphany as he is looking at this young, beautiful woman he would never be able to posses—never could have possessed—and there's a shocking juxtaposition with Emilia on the dock and with Desdemona and myself because you have to remember that nobody loathes Iago more than himself. And it's a stark realization to see Cassio come up and take her by the palm, to witness this suave, slick Florentine work his magic on women. It suddenly shifts into something much uglier, and so Jim and I wanted to make this scene with Desdemona a real turning point in the production.

FLACHMANN: That section is often cut in production, isn't it?

NEWCOMB: Yes, that part is generally cut. Jim wanted to delete it initially, too, but we had a talk about it and reinstated it in that context.

FLACHMANN: Corliss, I'm assuming you'd like to respond to that.

PRESTON: If rehearsals are a true collaboration, you start to find out why these scenes are necessary. Even if you decide to cut them, you need to know why they are there. You have to at least understand what you are missing. In rehearsals Jim spent a lot of time trying to guide me away from certain character strengths so I could save them for the end. When you are first in rehearsals and you're reacting to everything, you're pretty much wearing your heart on your sleeve. So Jim would try to say, "Yes, that's all underneath. Now let's try to put something on top of it." So I think it was a true collaboration in the creation of my character between the playwright, the director, myself, and the people I was onstage with.

FLACHMANN: Thanks, Corliss. Justin, any epiphanies for you during the rehearsal process?

GORDON: Absolutely. In [act] 2, [scene] 3 when I lose my lieutenancy, my initial approach to it was complete shell shock, and I think the first choice I made was to underplay it too much. And then Jim and I talked about his youth, and it's almost like he has a temper tantrum that an adolescent would throw when he disappointed his parents, which felt a lot more right, especially with everything Cassio has on the line up until that point and how embarrassed and ashamed he feels for failing Othello. So that was a definite change for me.

FLACHMANN: Jonathan?

PECK: I talked earlier about the production I did in Tennessee, which toured through a lot of small towns. One morning we're in Maresville, Tennessee, and the director says when we go into these rural high schools, we want to be very careful with the kiss. If you've ever been to a high school assembly, the football team always sits up front. So we do the kiss, and we're used to high school kids kind of rumbling, but we heard this sort of low growl come out of the football team during the kiss. [laughter] So I looked around for an exit, [laughter] and I walked over and said, "You guys crank up the van and keep that motor running because if I have to leave, you're on your own." [laughter]

I like what Jim has done in that opening scene because it's clear from the staging that the marriage has been consummated. We got that whole question out of the way early so people could focus on the story. During the Renaissance, to prove your newly wedded wife was a virgin, you'd go to the window and hang out the bloody sheet. Rather than do that, we have a moment with the handkerchief that says they've consummated the marriage. I agreed with Jim that we needed to communicate that at the top of the play. Let's get the kiss out of the way, too. Let's just tell the story.

FLACHMANN: I'm glad you brought that up, Jonathan. What about some of the other backstories? Would any of you feel comfortable talking about extratextual decisions you made about your characters' lives before the play begins?

PRESTON: Well, we've already discussed certain moments that changed in rehearsal because once you get onstage with each other, you start to create this whole other universe. One decision, which was actually determined in the casting, was that Iago and Emilia are a middle-aged couple as opposed to a younger couple, which helped us heighten certain aspects of the roles. Jamie and I started talking about how they were two kids from the Bronx, [laughter] and they had a lot of potential. They were both ambitious, and they thought they were going to achieve all these dreams and go all these places, and then they end up twenty years later, and none of these dreams have happened. Their great potential has gone nowhere, which is a real disappointment to them. Nor have

35. *Othello*, 2008. Lindsey Wochley as Desdemona and Jonathan Earl Peck as Othello. Photo by Karl Hugh. Published with permission of the Utah Shakespeare Festival.

they any hope of a future generation fulfilling their fantasies because they are childless. We also discussed the possibility of a physically abusive relationship, but the more we talked about it, the more interesting the emotional abuse seemed. [laughter] I know so many marriages that are messed up on that level: how many buttons you push and how you can manipulate each other and how you can still want that person to love you, even though they don't give you anything you need. Dysfunction is always fun…when it's not your own life. [laughter]

NEWCOMB: There's a codependency in this relationship, and of course we're living in a patriarchal society. Iago is undeniably intelligent, but he's not very savvy politically. He's never risen above anything but an ensign, and he's forty-seven years old (as we say in the play). So we hit upon this idea that Emilia is desperate for some kind of affection from him, which I can give her on occasion, but I can also pull it away. After Othello is sent to Cyprus, our station is elevated. Othello has put Emilia in charge of his wife, which means we are going to make ourselves collectively indispensable to Othello and Desdemona, which will help me in my attempt to get the lieutenancy from Cassio. We were probably pretty sharp cookies early on, pretty hip, and saw the world in that light. We were smart, and the rest of the world wasn't. That kind of conceit ultimately becomes quite toxic.

FLACHMANN: Thanks. I want to get Jim in on that question. So these guys go out to breakfast and come back to rehearsal and say they've got this play all figured out. [laughter] What role do you have in these decisions? Were you keen on this concept?

SULLIVAN: That's what I expect them to do. Because of our repertory rehearsal schedule, we don't get to the play more than sixteen guaranteed hours a week. It's difficult to build momentum in rehearsal for something that's as complex and rich as this play. For me it's largely a matter of taking what they bring to the room and shaping it. But you expect them to investigate the script on their own. That's what they do. Through the words in the text, they make relationships with each other that are authentic and honest. They avoid the actor's nightmare by knowing who they are and what they're about. The combination of this level of talent at the festival and the difficult rehearsal schedule always makes the work richly fulfilling for me and hopefully also for our audiences.

NEWCOMB: Yes, I'm just so proud of Emilia for what she's done. Getting Desdemona to plead for Cassio fits in perfectly with my plan.

FLACHMANN: While Jamie has the mic, I wonder if we should talk a little bit about the soliloquies in the play and especially about the relationship between the characters and the audience. What kind of special bond is that? I'd be interested in hearing from Jamie and Jonathan on that question.

NEWCOMB: I find direct address in Shakespeare fascinating because I know there's a dramatic convention in which the character is speaking to the audience, but in the world of the play, whom is he really talking to? I have a line early in the first scene with Roderigo where I say, "Heaven is my judge," and I sort of laugh at the idea of it because I don't think Iago is a very religious character! [laughter] Since Iago is a pragmatist, there isn't any empirical proof of God in a staunchly Catholic world. One day in rehearsal, I had a wonderful idea: What if God was right in front of me? What if all these people in the audience are God? And I'm going to tell you exactly what I plan to do. To date nobody has stood up and said that's enough of that. [laughter]

During the course of the play, I have the three direct-address soliloquies in a row which get progressively meaner, and I'm looking right at you as I'm saying all these horrible things and asking you an implied question: "Are you going to do anything about this?" [laughter] Near the end of the play, when I have the scene with Desdemona and Emilia and say everything's going to be all right, I have a silent soliloquy, which was an idea Jim and I had about turning to the audience and not saying anything, just letting the thought sit there unspoken. At that point, I don't have to say anything to you anymore. And I actually wonder if God is going to do anything to help these characters. I guess not. [laughter] So that is the context for my direct address, and I think it's important for the actor doing the soliloquy to have a very specific idea about whom he is talking to.

FLACHMANN: Lovely. Jonathan, do you want to add anything to that?

PECK: I see many of my soliloquies as "interiors" rather than direct address. For example, when I say, "Haply, for I am black/And have not those soft parts of conversation/That chamberers have," I think this is a thought rather than a statement directed to the audience. However, there is something I'd like to say about Jamie's direct address. [laughter] He has a moment…let's get this out now. [laughter]

NEWCOMB: Just before Othello enters in one scene, I do an impression of a monkey. And the audience always responds strongly. Sometimes they even laugh nervously.

PECK: And sometimes, I think most times, there is an audible gasp. Since we know that what he's doing is horribly racist, the question becomes, "How complicit is the audience in Iago's racism?"

NEWCOMB: Yes, that's the first moment of complicity. Anybody who laughs at that extremely rude gesture is implicated in the play's racist attitude.

PECK: It's one of the reasons things deteriorated in Germany in the thirties. Does your silence make you complicit? If you guys would like to talk about it later, I'd sure like to do that. [laughter]

FLACHMANN: Let's discuss character arcs a little more—how the characters change as the play progresses. Jonathan, do you want to start?

PECK: I think this play is where Shakespeare shows his maturity in writing characterization. Othello's arc to me is so clear. It begins with his new love and his joy in his marriage. Then he descends from that love to suspicion and then to outright jealousy and then to my favorite part: the madness that comes with jealousy. At my house on the back of my bedroom door, I have a growth chart for my daughter. "Look at you: you grew five inches last year." [laughter] In a sense, this play is like that for me. You learn how to deal with the verse; then you figure out the character arc, which goes from happiness to jealousy to madness and finally to death. As an actor, you learn how to tell the story, and then you start to fill in the blanks with all the little details. I've never been jealous before because I am not that kind of person. And when you finally feel that and the attendant madness, it *is* the green-eyed monster. The madness that comes with that discovery makes the story just so much clearer!

FLACHMANN: Good job. Lindsey?

WOCHLEY: I think the moment my arc changes is when he asks me for my handkerchief. When he starts telling me this story about the sibyl who, "in her prophetic fury sewed the work," it all starts going downhill because I don't know what's wrong. I don't know what's happened to him. He won't tell me; he won't talk to me. All I know is that I lost his handkerchief, and he's livid about it.

FLACHMANN: Jamie, we talked about a moment at which you lose control in the play. I wonder if that's part of your character when things begin to spiral downward?

NEWCOMB: For Iago there's a very clear dramaturgical arc. I trick Roderigo, then do the gulling of Cassio, and then move on to the big guy. And I drive him all the way until he falls to the ground in a fit, and that's a huge moment of triumph for Iago. Up to that point, I've done my work mostly in two-person scenes: Iago/Roderigo, Iago/Cassio, or Iago/Othello. Suddenly, Cassio comes in during the fit, and three people are involved. And I say now I'm going to bring Bianca into it, and I'm going to have Othello stand behind this screen and watch the action, so it starts to get more complicated. Later—when Lodovico comes in with Desdemona—I have to orchestrate even more people. In [act] 5, [scene] 1, Iago is dancing as fast as he can; luckily Bianca shows up at the wrong time, and I blame it all on her.

FLACHMANN: Corliss, what about your character arc?

PRESTON: I was fascinated throughout the rehearsal process with the idea of Emilia's identity and how she discovers who she is through the course of the play. I read an article by Simone de Beauvoir about the role of women in a patriarchal society. What was really fascinating to me is that women will bond with males of their own class before they will bond with another woman. I come from a working-class environment; based on my own experience, I think that insight is true.

I have no problem stealing the handkerchief. For Emilia the problems in the play are always somebody else's fault until she takes responsibility for her own actions at the end of the production and chooses to tell the truth. There's a level of enlightenment there. She's starting to discover who she really is, and she's willing to risk death to find herself. But I'm also intrigued when Desdemona lies about the handkerchief. I'm ready to fess up, and then you lie about it, and I think, wow, this is interesting. Then all of a sudden Emilia starts to bond with Desdemona as one woman to another, and that progression continues when she starts to reveal what she thinks. The ultimate betrayal is the realization that her husband set her up through the whole thing.

FLACHMANN: Thanks. Justin?

GORDON: If you listen to Cassio's language early on, he's very courtly in the way he praises Desdemona and when he talks to Othello and Iago. Cassio is rigid when he describes Desdemona because he's being very careful to do a good job as the lieutenant. He has the office, but I don't think he fully owns it yet. And then when he loses his office, he almost looks to Iago as a kind of mentor, as a guide: "He's helping me; he's teaching me how to be more like one of the soldiers."

And I think he finally becomes a man when he walks into [act] 5, [scene] 2 and sees the carnage. He sees his best friend kill himself. The man whom he has trusted has betrayed everyone. The woman he has loved on a variety of levels is dead before him. Everything that he knows is gone. And when he becomes governor of Cyprus, he's attained the highest status, but he's had to lose everything to get it. I think that's when Cassio becomes a man. There's even a shift in his language at the end when he says very simply, "Dear General, I never gave you cause.…I found it in my chamber." Everything is very direct at this point; he has lost all the airs he had at the beginning of the play. So for me, that's the arc. He goes from being an eager, officious upstart, wanting to prove himself, to a real man by the end of the play.

FLACHMANN: Great, thank you. Jim, you have the responsibility, of course, of coordinating all these characters' arcs. Do you feel like a juggler in a three-ring circus?

SULLIVAN: No, I'm an audience for them throughout the process. When these events happen in rehearsal—moving to the point where you can have all these arcs interacting with one another and interacting with an audience—it's a real miracle. That's why we do it.

FLACHMANN: I wonder if Jonathan and Lindsey could say a few words about their relationship, particularly the age and ethnic differences? What is it, Lindsey, that attracts you to Jonathan's character? "She loved me for the dangers I had passed, / And I loved her that she did pity them." I wonder if that's a solid foundation for a marriage. [laughter]

WOCHLEY: For Desdemona it is. The script explains that she has had all these suitors and that she didn't want to marry any of them. And then Othello comes along and tells her these fantastical stories; it's a dream world, and he's my knight in shining armor. With reference to the age difference, I also see him as the father figure I never had, which adds so much more to my love for him. It's only two days before he kills me, right? We really don't know each other at all. Our relationship at the beginning, in fact throughout the whole play, is purely based on attraction, and I don't really know him as a man. So when he switches from "I love you" to calling me a whore, I think this isn't the man I married. This isn't the man I fell in love with. I keep thinking it's a little bump in the road. We'll get through this. I don't have any family or friends. Emilia is the only woman I've ever been close to in my life, and I've only known her for a few days.

FLACHMANN: Jonathan, anything to add?

PECK: Yes. Othello is basically used to protect trade routes and the economic viability of Venice. But Desdemona is the one who has actually listened and who has an idea of who I am and what I've gone through in life. When you find a person like that, they are very special to you, particularly when you are a stranger in a strange land. Justin and I have talked about this a lot. What Othello really does is send Cassio to talk to her.

Now as I think back on my life, I remember doing that in ninth grade. [laughter] I sent Cedric to talk to Debra, and the next thing I know, they're going out. "Why'd you do that, man?" [laughter] Cassio is suave: he's a Florentine, and he's good looking, and he's of her own ethnicity and class. So it's easy to take that to the next level and say, "What did he tell her when I sent him to talk to her? Why wouldn't she fall in love with him? He is familiar to her, and I am not."

I look at her father and say, "She thanked me." I work for these other guys, and they never thank me. They write me a check, and I'm gone. The woman actually looks at me and says "thank you for telling me these stories. Thank you for entertaining me." And I think that's the basis of his love for her.

FLACHMANN: Thanks, Jonathan. What about the balance of the characters in the play? Whose play is it?

SULLIVAN: That's a very good question. I never think of a play, even *Hamlet,* as dominated by one character. To me the ensemble makes it happen. But the weight of this play, the spring of action, is certainly with Iago. I'm reminded of a phrase from Melville's *Billy Budd*—"the mystery of iniquity"—and I think that's the compelling aspect of the play. And it's the one that compels us still. We've created pop entertainment around it, certainly. Mass culture broods about it. The nature of evil is the meditation of the play, and that makes it the catalyst for the action of the play. Iago works through other people's hands until the very end. When he's caught and brought back, he has a kind of stoicism which turns the final act into his ultimate creation at this point. Consequently, I have shifted the production to that focus because that's what I find most intriguing.

FLACHMANN: That's part of the enigma of Iago not speaking at the conclusion, isn't it? One of the definitions I love of great art is that it is inexhaustible. We keep looking into it and finding new and wonderful discoveries. Jamie, anything to add here?

NEWCOMB: I think Iago starts bad and gets worse as the play progresses. He's one of those unfortunate individuals who have very large egos and terrifically low self-esteem. It's all a sport for him. When someone loses his scruples and his ethics, the world gets out of his way because we depend on each other's innate goodness. When somebody can take advantage of that and see what a person's weakness is and manipulate it, that's a pretty scary prospect, and it's empowering in a very negative way.

As I worked on the role, I found there was a kind of quirky "slouchiness" that Iago has early in the play; as he gets more successful, he becomes more still, upright, and powerful as the play progresses. So by the end of each performance, of course, we find there wasn't ever any core to Iago. There's no "there" there. He's the nowhere man. By the end of the play, what you see is emptiness. His last line is "from this time forth, I never will speak word." There's a terrible stillness in that moment.

FLACHMANN: Jonathan, how does your descent into madness happen? What percent is your own gullibility, and what percent is Iago's brilliance at manipulating the people around him?

PECK: Iago says, "The Moor is of a free and open nature / That thinks men honest that but seem to be so, / And will as tenderly be led by the nose / As asses are." He assumes that everyone around him is honest and truthful and that we are all working toward the same goal. This realization allows this Machiavellian ensign to create a web that ensnares Othello. In society, in politics, we often see people who cannot stand watching someone else who is truly good. They have to tear them down because it makes them feel like a lesser entity.

FLACHMANN: Jim, a closing comment from you?

SULLIVAN: Iago's words are an infection in the ear of Othello. He unleashes a disease that turns this man of elegance and accomplishment into a monster; he destroys a marriage and turns rapturous love into murderous jealousy. As the catalyst, as the infecting agent, he stands back and is astonished and delighted by his own creation. That way he's an audience within the audience sometimes.

FLACHMANN: What a lovely comment to end on! Please join with me in thanking these wonderful actors and this brilliant director for spending so much time with us this morning. [applause] We appreciate the opportunity to gain some insight into your art and lives. My thanks also to the organizers of the Wooden O Symposium, especially to Michael Bahr, Matt Nickerson, and Jessica Tvordi; to Scott Phillips and the Utah Shakespeare Festival; and, finally, to all of you in the audience who support this beautiful theatre. You are the most important ingredient we need to make these plays come alive each year. [applause]

Henry V AT THE 2009 UTAH SHAKESPEARE FESTIVAL

Featuring Jim Sullivan (director), Brian Vaughn (King Henry V), Corliss Preston (Chorus), Phil Hubbard (Exeter), Rick Peeples (Fluellen), Will Zahrn (Pistol), Emily Trask (Katharine), Ben Cherry (the Dauphin), and Michael Flachmann (festival dramaturg)

FLACHMANN: Welcome to the culminating event in our Wooden O Symposium, the actors' roundtable discussion on *Henry V.* I'd like to begin with a question for Mr. Sullivan, and then move on to the actors for their opinions on the same topic. The primary criticism levied against history plays is that they are often boring recreations of mundane historical details, but anyone who has seen your wonderful production of *Henry V* would certainly disagree with this statement. So I'd like to know your secret for making this play so accessible, so immediate, and so alive.

SULLIVAN: It's like what happened in school, isn't it? If you had a history class that was simply dates and battles and the important reigns of kings or presidents or prime ministers, it could be awfully dull. But if it's a story, as history really is, then you are talking about an entirely different situation. Of course, in the theatre, storytelling is what we're about. Shakespeare's histories are not so much recitations of history as they are stories about human behavior in crisis.

FLACHMANN: So these plays are really about people and what they must do to survive.

SULLIVAN: Absolutely. Shakespeare certainly gives us a national impression about Henry the Fifth, something that was received by his audience from generations before. We have the same in that we as a nation have received impressions about Abraham Lincoln, for example, or George Washington or Amelia Earhart. People may not know the whole story about these heroes, but they usually know something about them: a picture of the person or a notion of that person's character, a sense of his or her impact on the planet. History is always subjective. It's never the whole story; it never can be.

FLACHMANN: Thank you, Jim. Brian?

VAUGHN: For me the main goal—the main objective in doing these plays—is to try and find as many of the human connections to the characters as possible so the audience can relate to them as people. History plays are more like a big family drama than a boring history lesson, a recital of kings and monarchs. Jim's vision was to make the play as human and as visceral as possible so the audience could strongly identify with these characters. The beauty of playing Henry is that you have three other plays in which he is mentioned or he appears, so you definitely get a thorough backstory for his character in the *Henry IV* plays. In *Henry V*, however, he's a different man; he's turned away from his former self and become a king.

I loved the journey of trying to find the heart of this guy, of discovering who he is as a ruler, as a king, as a lover. There's lots of theatrical language in the play about becoming one person and then putting on a mask to be an entirely different character, and I think that's the journey for Henry. He plays the politician in the first scene, then the defiant ruler punishing the traitors, then the angry soldier, then the trickster, and finally the lover. So the challenge is in discovering who he is beneath all these personae, which is his own spiritual journey of finding himself in the play. Much of this culminates in the prayer scene before the Battle of Agincourt, when he discovers that all these different aspects lie within him. After this pivotal moment in the play, he is no longer concerned with trying to play all these separate roles. He can be the role itself.

FLACHMANN: Thanks, Brian. Corliss?

PRESTON: At the first read-through, Jim told us that this is a play about language—about the ability to communicate or miscommunicate—and it's also very muscular. So all of a sudden, he gave me two things that helped me greatly as the chorus. I knew instinctively that I could move around, that I didn't have to stand there and just say the words. I was given freedom to embody the action, and that made a lot of sense to me personally. I also know that you [gestures to Michael Flachmann] and Jim broke up some of the speeches, which allowed me as chorus to remain present throughout the entire play. I love watching the action onstage, which keeps me connected to the play. I invite the audience into a world of imagination that I truly believe in. And it's not easy language; there's a density to it. We really tried to make it accessible to the audience.

I also immediately identified with the war effort in this play because I had just finished working with returning veterans from Iraq and Afghanistan, and the stories these soldiers told gave me a strong emotional connection to Shakespeare's script. This role is sometimes divided into an ensemble with many people doing it. I knew we didn't have time for that here. Choral work takes an enormous amount of rehearsal time to do well. What I found playing the role as one person was that I felt emotionally connected to the characters onstage, which was a wonderful surprise for me.

FLACHMANN: Thank you, Corliss. Phil?

HUBBARD: I play the Duke of Exeter, which is a lovely supporting role. He's a bit of a father figure, I think, to the king, a confidant, a huge fan and supporter. In a role like this, what's important is finding out where my character fits into the story. It's easy to admire Brian because he's a friend of mine and I love his work, so it's simple to play Exeter for that reason. I played Cominius in *Coriolanus* a few years ago, who is also a huge supporter of the key figure in the play. I tend to play roles like that. [laughter] Exeter is also somewhat ambassadorial. The scenes with the French are a little bit like United Nations meetings—well, we've talked about Colin Powell bringing those satellite photos to the UN and proving why we should go to war. That aspect of Exeter is in there, too. He's like a secretary of state.

FLACHMANN: That's excellent. Rick, how about Fluellen?

PEEPLES: He's been a problematic character in productions because he's really hard to understand and often gets cut a lot. [laughter] I had the experience as a younger actor of being in a couple of different productions of *Henry V* and almost feeling sorry for the poor actor playing Fluellen. I could never understand what he was saying, and neither could anybody else. So I was resolved coming into this production that my main goal was to make Fluellen understandable and accessible so that the language was at least clear. After that—if he was funny or engaging or interesting—that was just going to be gravy. [laughter]

Fluellen's a clown, obviously, but he has his serious side, too, because he's kind of like Lear's fool. He's also like a new Falstaff. It's really interesting, in fact, that Falstaff dies early in this play without ever having his name mentioned. So we had some discussions about whether Fluellen is a reincarnation of Falstaff for Henry, who needs a new common man to be a reference point for him. I'm fascinated with how Fluellen has these hilarious scenes and then turns on a dime when we're counting the French and English dead. It's really an intriguing role for me to play. I'm having a lot of fun doing it.

FLACHMANN: Thanks, Rick. We've got Will down there who, as Pistol, is our working-class representative.

ZAHRN: Yes, but I think Pistol and his Boar's Head buddies are even lower than working class. [laughter] They won't work! [laughter]

FLACHMANN: They're the stealing class. [laughter]

ZAHRN: That's right, the stealing class. Nym, Bardolph, the boy, and I go to France to steal. We're like mercenary soldiers who are going over there to glean what we can off whoever happens to be dead or dying or not looking. [laughter] When we started working on the Boar's Head scenes in rehearsals, Jim Sullivan equated us with the Three Stooges, and we kept shifting who was Moe and Larry and Curly. [laughter]

But I feel really special because this is my second season in Utah and this is my second Shakespeare play, and my GI bill ran out before I got to the third year at the Goodman School of Drama, and that's when you learn Shakespeare! [laughter and applause]. So it's taken me a while to figure out what we're talking about. [laughter] It's a joy at this late date for me to get to work on the real stuff. I'm in hog heaven! [applause]

FLACHMANN: Thank you, Will. Now let's move down to the French characters, who are already giving me trouble for having marginalized them on the dais. [laughter] I apologize. Emily, talk to us about the beautiful Katharine, please.

TRASK: The word "beautiful" is a good introduction to Katharine. I have the pleasure of providing a dash of estrogen in a very testosterone-heavy play. [laughter] It's certainly only a dash, but I think it's a very potent dash. When I approach a history play, I see it first as a story involving real people and real lives. I feel like there's a greater charge to it, a greater sense of responsibility—almost an amplification of life—especially since these people have actually lived and breathed historically. So I think the story is especially alive, and that's the way I've tried to approach Katharine. It's a lovely, lovely challenge. French is such a beautiful language, and I think it's perfect for the separation between the men and women in this play. Like Henry, Katharine is also coming of age through the play, and so her journey through those two scenes kind of mirrors Henry's through the feminine aspect.

FLACHMANN: That's excellent, and if I might ask while you have the microphone, Emily: you had some prior experience with speaking French, isn't that correct?

TRASK: I took French starting in junior high through high school but wasn't a very good student. To pass I ended up having to do some extra credit, which was a French forensics competition. My French teacher asked if I would get a group of friends together to do a play, and we did a little five-minute farce. It was so much fun that we continued doing it every year until I was a senior in high school, when we put on a production of *Waiting for Godot* in French. We took Nationals, which sounds pretty impressive, but French forensics competition isn't too stiff. [laughter] That's actually how I got into theatre: doing extra credit for my French class. [applause]

FLACHMANN: *Très bien,* Emily. Ben, tell us about the dauphin.

CHERRY: Emily speaks beautifully in the show, by the way. I, on the other hand, got a C both times I took French in high school, so I apologize to you and everyone else who has to hear me speak French onstage. Often when this show is produced, the dauphin and the French court are very stylized—covered in pounds and pounds of frills and bows and lace with really high heels—so the audience sees this masculine English court and these frou-frou French people, and it's obvious who's going to win. [laughter] Jim decided to stay away from that interpretation. He wanted the audience to see the French as equals to the English, though he certainly didn't take away their boastfulness. He also didn't want the dauphin to be evil but rather realistic, just like all the other characters.

FLACHMANN: You're not evil; you're just misunderstood. [laughter]

36. *Henry V*, 2009. Brian Vaughn as Henry. *Photo by Karl Hugh.* Published with permission of the Utah Shakespeare Festival.

CHERRY: Totally misunderstood!

FLACHMANN: Lovely. So is this play pro-war or antiwar? That's a hot scholarly topic these days. I wonder if anyone has an opinion about that? Jim?

SULLIVAN: I don't think Shakespeare takes a political view on that. He just presents the situation as it is and lets his audiences respond to it. I think he gives us both sides of the question. Soldiers will go to war for a phrase. So that makes language powerful and also potentially dangerous. Some productions of *Henry V* explore Henry's Machiavellian nature and emphasize his manipulative side, but I don't see the play that way. These characters are all actors in life. Like Hamlet, he is the most observed of all observers. He has public speech and private speech. That was rather new for Elizabethan drama, and that created the theatre we have today. As Harold Bloom would argue, that created human beings, the consciousness of self. We all have an inner life that we can connect to the inner lives of the characters while our outer lives are connecting to their outer lives as well.

FLACHMANN: Very good. Phil?

HUBBARD: I think a play always resonates within the period in which it is performed. In other words, we are doing this play in 2009, so it's appropriate for us to ask that question about our world now. Over the past few years in the United States, there's been an antiwar sentiment about conflicts we've been involved in, so the topic of war is certainly on the minds of everyone who sees this production. I definitely think our show deals with the cost of war and whether war is ever justified. When Brian is speaking to the mayor of Harfleur, what he says is really horrible, and that resonates within our antiwar sentiment today. We don't want to go in there and do the things he is saying we will do if they don't surrender. I wouldn't personally classify it as an antiwar play, but this is certainly one of the voices we listen to and deal with when we perform the play.

FLACHMANN: Brian?

VAUGHN: I agree with Phil completely. I think our production takes both sides of the question during the course of the play. One of the beauties of its dramatic structure is that all these contradictions are represented within the script, and the audience gets to walk away from it and ask themselves what they think. "Conscience" is a word that comes up frequently during the play. I think the cost of war is represented clearly. We found it much more interesting to portray Henry as a guy who has a great deal of trepidation about going to war and a lot of guilt about making this fatal decision. That first scene with the archbishop of Canterbury really has to set that up. After the dauphin's insult involving the tennis balls, Henry doesn't have much choice but to attack France.

FLACHMANN: Corliss, would you like to weigh in on this question, too? You and I have talked a lot about how a female narrator influences the audience's perception of the play.

PRESTON: Well, it certainly influences me personally. I believe the play is about the emotional and political necessity of having a leader, someone you can believe in and follow. That's the journey I see. As a female watching all that testosterone onstage getting ready for war, I am acutely aware of our current conflicts around the globe, and I feel a profound responsibility to help the audience connect to that awareness as well and buckle their seatbelts! [laughter]

FLACHMANN: The play is obsessed with war for such a long time, and then, interestingly enough, it veers near the end toward more comic scenes with the duping of Williams, Fluellen making Pistol eat the leek, and the wonderful wooing scene with Katharine. I wonder if I could get Brian and perhaps Emily to talk a little bit about that shift and especially the purpose of the wooing scene.

VAUGHN: The wooing scene is almost a retelling of what Henry has been going through emotionally during the whole play. The last scene is a through line for Henry. When he says to her, "Shall not thou and I, between St. Denis and St. George, compound a boy, half French, half English, that shall go to Constantinople and take the Turk by the beard?" that's the ultimate goal for Henry: future generations of England and France walking together in the realm. That to me is what Henry is ultimately trying to accomplish in this play.

And I think this scene is a relief for the audience. They can see these people not as leaders involved in a bitter war but as human beings pursuing love and peace. This is Henry's discovery in the play at the end. From the prayer scene in [act] 4, [scene] 1—what Jim has called the "Gethsemane moment"—the play is about brotherhood. Henry never again mentions conscience after the victory at Agincourt. All of a sudden, he begins to delegate all these tasks to different people. He tells the French

King and Exeter to go make the final decisions on the peace treaty. "I'm going to woo Katherine," he says. [laughter]

FLACHMANN: Emily, Henry really doesn't have to woo you. You are his principal demand, to which your father has already agreed. How do you see that wooing scene?

TRASK: Well, Henry and I shift into prose in [act] 5, [scene] 2, which makes the scene all about communication. Perhaps he moves into prose because he's more relaxed, but Katherine speaks in French prose, too. I love the fact that he doesn't have to fight this battle, but he chooses to anyway. That he continues to say all these beautiful things, knowing full well that she doesn't really understand him, is highly romantic. It's a lovely release for all of us, I think, especially during the kiss.

In some productions, she is played as a pawn, a pushover, but one line in there is quite wonderful. When she asks, "Is it possible dat I sould love de *ennemi* of France?" that takes some pretty serious guts for this little French princess to say to the king of England. I think it's a meeting of the minds, even though the minds speak different languages.

VAUGHN: Yes, she brings him down a peg, which is a stripping away of ceremony, of royalty, and reveals the core of these two wonderful characters, which again is what makes a history play like this so human and alive for its audience.

FLACHMANN: I think you get a different type of love in the scene when Bardolph is being led off for execution. Pistol is the only one of the Boar's Head crew who survives all of this. How painful is it for your character, Brian, to watch this?

VAUGHN: It's incredibly difficult but also incredibly necessary. If Henry doesn't have Bardolph killed, his army would be out looting and pillaging with no code of conduct at all. This is just as painful as saying good-bye to Falstaff at the end of *Henry IV, Part II*. Henry has to get people to see a new way of thinking, and Bardolph doesn't inhabit that new worldview. I've heard of productions where Henry just turns his back on Bardolph as he is led away with no emotional connection whatsoever, but I find that personally wrong.

FLACHMANN: I agree. Let's get back down to Ben with a question about the difference between the real history upon which the play is based and Shakespeare's dramatic, imaginative version of that historical past. For example, the dauphin was actually dead at the end of the play, and yet Shakespeare has your character appear in the final scene. In the same fashion, your father in the script—played beautifully in this production by Mark Light-Orr—was mentally ill, but Shakespeare does not choose to bring that aspect of his life into the play.

CHERRY: The French king was certainly mad. He believed he was made of glass. So we have taken that historical reality and used it to inform his scenes. Rather than being insane, he's very sad and passive as if he might break if he did anything too large or alarming. So we have taken all the research work Michael [Flachmann] has done for us and used it in our own way throughout the production.

FLACHMANN: Brian, another notable departure from historical reality involves the killing of the prisoners, which was strategically done to free up the soldiers because the French were massing together for another assault. Historically—and in Shakespeare's play—the prisoners are killed before the massacre of the boys guarding the luggage. In our cutting of the script, however, the murder of the boys happens first, which so angers Henry that he orders all the French prisoners killed.

VAUGHN: This was something that Jim and I talked about a lot before we began rehearsals. I was drawn to this new cutting because I thought it made Henry a little more sympathetic. Killing the prisoners was a tactical move on Henry's part: he needed the men who had been guarding them because the French were regrouping, and the odds were still over five to one. This one decision has weakened Henry's historical reputation and made him seem more merciless, but it's just one of those orders made in the heat of battle. He had to protect his troops, and this was an action that saved many lives for him, which goes back to the role of conscience in warfare. I'm particularly fond of the way we've arranged these scenes, because I think it helps soften Henry's character a bit. It was just something he had to do.

FLACHMANN: Will, I think you lose two hundred crowns when you're forced to kill your prisoner.

ZAHRN: Yes, it's a bittersweet moment for me. That's more money than I could make in a lifetime.

FLACHMANN: That's a lot of pockets to pick! [laughter] How do you think the Adams Theatre lends itself to a show like this? Corliss, you've got a particularly acrobatic role going up and down those ladders. How do you feel about that?

PRESTON: Well, of course, it's a joy. If you're going to do the chorus in *Henry V*, it's nice to have a Wooden O to do it in! [laughter]

VAUGHN: I believe the play was written for the newly rebuilt Globe Theatre. It was the first play presented there. So performing this show in a replica of Shakespeare's theatre really presents us with some wonderful opportunities. When you see the play on film, it takes away all the audience's imagination, and that's the beauty of Corliss's role as the chorus: painting a picture so the audience can see the proud hoofs, the receiving earth, the magnificent horses.

For a war play, there is actually very little fighting in this production. You principally see the aftereffects of the battles. The only actual fighting you see is the Pistol scene with the French soldier. The scene with the archers above is not in the original script. We put that in our production because the English longbow was so crucial in winning the battle. That and the rain and muddy fields, of course!

FLACHMANN: Rick, there are so many different kinds of language used in this play. We have aristocratic language; we've got working-class or tavern language; and we've also got Welsh, French, Scottish, and Irish. What does such linguistic profusion say about bringing this country together?

PEEPLES: One of the main themes of the play is how Henry is going to unite not only France and England but all these separate nationalities within England. Remember the hilarious scene between Captains Jamy, Macmorris, and Fluellen? They can't even understand each other. Henry's most important job is to unite all these people, which he does by the end of the play.

SULLIVAN: Absolutely right. It's interesting to me that at the conclusion of our part one, Henry's soldiers have just held the bridge. I think that's a poetic idea in the play and a metaphor for connecting two different points of view. Henry rouses his soldiers to magnificent deeds simply by helping them understand that their mortal bodies carry a profound, deep, and enduring spirit. Because of what they are going to do that day, they will live forever.

His ability to connect to his people is extraordinary, but the whole play is really about people connecting with each other. Henry has to build a bridge to Katharine by virtue of his own character and his mind. That scene in our production is staged around a simple wooden table, which is, in effect, a bridge between nations. Even the scenes involving Pistol and the Eastcheap gang help deepen this important theme in the play. They have a very colorful vernacular, and their scenes are filled, particularly for Mistress Quickly, with the misuse of language. Thematically Shakespeare is exploring the use of language in every scene in the play.

FLACHMANN: What about the relationship between religion and history in the script? Do you feel manipulated by the archbishop of Canterbury at the outset of the play, Brian?

VAUGHN: I don't see Henry as being manipulated by the archbishop; rather, I see them manipulating each other: "You scratch my back, and I'll scratch yours. If you fund this war for me, I'll forget about the tax." This political maneuvering helps both their agendas. That's why the first scene is so public: he wants support from all the constituents in the kingdom. There was a massive snowstorm during Henry's coronation, which is a wonderful metaphor for this guy. He comes out of this storm and makes a personal journey of self-discovery throughout the play. During the prayer scene, he realizes that he doesn't have to live in the past and continue paying for the mistake his father made in seizing the throne from Richard. He realizes that success lies within him, which is very Christlike. He's very much like Hamlet, who goes to England and comes back a changed person.

FLACHMANN: What a brilliant, articulate, thoughtful panel this morning! Don't you all think so? [applause] As you can tell, we only hire really smart actors here at the festival. [laughter and applause] Before we come to a close, I want to thank Mr. Sullivan and the actors for spending so much time with us this morning. What a thrill to have them all to ourselves. And thanks especially to our wonderful audience. We couldn't do any of this without you! [applause]

Acknowledgments

DRAMATURGY

"Dream Making in Cedar City," originally published in *Articles: A Publication of California Institute of the Arts* 3, no. 1 (spring 1987): 28–32.

"The Merchant of Ashland," originally published in *On-Stage Studies* (1992): 17–35.

"Rehearsing the Audience," originally published in the Utah Shakespeare Festival program, summer 1989, 22–23.

"Designing the Script," originally published in the Utah Shakespeare Festival program, summer 1990, 26.

"*Cymbeline* in the Wooden O," originally published in the *Journal of the Wooden O Symposium* 2 (2002): 82–88.

"The Kindest Cut of All," originally published in *Stage Directions,* January 2009, 10–13.

THE COMEDIES

"The Errors of Comedy," originally published in *Shakespeare Edition: A Publication of the Utah Shakespearean Festival* 51 (spring 1987): 51.

"'Touches of Sweet Harmony,'" originally published in the Oregon Shakespeare Festival program, summer 1991, 5–7.

"The Forest of Arden," originally published in the Oregon Shakespeare Festival program, summer 1992, 20–21.

"'Swear by Your Double Self,'" originally published in *Shakespeare Bul-*

letin: A Journal of Performance Criticism and Scholarship 11, no. 2 (spring 1993): 46–48.

"Festive Comedy," originally published in the Oregon Shakespeare Festival program, summer 1995, 4–7.

"The Sins of the Father," originally published in *Insights: A Guide to the Utah Shakespearean Festival* 22 (summer 2000): 7–8.

"The Two Comic Plots of Verona," originally published in *Midsummer Magazine: The Magazine of the Utah Shakespearean Festival*, summer 2001, 22–25.

"My Daughter, My Ducats," originally published in *Insights: A Guide to the Utah Shakespearean Festival* 28 (summer 2006): 24.

"'This is Illyria, Lady,'" originally published in *Midsummer Magazine: The Magazine of the Utah Shakespearean Festival*, summer 2007, 10–13.

"Love's Labor's Won," originally published in *Midsummer Magazine: The Magazine of the Utah Shakespearean Festival*, summer 2005, 16–18.

"The Taming of the Script," originally published in *Midsummer Magazine: The Magazine of the Utah Shakespearean Festival*, summer 2008, 19–20.

"Much Ado about Something," originally published in *Insights: A Guide to the Utah Shakespearean Festival* 32 (summer 2010): 26.

THE HISTORIES

"Parrot, Parody, and Paronomasia," originally published in *Journal of the Wooden O Symposium* 4 (2004): 45–52.

"Historical Narratives," originally published in *Midsummer Magazine: The Magazine of the Utah Shakespearean Festival*, summer 1993, 15–16.

"Richard III and the Theatricality of Evil," originally published in *Midsummer Magazine: The Magazine of the Utah Shakespearean Festival*, summer 2003, 16–19.

"Poetic History," originally published in *Midsummer Magazine: The Magazine of the Utah Shakespearean Festival*, summer 2004, 13–15.

THE TRAGEDIES

"The Medieval Heritage of Iago," originally published in *Midsummer Magazine: The Magazine of the Utah Shakespearean Festival*, summer 1988, 21–22.

"Family Matters," originally published in *Midsummer Magazine: The Magazine of the Utah Shakespearean Festival,* summer 1998, 32–33.

"Lear's Mythic Journey," originally published in *Midsummer Magazine: The Magazine of the Utah Shakespearean Festival,* summer 1992, 22–24.

"Biological Finance," originally published in the Utah Shakespeare Festival program, summer 1993, 27.

"The Scottish Play," originally published in *Midsummer Magazine: The Magazine of the Utah Shakespearean Festival,* summer 1996, 14–18.

"The Art of Dying Well," originally published in *Midsummer Magazine: The Magazine of the Utah Shakespearean Festival,* summer 1997, 30–34.

"All My Travels' History," originally published in *Insights: A Guide to the Utah Shakespearean Festival* 24 (summer 2002): 16–18.

"The Rhythm of the Kiss," originally published in *Inside English* (forthcoming).

THE ROMANCES

"All Corners of the World," originally published in *On-Stage Studies* (1989), 73–76.

"This Rough Magic," originally published in *Insights: A Guide to the Utah Shakespearean Festival* 17 (summer 1995): 12.

"'It Is Required You Do Awake Your Faith,'" originally published in the Oregon Shakespeare Festival program, summer 1990, 19–22.

SHAKESPEARE'S CONTEMPORARIES AND OTHER PLAYWRIGHTS

"Food for Thought," originally published in the Utah Shakespeare Festival program, summer 1991, 27.

"Awl's Well That Ends Well," originally published in *Midsummer Magazine: The Magazine of the Utah Shakespearean Festival,* summer 1994, 35–37.

"The Heart of the Matter," originally published in the California State University, Bakersfield, program, fall 2006, 2–3.

"Invalids, Real and Imaginary," originally published in the Utah Shakespeare Festival program, summer 1989, 8.

"A Modern Jacobean Comedy," originally published in *Performing Arts: California's Theatre and Music Magazine,* July 1983, LPH 4.

ACTING SHAKESPEARE: ROUNDTABLE
DISCUSSIONS WITH ACTORS AND DIRECTORS

"*Measure for Measure* at the 2003 Utah Shakespeare Festival," originally published in the *Journal of the Wooden O Symposium* 3 (2003): 94–111.

"*Henry IV, Part I* at the 2004 Utah Shakespeare Festival," originally published in the *Journal of the Wooden O Symposium* 4 (2004): 150–64.

"*Romeo and Juliet* at the 2005 Utah Shakespeare Festival," originally published in the *Journal of the Wooden O Symposium* 5 (2005): 171–82.

"*Hamlet* at the 2006 Utah Shakespeare Festival," originally published in the *Journal of the Wooden O Symposium* 6 (2006): 100–115.

"*King Lear* at the 2007 Utah Shakespeare Festival," originally published in the *Journal of the Wooden O Symposium* 7 (2007): 97–112.

"*Othello* at the 2008 Utah Shakespeare Festival," originally published in the *Journal of the Wooden O Symposium* 8 (2008): 102–14.

"*Henry V* at the 2009 Utah Shakespeare Festival," soon to be published in the *Journal of the Wooden O Symposium* 9 (2009).